THREE AGAINST
the Wilderness

Eric Collier

VICTORIA • VANCOUVER • CALGARY

Originally published in 1959 (E.P. Dutton & Co., New York)

TouchWood Editions   TouchWood Editions
#108 – 17665 66A Avenue   PO Box 468
Surrey, BC V3S 2A7   Custer, WA
www.touchwoodeditions.com   98240-0468

Library and Archives Canada Cataloguing in Publication

Collier, Eric, 1903-1966
    Three against the wilderness / Eric Collier. — 1st TouchWood ed.

ISBN 978-1-894898-54-6

    1. Collier, Eric, 1903–1966.   2. Frontier and pioneer life—British Columbia—Chilcotin
River Region.   3. Chilcotin River Region (B.C.)—Biography.   4. Trappers—British
Columbia—Biography.   5. Conservationists—British Columbia—Biography.   I. Title.

FC3845.M44Z49 2007   971.1'75   C2007-900761-9

Library of Congress Control Number: 2006940188

Cover design by Jacqui Thomas
Cover and all interior photos from the collection of Eric Collier

Printed in Canada

TouchWood Editions acknowledges the financial support for its publishing program from the
Government of Canada through the Book Publishing Industry Development Program (BPIDP),
Canada Council for the Arts and the province of British Columbia through the British Columbia
Arts Council and the Book Publishing Tax Credit..

The Canada Council | Le Conseil des Arts
for the Arts | du Canada

BRITISH COLUMBIA
ARTS COUNCIL
We acknowledge the support of the Province of British Columbia
through the British Columbia Arts Council

Eric Collier in 1959

Chapter 1

It seemed that the whole world was ablaze when first I saw Meldrum Creek. From where I sat in temporary safety on the knoll, I could hear the fire move toward the creek from the north. When it reached the meadow beneath the knoll, the flames hurled themselves at the tinder-dry grass with a crackling roar and in scarce two minutes the whole meadow was ablaze. The flames cleared the creek channel at a bound and raced toward the spruces beyond. Within a half-dozen minutes the meadow lay black and smouldering. Though the needles of the spruces were still on fire, I knew that the trees were dying. And suddenly I thought, "The creek is dying, the trees are dying, the land everywhere is dying."

Yet this was the very land that soon Lillian and I were to share. There in that barren, burned-over primitive wilderness that has been home to us for almost thirty years, we were to raise our son Veasy to manhood. There we tasted all of summer's searing heat and winter's penetrating hostility, our only neighbours the moose, bears, timber wolves and other wildlife of the muskegs and forest, some of whom seemed ever ready to dispute our right to be there at all. There we learned to accept the mosquitoes and deer flies that often drove us, our work horses and saddle stock almost crazy with their persistent thirst for blood, even as we accepted all that was good in the wilderness around us.

There we were to share moments of tranquility—overnight camps in the deep moss-carpeted forest, or by some quiet sparkling pond whose privacy had been disturbed before only by a flock of migratory waterfowl or some sour-tempered bull moose. Pleasant enough in summer, but in winter, when the floor of the forest hibernated beneath a shroud of three or more feet of snow, life in the woods and around the ponds was a matter of spartan endurance, a time when our breath frosted almost as it came from our lungs, and the cold pried at our flesh with the edge of a keen-bladed skinning knife. It was then, when winter held the wilderness in its hard grip, that Lillian would spend many moments of watching and waiting outside the cabin, standing bareheaded in the moonlight, indifferent to the vicious stab of the sub-zero temperature, so very still, listening for the soft swish of snowshoe webbing on ice, or the heavier step of a saddle horse as it broke the snow's crust, her lips mutely wondering, "Why aren't they home yet? What is keeping them out in the snows at this hour of the night?" Here in the country that was now becoming a charred, smouldering ruin even as I watched, we were to endure too many a moment of bleak despondency when all our hopes seemed to have gone so calamitously astray. Here we were to savour gratefully the moments of supreme happiness, accomplishment and satisfaction that were ours when finally some of those hopes bore fruit.

This was the Meldrum Creek where, when Lillian's Indian grandmother was a child, the elk and deer herds came to quench their thirst, where beavers splashed their tails, trout leaped for the mayfly, and ducks and geese in their thousands glutted themselves at the pondweed beds. But now the water was stagnant; in spots there was none at all. Fire was sweeping the forest, the trees were already dead, and from my vantage point of safety on the knoll, watching the agony of it all, I could only think that the land was dying and there was not a soul to save it.

∿

It was in the late spring of 1922 that I first saw the creek. Its headwaters, that is. I didn't see its mouth, where it drains into the Fraser River three hundred-odd miles as the goose flies north of Vancouver, British Columbia, until the fall of 1926.

I was riding a pinto gelding, six years old, innocent and tame enough without, but treacherous as shell ice within. If now he slouched along the trail at a slow lazy jogtrot, ears back, eyes partly slitted, the pinto could become a whirlwind of swift and furious activity should a willow grouse suddenly take wing from beneath his feet, or a deer heave wildly away from its bed in the thickets of second-growth jack pine alongside the trail. He'd bucked with me before, had the pinto, and on two occasions anyway thrown me clear out of the saddle. Right now, I guessed that I was at least thirty miles from another human being, and should the pinto and I part company, it might be many a long day before I saw hair or hide of the rascal again. So, while my left hand held a firm grip on the bridle lines, my right hovered just above the saddle horn, ready to grab it and hang on for dear life.

Having lived in the remote Chilcotin district of interior British Columbia now for all of a year, and having absorbed much of the ways of this strange untamed Chilcotin country into my bloodstream, I was uneasily aware of the fact that it was the matchbox carried by man himself rather than any act of God that was responsible for most of the forest fires that were now burning unchecked over so much of the land. Here it was quite orthodox for anyone wishing to cut slough-grass hay for his cattle on some as yet unmowed wild hay meadow to ride out into the meadow on some sunny day in late spring and toss lighted matches into the dead grass of yesteryear and get rid of it, so that at a later date in summer, when the hay was ready to cut, it would not clog or impede the sickle bar of the mowing machine. Perhaps the total area to be shorn of its natural grasses comprised but twenty or so acres, but in order to rid its bottom of the litter, hundreds of acres of surrounding forest fell prey to the flame.

But that didn't matter. In a land where fir, pine and spruce forests rolled away for mile after endless mile, and ending no one quite knew where, timber was a natural resource without economic value, save

3

perhaps for the cutting of fence rails, logs for the quick throwing up of a sod-roof cabin or a winter's supply of firewood.

I think the idea was first conceived when I steered my horse across the headwaters of the creek and continued downstream parallel to its flow. It was conceived in much the same way as one who hopes someday to have a home of his own might view a vacant lot upon some street or avenue, and wishfully think, "This is where I would like to build a home." Almost subconsciously the thought crossed my mind, "Someday I'd like to come to this creek and live." In a few years' time, when that idle thought became sober concrete fact, I was to lie awake many a night, turning restlessly in bed, debating the wisdom of it all, wondering was it worthwhile. But I had Lillian with me then, Veasy too, for that matter. And they, between them, were the anchorage that held me there to the creek in fair weather or in foul.

Across the creek was a small meadow, perhaps a half-acre of it, girded by spindly willows. Beyond the willows the everlasting jack pine again came into its own. At the meadow's edge I eased my lank six feet one and a half inches out of the saddle, tied my lasso rope to the end of the halter shank and, unbuckling the throat latch and taking the bridle off, allowed the pinto to crop the knee-high grass.

Deer had recently bedded down in the meadow. I had cut fresh deer sign several times since nearing the creek, as well as surprising a large black bear, who was so busy tearing a log to slivers in search of succulent grubs that he neither winded nor heard my approach. I brought the pinto to a stop when finally the bear did sense my presence. I sat very still in the saddle and watched the animal break at a clumsy gallop for the closest patch of second growth in which he could speedily hide himself. At that moment, I hadn't too much interest in the bear. A day was to come when a black bear, heavy and round with fat, was of great and vital significance indeed. But the tracks of the deer and their sign in the meadow were something for sober contemplation; there'd be no shortage of meat here anyway, if one knew how to hunt it.

After the pinto had eaten a while, I followed the water upgrade for

4

a half-mile. The creek sneaked away from a narrow sliver of lake a half-mile wide, maybe three long, as if shameful of its presence there in the first place. For the level of the lake was so low that only a dribble of water flowed from its mouth. The sun, now nooning, was a blood-red ball seemingly supported in the heavens by the dense smoke that plumed up from the burning forest. It was the acrid taste of the smoke on my tongue that warned me I must soon turn back. I was not far from the flames.

Curiosity now tugged me farther down the creek. The water seeped downgrade through the gravel and boulders as if it were spent of either hope or ambition of eventually getting somewhere in its travels. About a mile below the crossing, the creek came to an old beaver meadow, and here the water became stagnant and smelly, scarcely hiding the black muck at the bottom of the creek channel. I reined my horse into the meadow; its matted, powder-dry grasses rustled beneath the gelding's hoofs like so much paper.

The crumbling façade of the beaver dam loomed up where the meadow ended, and beyond the remains of the dam the watercourse fell away through a healthy stand of mature spruces. There was little life to the creek where it escaped through the breach in the dam. The water barely trickled over the gravel and slowly seeped into a small pond beyond. Here was a creek that was sick; that was as plain as the nose on my face.

It was then that I actually heard the fire as it moved down on the creek from the north, and caution told me I'd best get my horse away from the meadow to the high knoll where I might watch the approach of the fire yet quickly get away. In another few minutes I had to.

Up there in the pine timber, with little in the way of underbrush to feed upon, the flames were unable to generate enough heat to crown in the tops of the trees. Not until they reached the meadow did they give frightful demonstration of their full appetite for destruction when bone-dry fodder was before them.

I knew not at the time how many years Nature requires to produce one mature spruce tree, sixty feet from root to crown and twelve inches in diameter at the stump, but across the meadow stood many such trees, each perhaps capable of yielding some one hundred and fifty feet of dressed lumber if called upon to do so. Their resinous branches thrust low to the ground, and so close was one tree to another that a moose or deer seeking the cool of their shade would surely have trouble passing between them.

When it came to the spruces, the fire crowned in their tops. Live sparks rocketed up into the smoky overhead were borne along with the wind and fell to earth a hundred or more yards away. And wherever a spark fell, a blaze was soon kindled.

I leaned forward in the saddle, both hands clasping the horn, and peered through the smoke at the remains of the beaver dam. And the gap in its wall, where the creek passed through, seemed to remind me of the gap in a fence that was once closed by a gate.

A moment ago the meadow was verdant green, but now it lay in blackened ruins, its peaty soil laid bare to the whims of the elements. I sat very still in the saddle, eyes on the breach in the beaver dam. If, I thought, but a single pair of beavers had been allowed to remain in the meadow, the gate would have been there, shut. And in front of the dam, and over the length and breadth of the meadow, there would now be water instead of highly inflammable slough grass. At water's edge the flames would have been halted, thrown back upon themselves, the spruces across the meadow spared. But there was no gate in the dam, for the beavers had long since gone, and with the beavers gone, all hope seemed to have gone from the land too.

Chapter 2

It was across the rough plank counter of a frontier trading post that I met the girl who was to share the wilderness with me. She came to the store leading an unbelievably aged Indian woman by the hand. It was this Indian woman, sightless and illiterate, yet possessing such a knowledge of the wilderness as few, if any, white men have, who was to tell me of Meldrum Creek as it was before ever a white man laid eyes upon the watershed, and urge me to go to the creek with Lillian and give it back its beavers.

I was working for an Englishman at the time, Becher by name, who had crossed the ocean some fifteen years before I was born to seek his fortune trading cheap trinkets to the northern Indians in return for costly furs. He stood six feet two in his stockinged feet and was a little the wrong side of sixty when I went to work for him. But despite the load of years he carried on his broad shoulders, his powerfully muscled frame wore little spare flesh, if any. A well-groomed moustache hid his upper lip, and when I first laid eyes upon him I thought that surely here was a man who only yesterday had stepped out of a guard's uniform.

Becher owned a sizable stopping house and trading post at Riske Creek, its hodgepodge of log buildings straddling the one and only government-maintained road to serve all the vast Chilcotin Plateau. Riske

Creek was a broiling stream that headed into the deep heart of the wilderness some thirty miles north of the trading post, and its waters too emptied into the Fraser River.

Among other chores at the trading post, I looked after the livery barn and clerked back of the counter when the Englishman had other matters to attend to. Across the plank counter I received a primary education in the fur trade. During late fall and winter, Indians from the nearby reservation brought in their coyote pelts and exchanged them for flour, tea, tobacco, calico and other trade goods. Occasionally a handful of muskrat pelts was hauled from a gunny sack and laid upon the counter, but seldom more than a dozen at a time. There were few muskrats left in creek or pond when I first dabbled in the fur trade.

Once in a remote while a sleek dark mink skin was held up to my eyes. "How much you give this kind?" its dusky owner would ask. And the price the trader told me to pay for mink pelts was never in cash, ever in trade. There was sense in this method of transacting business, too, for if the Indians received cash for their furs every penny of it was sure to be exchanged for trade goods. Money was of no use to an Indian unless he could immediately spend it.

England was only two years behind me when I went to work for the trader. Even the ripe old age of nineteen has advantages all its own, particularly the ability to shed one garment, hastily step into another and become perfectly attuned to its fit. I took to the sparsely settled outlands of interior British Columbia as the sunflower takes to the sun. The hedgerows and brooks of England had always attracted far more of my attention than the wearisome matters of algebra and Latin that an equally weary schoolmaster tried to coax into my unreceptive head at Northampton Grammar School. Northampton was a manufacturing town in the Midlands of England. At fourteen years of age I was already owner of, and intimately acquainted with, the doubtful mechanism of an ancient muzzle-loading shotgun that was as likely to knock me flat on my back as the rabbit or hare at which I aimed.

But I didn't mind that. The hunting of rabbits and hares, plus

8

occasional cock pheasants thrown in, soon became my real schooling grounds, the only ones I wanted, the only ones where I could learn anything.

If my father had had his way about things, he would have made a lawyer of me. Indeed, he had in 1919 articled me to a prominent firm of Northampton solicitors, and for twelve months anyway I had wasted my time, his money and the total patience of the two partners in the practice as I applied a fractional part of my mind to the matters of conveyancing, mortgages, divorce and bastardy cases.

But even when sitting in Borough Police Court listening to counsel for the plaintiff eloquently trying to prove beyond all reasonable doubt that the defendant was indeed the father of a child born out of wedlock, my mind was searching for some legitimate excuse whereby I could get out in the open fields, or merely tramp the hedgerows.

One morning in mid-May of 1920 my father addressed me in his roomy office. The manufacture of boots and shoes was Northampton's basic industry, and my father was managing director of a company that supplied the machines used in making the footwear.

I perched myself on a stuffed leather chair opposite his own and sat there very straight and still. My father studied me silently for a few moments.

"Tim Kingston and I were talking about you the other day," he stated, a trifle too casually. He seemed somewhat uncomfortable and unhappy. I sat very still in the chair. Williams and Kingston was the firm of solicitors with whom I was articled. "He informed me," Father went on, "that in his opinion it's a complete silly waste of time for you to continue with your law studies. You simply lack all interest in the profession."

I felt like crying out in exasperation, "Bastardy cases!" but kept my mouth tightly closed. My father had spent quite a sum of money in trying to make a lawyer of me, and it was hardly his fault that I had little appetite for the profession.

"You could, of course, come here," Father went on, but without much zest in his voice. "But I don't think you'd like this business either."

I knew perfectly well that I wouldn't. I had two older brothers in the business, but the manufacture of machinery held no enticement for me.

After a moment's pause Father mused, "There's your cousin Harry Marriott over in Canada. He went out in 1912, learned the ranching business and now has cattle of his own."

I suddenly came to life. Leaning forward with interest, I placed both elbows firmly on the desk, cupped my chin in my hands and asked, "Harry Marriott is out in British Columbia, isn't he?" I leaned still farther over the desk. Although I knew little or nothing of Canada's westernmost province, I had read in school with keen interest of Mackenzie's overland journey to the Pacific and Simon Fraser's perilous descent of the river that now bears his name.

Sensing my sudden interest, Father struck quickly. He nodded, "He's at Big Bar Lake, Clinton, British Columbia. You'd get plenty of shooting out there. Fishing too. There's capital deer hunting around his properties. Bear too, I believe. And trout in the brook that flows by his door. And of course you'd learn to ranch and perhaps in four or five years' time—" He broke off, thoughtfully closed one eye (Father ever had one eye on finance), then quickly opening it concluded, "It would have cost more than a guinea or two to set you up in a law practice. Maybe the price of a ranch and small herd of cattle out there wouldn't come too high if the investment was warranted."

Now that was two years ago, although to me it seemed all of twenty-two. I'd stayed a year with Harry Marriott, whose ranch was twenty-five miles from Clinton, a very small settlement of farms and log buildings, with one hotel and livery barn, tucked away between two mountain ranges and lying some thirty miles north of Ashcroft on the main line of the Canadian Pacific Railroad. I stayed long enough first to blister and then to harden the palms of my hands on the handle of a double-bitted axe, long enough to become fairly proficient in the tricky art of loading a pack horse and then firmly securing the pack with a diamond hitch. Long enough to recognize a buck track when I saw it on the muddy shoreline of Big Bar Creek. And long enough to realize that there was no proper anchorage for me at Big Bar Lake, or, for that matter, in the ranching business anywhere. It wasn't so much that I minded the work. But raising cattle, like studying law, just plain didn't interest me. So in the late spring of 1921 I threw my riding saddle on the pinto, loaded almost all my belongings on a pack horse, said "so long" to Harry Marriott and neck reined the gelding northward, feeling that surely somewhere in this wild, sprawling province there must be a spot in which I could settle down and take root, some endeavour that would hold me. A hundred miles north of Big Bar Lake, west of the Fraser River in the Chilcotin district of interior British Columbia, I eventually found both.

:~

The girl wore a blue print skirt, which, I thought, had not been bought at any trading post or, for that matter, selected from the pages of a mail-order catalogue. It was homemade, I judged, yet it seemed very neat, was spotlessly clean and fitted her like a glove. Her blouse, however, might have come from the mail-order book. It was an affair of georgette crepe, and its sheer whiteness accentuated her dark shingled hair. I noticed that she walked with a slight limp and thought at the time that maybe one of her black leather shoes had given her a sore heel. It was no sore heel that caused the limp. Her face was slightly oval, shaped like the egg of a plover, and freckled like one too. It had such an attractive quality to it that it acted like a magnet on my eyes.

Then I looked at the old Indian woman by her side, and with little shyness either. Surely there stood the oldest human being I'd ever set eyes upon. Her face was wrinkled like a prune, and almost as dark too. She wore a black silk handkerchief in lieu of a hat, and two long braids of gray hair escaped the confinement of the handkerchief to hang almost at her waist. She wore a black calico dress with a blouse of similar material, and despite the warmth of the day—June had been torn from the store calendar just that very morning—a heavy woollen shawl was thrown across her shoulders. In place of leather shoes, her small, almost childish feet were laced in coarse Indian moccasins.

Once more I looked at the girl. "Who," I asked with rude curiosity, "is she?"

She studied my face a moment before replying, "My grandmother."

"Your grandmother!" I blurted out. Then, unable to halter break still less bridle the words that leaped to my tongue, I exclaimed, "But she's a full-blooded Indian!"

Those probing hazel eyes never left my face. "Yes," came the measured retort. "I am part Indian myself." And with a faint smile playing at the corners of her mouth: "I am a quarter-breed."

I was busy studying the old one's shrivelled face. "She must be very, very old," I remarked.

With a slight nod of the head: "Lala is ninety-seven."

"Lala?" There was a musical if unfamiliar ring to the name.

"Lala is an Indian name," she quickly informed me.

Taking a pencil from the counter, I did a simple sum in arithmetic upon a piece of blotting paper. The answer told me that Lala must have been born around the year 1830. There could not have been many whites in the country then, for there weren't very many now.

Youth has its own bold way of getting at the root of matters. There was something about the girl that not only aroused my curiosity, but also invited further acquaintance with her. So: "Where do you and Lala live?" I asked.

"A couple of miles up on the hill," she told me, gesturing northward toward the slope of the hill leading away from the store.

My gaze returned to Lala. It was all very perplexing, for the Indian reservation was three miles south of the trading post.

Evidently the old one's grandchild easily read my thoughts, for she quietly went on to explain, "A white man took Lala away from her family when she was fifteen years old. She hasn't lived with the other Indians since."

I had a saddle horse of my own in the pasture that wasn't getting the exercise he should. The old one presented an opportunity, so I grabbed it. "Could I ride up and visit Lala some evening when the chores are finished here?" I asked.

"I don't think Lala would mind," came the smiling response. "Lala is too old to mind anything now. She might even like you if you bring her a sack of tobacco once in a while."

That is how I first met Lillian, who for so much of a normal life span has been there at my side, taking the good with the bad, and with never a grumble either. The more I saw of her, the oftener did my thoughts return to the headwaters of the creek I had visited in the spring of 1922. I wanted to go back to that creek, not merely for a fleeting visit, but to stay. Furthermore, I wanted Lillian to be there with me, and had more than a sneaking suspicion that she would be willing. It was Lala who brought matters to a head.

Tucked away within the recesses of Lala's wise old mind was a veritable storehouse of knowledge concerning the land as it was when the white men first came to it. Though she knew nothing of biology as printed in any book, the everyday chores of an era when she and the others of her tribe were entirely reliant upon the wildlife resources of the land had brought her into almost daily contact with the complex laws of Nature. Lala knew well of the seven kind years and the seven lean years, and her knowledge was not gleaned from a Bible. The interplay of the cycles that have such paramount bearing upon the fortunes of all wildlife communities was as familiar to Lala as the letters of the alphabet to a child of civilization. If Lala's biological knowledge came to her from the campus of the wilderness itself, she could not perhaps have attended a better school of learning.

It was difficult for me to converse freely with Lala, to pump her of all she knew, for only by use of a crude form of pidgin English was she able to answer the thousand and one questions my inquisitive mind demanded of her. Her jumble of words flowed most prolifically, and her memory was most active when, together with Lillian, I talked to her over the smoke of a campfire. While she had a small log cabin of her own, Lala often asked Lillian to kindle a fire outside. Over the coals of the fire she would pass many a long hour, puffing slowly away at her pipe and gazing pensively if unseeingly into the flames. Lala had been totally blind for the last twelve years.

Across these frequent campfires, Lala told me much of the creek as it was when she was a little girl, before ever an Englishman named Meldrum moved in on the scene to give it the name it bears today.

"Some elk stop then," she recollected. "Lots tam' I watch him stand in beaver water and drink."

Yes, there had been elk in the country once upon a time, large herds of them. I'd seen their shed horns with my own eyes, bleached and crumbling in the forests where they were shed. No one seemed to know what had happened to the elk herds of the Chilcotin, or why they had disappeared. But Lala had a possible clue.

"Me remember one winter—me just little girl—when snow never stop fall all of two moons. Bimeby just tops of little trees stick above snow." And she measured the depth of that snow by holding her bony hand high above her head. "Lots Indian starve and die that winter," she clucked on, "'cause pretty soon dry fish and berry all eaten and deer nobody can find. For five moon that snow no melt at all, and when warm weather come back, pretty near half Indian people be dead."

I judged that this exceptionally long and ferocious winter sank its vicious claw into the land somewhere around 1835 or 1836. True or not, when the whites began dribbling into the Chilcotin a year or two later they encountered no living sign of elk.

Lala's words flowed freely when she talked of the creek. In the days of her childhood, it was tribal custom for each Indian family to have their own privileged hunting preserve where they trapped the fur-bearers and hunted the great herds of mule deer migrating from the higher altitudes to their wintering grounds along the Fraser River. The headwaters of Meldrum Creek were the hereditary hunting preserve of Lala's family, and the long and changing years between that day and another when I first laid eyes upon her had been unable even partially to cloud Lala's recollection of all that had been there then.

She delved back into the pages of her fertile mind to tell of the honking of thousands of migrant Canada geese resting their mighty wings on the lakes, and of mallards and other ducks lifting from the marshes at sundown in flights that hid the skyline. The creek below the beaver dams teemed with monstrous trout, resting there a moment in order to gain strength for the effort that would carry them over the dam itself and into less turbulent waters beyond. She'd suck in her breath and clack her tongue when telling of the noisy splash of a beaver's tail at the cool hush of eventide, point and gesture with her hands in an effort to convey the proper mental picture of the muskrat dens in the banks, or of dark furred mink and otters sunning themselves on the beaver lodges.

One evening while I squatted by her campfire, studying her wrinkled face, I said, "No trout stop now, Lala. Just suckers and squawfish. And now the Indians never bring beaver pelts to the store to make trade."

She shook her head. Her scraggy hand sought and found my arm. Her fingers gouged into its flesh. Lifting her blank eyes to my face she said swiftly, "No, not'ing stop now." Her fingers relaxed their grip. Suddenly she demanded, "You know why?"

I pondered this a moment, then hazarded, "Is it because of the beavers?"

"Aiya, the beavers!" I filled her pipe from the sack of tobacco I had fetched her from the store, passed it over to her and held a faggot to its bowl. She sucked deeply at the stem, imprisoned the smoke in her mouth and then slowly expelled it. "Until white man come," she then went on to explain, "Indian just kill beaver now an' then s'pose he want meat, or skin for blanket. And then, always the creek is full of beaver. But when white man come and give him tobacco, sugar, bad drink every tam' he fetch beaver skin from creek Indian go crazy and kill beaver all tam'." Again her fingers clawed my arm. Harshly she asked, "What's matter white man no tell Indian—some beaver you must leave so little one stop next year? What's matter white man no tell Indian—s'pose you take all beaver, bimeby all water go too. And if water go, no trout, no fur, no grass, not'ing stop?"

After a few contemplative moments she suggested, "Why you no go that creek and give it back the beavers? You young man, you like hunt and trap. S'pose once again the creek full of beavers, maybe trout come

15

back. And ducks and geese come back too, and big marshes be full of muskrats again all same when me little girl. And where muskrats stop, mink and otter stop too. Aiya! Why you no go that creek with Lily, and live there all tam', and give it back the beavers?"

Thus the logic and advice of this ancient unlettered Indian woman, who was there to watch the first of the white men come to her land, and who shared the blankets with one when she was but fifteen years of age, who died a twelvemonth past the hundred mark without having lost a single tooth from her head, or endured a single ache in them. When Death finally crooked a finger, Lala knew naught of the gesture. No spasm of pain pricked her tired wrinkled flesh. She died as some ancient oak might die that has stood too long in the forest. A moment or so ago she was resting comfortably upon her straw-filled tick, puffing serenely away at her pipe. When the tobacco ceased to smoulder, and the bowl of the pipe grew cool, she placed it carefully on the stool by her bed and sighed, "Me tired now, bimeby me sleep." And that's how Lala died.

She was buried on the spine of a bunchgrass-covered ridge above the little log cabin in which she had lived out so many of the declining years of her life. A little girl broke from the ranks of the impassive-faced Indians about the grave as the rough board coffin was lowered on its ropes. The Indian child ran to the grave, looked down into it and said simply, "Lala all gone now." I was at the grave, reading a bit of the burial service from the Book of Prayer that had come with me from England. "Earth to earth, ashes to ashes, dust to dust—" A princess of the royal blood could not have wished for more.

∿

At the time of Lala's passing, there were few registered traplines in the Chilcotin, as indeed there were not many in the whole province. Hitherto the trapping of fur-bearing animals had been carried on upon a catch-as-catch-can basis, with every man for himself and the devil take care of the hindmost. The word "conservation" was not to be found in the lexicon of the fur trade. That the water tables of the land were slowly but inexorably

16

shrinking was plain for all to perceive, yet no one had vision enough to couple this calamity with a complete decimation of the beavers that had taken place upon so many of the watersheds, except perhaps Lala, and a few other oldsters of her race. But no one sought the advice of any Indian upon such matters, least of all the government agency responsible for the administration of the water resources of the province. And of course no one would have heeded their advice had it been offered—except Lillian and I.

Together we pondered the pros and cons of such a questionable venture. To me it presented a challenge, and offer of a life I loved to live. I had already trapped a little, although the trapping was confined to the coyotes that came down from the timber at nights to prowl the creek bottoms by the trading post. To Lillian it meant a home of her own, and all that this means to a woman. While I was earning only forty dollars a month and board at the trading post, I might in two or three years' time save enough to purchase the bare rudiments of the outfit we must have before starting out. There was no lack of obstacles, but what are obstacles to the young? So our minds became set on the purpose; together we'd go to the head of the creek and let God take over from there.

I applied for, and was given by the British Columbia Game Department, sole trapping rights over some one hundred fifty thousand acres of wilderness that embraced all of the Meldrum Creek watershed from its headwaters to within a mile or so of its mouth. It wasn't a bad bargain as bargains go. In return for such trapping privileges I must pay the Game Department the huge sum of ten dollars per annum plus certain royalty money upon each pelt trapped. In return I must undertake to "conserve and perpetuate all fur-bearing animals thereon." But alas, Lillian and I were very soon to discover that there was little fur left there to conserve.

For one quick moment I did allow my thoughts to dwell upon England and possible financial help from that quarter. My father had certainly hinted that he might supply the money necessary for the purchase of a small cattle ranch in British Columbia. Cattle ranch! There was something substantial, which if managed properly could be expected to yield certain annual dividends. Whereas the project filling my thoughts was as bizarre and uncertain as the tracks of a mousing weasel. My father had ever been a cautious man with his pounds, shillings and pence. If he invested a farthing in a seemingly hairbrained enterprise that offered no prospect of financial return, it would be unwillingly. I dismissed the idea of seeking financial help from England almost as quickly as it occurred to me.

In September 1928, Lillian and I were married by an itinerant Church of England clergyman. A roly-poly sort of a fellow was the parson, short in stature, broad in girth and as good-humoured and contented as a porcupine sunning itself on a treetop. There was a warm smile on his smooth round face as he began the ceremony and it was still there when he finished. The wedding took place in the spacious sitting room of the trading post, and went off without a hitch save perhaps for the moment when the trader's red cocker spaniel scratched and whined at the door, seeking his master. Both Becher and his wife were present, dressed in their Sunday best.

Lillian had given meticulous attention to her toiletry. Her wedding dress was of some flimsy white lace material, tied at the waist with a pale blue sash. She wore a veil of white netting, and I heard Mrs. Becher whisper to her husband, "My, how charming and sweet she looks!" Joe, the Chinese cook, had gone to supreme culinary effort to provide a feast worthy of such a momentous occasion. "Elic," meaning Eric, "him catch woman now," said Joe to Wong, the Chinese irrigator. "Boss woman (Mrs. Becher) tell me, 'Joe, you fix hi-u muck-imuck so ev'lybody have gleat big feast.'"

There was cold roast chicken and salad and potatoes and sweet corn fresh from the garden. And there was a large pink sockeye salmon, which, if illegally "dipped" from the Chilcotin River while innocently journeying to its spawning grounds upstream, certainly tasted none the worse for the fact. There was blueberry pie, and pumpkin too, and homemade ice cream and a large wedding cake, which, after the chicken, the salmon and desserts, hardly got sliced at all. Becher had unearthed two bottles of sherry from somewhere, and by the time all the customary toasts had been quaffed, the parson was as jolly as two porcupines sunning themselves on a treetop.

:~

In 1906—Lillian was two years old then—an elder sister tied a cushion on the back of a gentle saddle pony, hoisted Lillian on its back, placed the halter shank in her pudgy hands and briskly shouted, "Giddup!" The pony—it had packed many a deer into camp in its day—moved off at a lazy, affable walk, and then, when the sister fetched it a good one across the rumps with a willow stick, broke into an unwilling jogtrot. All might have been well if right that very moment a couple of Indian riders had not seen fit to pop over a nearby hill, their horses at a gallop. At sight of the two riders, Lillian's pony pricked up its ears and stopped dead in its tracks, throwing its tiny jockey clean over its withers to land kerplunk on her back in the dirt. If impact of soft baby flesh and bone against stubborn ground resulted in Lillian's moving with a pronounced limp when she toddled from here to yon, no one paid any attention at the time. Anyway, the nearest doctor had his shingle up at Ashcroft, over a hundred and fifty miles from the scene, a round trip of at least twelve days with team and buckboard.

If in the course of time the limp became less pronounced, it never altogether disappeared. Lillian's spine was affected by the fall, her right hipbone too. If in years to come both medical doctors and osteopaths were to examine her (as was the case shortly after we were married), it was now too late to repair the damage that had occurred such a long time ago. From the moment of the fall, the limp would be with Lillian to the end of her days.

It was this slight deformity of the spine that upset all our plans for moving back to the headwaters of the creek in the spring of 1930, and delayed everything for another year. According to all our calculations, if I remained working at Riske Creek until April of 1930, and saved every cent that I could from my wages, we'd then have sufficient money to buy all that was needed at the start of the venture anyway. But six weeks after our marriage an event came about that was to make impelling demands on no small portion of the money I had saved. Lillian was pregnant.

After digesting this breathtaking piece of news, I said soberly, "You'll have to go away to a hospital and a good doctor."

"That," she cut in quietly, "will cost too much money. After all, lots of women in this country have their babies in their own homes and—"

"But you're not going to," I interrupted. And after unsuccessfully fumbling for the right words: "Don't you see, with the shape your back is in, this might not be so easy for you as it is for some of the Indian women."

Shortly after, I packed Lillian off to Quesnel, a small village perched on the banks of the Fraser ninety miles north of Riske Creek, which not only boasted a doctor but a fairly modern hospital too. After examining her, the medical man's advice was blunt. She must be in Quesnel, where he could look after her, at least a month before the baby was born. Owing to the defects in her spine and hipbone, it wouldn't be an easy delivery. It was quite possible that he would have to take the child from her by caesarean operation.

As things turned out, by the grace of God and skill of the doctor, on July 28, 1929, Veasy Eric Collier was brought into the world naturally. But the following fall I met the doctor in person at Riske Creek, where he had come to hunt ducks and geese. After casually asking about the health of Lillian and our child, he stared me straight in the face and reflected, "Young man, you're fortunate. It wasn't an easy birth by any means." Then, completely serious, he warned, "I think you'd best settle for just the one."

It cost us close to one hundred fifty dollars cash money to bring Veasy into the world, and even if this did delay everything for another year, we were far, far richer for the delay.

:~

June 2, 1931. Eleven years ago to this very day, England became a memory. The sun, airborne now for all of four hours, stared cynically down from an almost cloudless sky. Swallows skimmed in and out of the high loft above the livery barn, building new nests or patching up last year's. Down the lane, a small flock of ewes snoozed beneath the shade of a lone cottonwood tree, lambs bucking stiff-legged on and off their as yet unshorn backs. In a log corral by the pigpens, a milk cow licked the membrane from her newly arrived calf.

The wagon stood in front of the store, stowed away within its high freight box the provisions, tools and other effects that we had been so long in gathering. Becher sat on the porch, stroking the ears of the cocker spaniel. "Look me up whenever you want a job," he said affably.

"There'll be work for me a-plenty, no doubt, back where we're heading," I tossed back.

He nodded. "But what about pay?"

I didn't know too much about that part of it myself.

I hitched the horses to the doubletrees, tossed Veasy Eric into the wagon box and then helped Lillian up to the high seat. I climbed up alongside her and said "Giddup," and flicked at the team with the whip. Bowing their necks to the collar the horses grudgingly tightened the traces. Slowly, and with a protesting creak, the wagon wheels turned. I followed the main Chilcotin road for a mile, then reined the horses away from the well-packed gravel, steering them due north toward the wilderness on the outline of a track almost hidden by grass and weeds. Lillian and I turned in the seat and looked down for the last time for many a month at the buildings of the trading post in the valley below. Then we shifted position again and faced the north.

Chapter 3

Open country, with its bunchgrass-clad slopes and its herds of white-faced range cattle, was behind us now. The everlasting forest and its litter of boulders, roots and blowdowns now held us in a grip that has remained unbroken from that day to this. Since leaving the open country and reining the horses through the timber, I'd had to jump impatiently down from the wagon seat a dozen times and heft the double-bitted axe and clear the right-of-way of some trees that had gone down before April's lusty winds. Yet blowdown or boulder, we could thank our lucky stars that there was such track to follow. Indians had originally blazed it out through the timber to get their horses and wagons back into the deep heart of the hunting country ahead. After the Indians, white men had followed this track in the forest, seeking wild hay meadows where winter feed for the cattle could be obtained in quantity for the cost of its cutting and stacking. Yet despite the hay that was annually cut upon these meadows, they knew no permanent inhabitants. A crew of men went out from the home ranches in late July to cut and stack the hay. Later on, usually in December, herds of cattle were driven north from the fall ranges to winter on it. From December until late March the small log cabins built on the meadows were tenanted by a couple of cowboys, usually bachelors, who fed and tended the cattle. But save for a month or six weeks in summer and three months in winter, the meadows got along nicely without the benefit of human presence at all.

We had no watch to tell us the hour of the day. Somewhere in the bowels of the wagon box a three-dollar-and-fifty-cent alarm clock was ticking off the seconds, if the jerk and the bounce of the wagon wheels had not yet ruptured its innards. The sun, now stooping down to the west, was our only visible timepiece, and for that matter the only one that counted. It had been rising in the east, bedding in the west, for quite some time before alarm clocks appeared on the scene.

Sweat dripped from the bellies of the team. In a sense, the horses themselves were a timepiece, and one that had to be heeded. They could pull the loaded wagon just so many miles in a day, but not an ell farther. You couldn't wind up horseflesh as you could the gears of a clock.

I half turned in the seat and glanced back at Veasy. He was cuddled up in a sort of nest that we had arranged for him among the bedding. His tiny hands were entwined in the rope binding the load down, and he lay on his back, face to the sun. His brow was moist with sweat, and his eyes were closed, and I wondered, "How does he manage to sleep through all this jostling and bouncing?"

Then I looked at Lillian. The whipstock was in her left hand, its lash trailing alongside the wagon wheels. "You're getting tired, aren't you," I said.

"A little," she acknowledged. Then with a mock grimace: "If only there weren't so many rocks!"

Rocks and roots! If the wagon wheels weren't climbing over the one, they were dropping off the other. It had been like that for the last few miles, and the lines were looped around my waist, leaving my hands free to grip the lurching wagon seat.

"We could keep on travelling north for a hundred miles without cutting the fresh tracks of another living soul," I remarked to Lillian.

But I don't think she heard me. For the last few minutes she had been leaning over the seat, staring down at the left front wheel.

"I declare it's coming apart," she now suddenly said. "One of the felloes is loose."

I hauled in on the lines. It wasn't much of a wagon anyway. I'd bought it from an Indian for fifteen dollars cash and one prime coyote pelt. At the time, I knew that its tires should be reset, and that it needed a new felloe here and there, but didn't feel like parting with the price a blacksmith would charge to make the necessary repairs.

Lillian's roving eye had spotted the damage in the nick of time. One more boulder, a couple more roots, and the wheel would have likely collapsed, and its tire gone rolling merrily off into the woods until halted by impact with a tree.

"Haywire," I jerked out. "Where did we stow that haywire?"

Here in these Chilcotin forests one could, if he owned any sort of a rifle and knew how to use it, get along nicely for day after day with no other food than that obtained with the gun. If one couldn't find a deer, he could almost always locate a porcupine. Or trail a band of wild horses and shoot a suckling colt whose pink tender flesh was as tasty as any veal. If dishes and cooking utensils were handy things to have along, they weren't really necessary. A hunk of deer ribs roasted on a spit before the open fire tasted perhaps a wee bit better than it would have had it just come from an oven. But haywire and pliers one must have somewhere in his kit if he wished to survive very long. With just a little haywire you could reset a fractured wagon reach, mend a shattered axe handle, brace an ailing pack saddle, make yourself a fish hook. Or if too much hard luck lay athwart the trail and misfortune had no end, you could as a last resort snip off a few feet of good pliable haywire, fix it with a noose and then go hang yourself from the sturdy limb of some nearby tree.

"Haywire," I repeated. "Where did we stow that haywire?"

"It's here, under the seat." Lillian handed me the wire.

Then: "Pliers," I sang out. "Now where did we put those pliers?"

"They're in your pocket, of course," Lillian laughed.

So I took the haywire and for the next ten minutes worked steadily and carefully on the wagon wheel. When at last satisfied that I'd done all that wire could do, I squinted toward the sun and said, "There's a lake up ahead a couple of miles and we'll camp there overnight. We can take the wheel off the hub there and give it an all-night soaking. That'll swell the wood and tighten it against the tire, and the wheel will be just like new until it dries out again."

The lake was over a mile long. At its north end where visible water halted and grassy marsh took over, a long sandy peninsula thrust out above the water. Pointing to the ridge with the whip, I told Lillian, "We'll make camp out on that point where there'll be nothing to break the wind. The mosquitoes will start coming out of the swamp in their millions as soon as the sun goes down, but the wind will keep them away from camp if we pitch our tent on the peninsula. If the wind drops we'll have to build a smudge, and keep the smoke rolling all night, or we won't be getting much sleep."

May had been cold and backward, and the pea vines and vetches of the timbered country were tardy in making growth. We had planned to start work on our cabin in mid-May so as to have it at least partially habitable by early June, when the stagnant waters of pond and creek would be hatching mosquitoes in their millions. However, a cold and unseasonable spring had delayed us and kept us cooling our heels at Riske Creek, looking for a warm-up in the weather that would ensure us plenty of green feed back in the woods for our horses.

As May gave way to June, the mood of the weather changed too. The nip of frost left the night, and the air became sticky and sultry. The mossy floor of the forest was still moist with winter's spent snows, and pea vines and vetches, wild columbines, fireweed and swamp lilies now clawed energetically up through the warming topsoil toward a sun that had been denied them so long.

Plants were not the only things to come up from the moss. This was the hour of the mosquito and deer fly, and for the next two months anyway, whenever human or other foot left an imprint in the wilderness, legions of bloodthirsty insects would question its right to be there. Yet somehow we must learn to get along with them if we were to become a part of that wilderness ourselves.

Out on the peninsula, the breeze coming in off the lake would push the mosquitoes back whenever they ventured away from the marsh. So on reaching the end of the lake, I pulled the harness from the horses, hobbled them and turned them loose to graze. Then I took the tent from the wagon, pitched it by the side of the wagon and, while Lillian cooked supper, jacked the wagon up, removed the ailing wheel and rolled it out in the lake, where it settled from sight.

The wagon bore all our worldly possessions, and though heavily over-loaded, the lot might have fetched only some two or three hundred dollars if one had to turn them in for cash. There were food, blankets and tents, pots and pans, axes and adzes, hammers and horseshoes, saws and nails, guns and traps, cookstove and heater; these and a score of other assorted items that had been gathered together over a period of two years completely filled the wagon box. Most of the tools were secondhand, but there on the headwaters of Meldrum Creek, twenty-five miles north of the nearest store, over seventy from the nearest railroad, they had a value that could hardly be computed in terms of dollars and cents. The .303 rifle in its buckskin scabbard was our passport to a certain meat supply when I was able to find time to hunt. The axes and adzes, nails and saws were essential tools when we began building the home.

Where we were headed there would be no neighbours to run to for loan of things—at least, not unless we wanted to undertake a fifty-mile round trip by saddle horse or wagon. And there was little money to replace any of the precious tools should they be broken or lost. Their purchase in the first place had about sapped us of cash. In fact, the pocketbook I had entrusted to Lillian for safekeeping now contained but thirty dollars and some odd cents, and neither of us quite knew how long that skimpy sum would have to last before more cash came our way.

We discussed this matter of finance as the wagon wheels jolted over the rocks and roots, each jolt taking us a little farther from Riske Creek, a little closer to journey's end.

"Discounting sickness or something like that," I remarked to Lillian, "that money should take care of us until fall, for there'll not be much use for money back where we're going. By the first of November we'll have a cabin and barn built, and hay of sorts stacked as winter feed for the horses. I guess the traps should take care of us then."

Lillian shifted position on the seat. She braced her left foot against the end-gate of the box. "My hip is beginning to ache a bit," she said. Then after a moment of thought: "I'm sure we'll get by, Eric." After a bit she went on, "It's likely to be quite some time before there's anything but coyotes to trap."

"Three or four years, maybe."

For if the activities of yesterday's fur trade had filched the very last beaver from the watershed—and the extermination of the beavers resulted in similar extinction of so many other fur-bearers—the coyotes had managed to survive. Trap and snare, rifle and hound dog—all had been employed by both white man and Indian in the effort to rid the coyote of his gray, silky coat. That is, since the fur trade found profitable use for his fur. There was a day when finer furs were so plentiful that the coyotes were only worth two dollars' bounty money that the government paid on their scalps. But today a prime silky coyote could be bartered at any trading post for eight or ten dollars' worth of groceries or other goods. Despite the fact that the hand of every trapper and settler in the country was raised against them, the coyotes somehow managed to hold their own.

Some forty or fifty assorted traps were in the wagon box, together with a hundred rounds of ammunition for the rifle. By tailing October the coyotes would lose their summer shagginess and their pelts would become prime. With November's first snowfall I could set and bait the traps, but not until then had we any hope of replenishing the lean contents of the pocketbook.

The water buckets filled, and wood cut and stacked alongside the fire, I sprawled on the ground, head on the wagon tongue, and watched Lillian make bannock (baking powder bread) and place it in pans before the fire. From somewhere on the lake a loon's dismal cry sang a song of loneliness. Perhaps according to some reckoning it might have been lonely out there on the point, a good many miles from anywhere and getting farther away all the time. But not according to mine. Resting there, listening to the jangle of the horse bells, and watching Lillian get the meal ready, I was contented, at peace with myself. Tomorrow we'd come to the headwaters of the creek, cross it and continue downstream a bit. By late afternoon we'd be home, and if for a week or two that home was a ten-by-twelve-foot tent stretched in the shade of the trees, it would be home just the same. And I'd have Lillian and Veasy, and a hundred and fifty thousand acres of wilderness, and as long as the three of us were together to share that wilderness, loneliness would never upset us. I was quite sure of that.

The sun was astir when I kindled a fire in the morning. A strong wind was still blowing in off the lake, keeping the mosquitoes out of camp. I waded out into the water and fished out the wheel. The soaking had swelled the felloe and it was again snug and tight against the spoke and tire of the wheel.

By the time I had wrangled the horses and harnessed the team, Lillian sang out, "Breakfast." Now the wind was dying, allowing the mosquitoes to move in on us from the marsh. And move in they did, in vicious humming clouds, forcing us to eat and drink with one hand as we fought them away with the other. For both us and the horses, there were only two possible avenues of escape: a huge smudge that would cover the peninsula with smoke, or a quick getaway from the lake. We chose the latter.

By ten o'clock we reached the headwaters of the creek, yet despite the fact that only some six or seven weeks ago there had still been snow in the forest, now only a thin trickle of water moved along the channel, barely enough to wet the tires of the wagon wheels as they bumped to the other side. "The whole creek will be dry in another couple of weeks unless it rains," I predicted to Lillian.

Beyond the crossing was a stretch of timber that had scarcely a mature tree still with sap in it. Here the fires of other years had destroyed almost all standing growth, leaving a debris of windfalls behind them. There had been no recent travel over the track, at least not since the previous March when cattle and sleighs had moved out from the hay meadows. Then, two or more feet of packed snow covered the blowdowns, and cattle and sleighs were able to get over them, hardly knowing they were there. But now every one had to be axed out before the wagon could get through, so building a smudge alongside the wagon, I unhitched the horses, leaving Lillian there to replenish the smudge from time to time while I hacked a right-of-way through the windfalls.

Their wood was dry and hard; a stifling noonday heat hung over the forest, and when I paused for wind and rest, every square inch of my exposed skin was quickly preempted by a half-dozen mosquitoes. I chopped steadily away at the windfalls, grumbling to myself about the fires that were responsible for their being there, grumbling at the mosquitoes, and almost regretting the impulse that had brought us back into this sullen, inhospitable wilderness to begin with. Yet two hours later, when I got back to the wagon, mosquitoes and windfalls were forgotten. And there was a whistle on my lips as I tossed Veasy up into the wagon box.

It was late afternoon when I braked the wagon to a stop at the edge of the aspen- and willow-clad flat that was to be the site of our future home. At that time in the Chilcotin one could still squat on a few acres of ground, throw up a cabin, plow up a garden patch and worry about legal title to the land at some convenient future date. Even if not recognized by any government department, squatters' rights were lawful rights in the eyes of all other residents of the country. Perched there on the wagon seat, flicking an eye over the half-dozen acres of ground before me, I now considered every square inch of it ours as if title deed were signed, sealed and delivered there in my hip pocket.

Ours to clear of its brush, to plow and seed down its soil. Ours to build a home upon, just as quickly as logs could be cut and snaked in out of the woods. It was ours from the moment the wheels of the wagon ceased turning, to have and to hold, today and tomorrow, down through the years, forever and ever, amen.

The Colliers' old wagon and the ten-by-twelve-foot tent that was their home until they finished building their cabin.

I jumped down from the wagon seat, fighting mosquitoes with one hand, trying to unhitch the stomping team with the other. "We're not getting much of a welcome, are we?" I said tartly to Lillian.

But she was far too busy to pay any attention to complaints from me. She was scurrying around like some busy squirrel, gathering punky chunks of wood for the smudge that was now a dire necessity.

Now when Lillian sits down at the kitchen table each spring to make out the list of groceries and other items needed to run us another year, the list always includes insect repellents of almost every brand and description. But at that moment when we perhaps needed them most, when we lacked even window or door to shut in self-defence, we had nothing. The only agent at hand with which we could battle the mosquitoes was the choking, eye-watering clouds of smoke that spewed up from the smudge. It is a debatable matter which was the lesser of the two evils, the mosquitoes or the smoke.

The third member of the family had his own answer to that question. Though Lillian might plump Veasy down on the windward side of the smudge, keeping him there was another matter altogether. As soon as her back was turned, he crawled away from the smudge into the hum of the mosquitoes. Since Lillian had to help with the unpacking of the wagon, give a hand with the stretching of the tent and begin getting supper, all at the same time, she sensibly decided that, in this moment anyway, the boy was master of his own destiny. If he preferred the mosquitoes to the smoke, that was the way he could have it.

Usually in interior British Columbia there is a brief period in the night when the mosquitoes retire into the moss and grasses, perhaps to rest and conserve their strength for renewed attacks at dawn. But every rule has its exception, as was the case now. Long after the campfire was a skeleton of graying coals, and we had retired to the tent and tied down its flaps in the foolish hope that somehow the tent would keep the enemy without, we lay wide awake, listening to the drone of their wings as they beat against the canvas. The hum of mosquitoes is almost as bad as their bite, and anyway, enough did manage to get inside that, despite the stickiness of the night, we were compelled to cover our heads and hands with blankets.

It was a night of little sleep. While Lillian lay awake trying to keep the covers over Veasy, I was wide awake with another serious problem. I could hear the harsh nervous jangling of horses' bells.

"The horses," I suddenly rapped out, sitting bolt upright. "The mosquitoes are driving them crazy."

I had hobbled all five of the horses and turned them loose to graze, not bothering to keep a wrangle horse on picket rope. Now I could hear the ring of their bells from somewhere off in the timber, and it wasn't the measured tingling that comes from the bells of horses contentedly grazing, but a brazen jarring ring that tells of horses steadily on the move.

"If they ever get started back on the wagon tracks ..." I muttered uneasily, turning on the flashlight and looking at Lillian. And she knew enough about horses to understand what was pricking me. Once they lined out on those wagon tracks, by daylight they'd be miles away, and it might take two days or more to track them down and bring them back.

That thought brought me out of the blankets. "I'd better go after them before it's too late and tie them up until it gets light."

Lillian was up too. "I might as well be outside too, building a smudge, as here trying to sleep." And she began dressing.

I shook my head. "Leave the smudge to me. They'll eat you alive out there." And I untied the flaps of the tent.

It still lacked a couple of hours of dawn and the tailing night was humid and pitch-black. At the opening of the flaps the drone of mosquitoes became a mounting ceaseless buzz.

The horse bells were fainter now. Ten or fifteen minutes ago they'd sounded from off in the west, but now they were only a tinkle, coming out of the south. "They've hit the wagon tracks!" I exclaimed.

Any horse accustomed to hobbles, as were ours, can clip along at a steady four miles an hour if determined to keep travelling. I judged from the sound of the bells that ours were already two miles south of camp.

Lillian picked up the flashlight. "You'd better take this and go after them, and I'll build the smudge."

I said, "I don't need the light. Not as badly as you'll need it hunting up stuff for the smudge." And taking the halters from the wagon, I slipped off into the darkness.

A horned owl hooted from the spruces across the creek. Seconds later, and from the same quarter, a snowshoe rabbit screamed. The drama being played there among the spruces was one without end, one that had gone on and on in the wilderness ever since there was a wilderness. At times, perhaps between sunup and sundown, there might be a truce of sorts, but it was one forever broken. Whoo-hoo-whoo-hoo! Not from the spruces this time, but from the jack pines back of the tent. Out of the nigrous overhead came the rustle of wings moving toward the creek. I paused a moment, listening to the screeching of two owls squabbling over a single kill. Then I quickly forgot about the owls and the fate of the snowshoe rabbit and thought of my own problems.

The east was graying when I got back with the horses. I hitched them to cottonwoods on the windward side of the smudge, then squatted on a log beside Lillian. Side by side we sat there in the smoke, with not a thing to say to each other, just watching the gray give way to a delicate rosebud pink. Pink became gold and sunlight suddenly flooded the treetops. The air became very still and the smoke plumed straight up. Now the mosquitoes were able to press home their attacks.

Then, with a faint trace of bitterness and half seriously, I broke the silence. "You know, Lillian, I have a strange feeling that maybe God doesn't want us here."

Lillian turned on the log. She looked steadily at me, and with all the depth that this wife of mine has, and meaning every word, said quietly, "Maybe He's just testing us, and seeing if we're worthy enough to stay."

But we weathered that first night of the mosquitoes as we have since weathered so many tribulations that have worried away at us while we tried to earn ourselves some sort of a living on the hundred and fifty thousand acres of wilderness that has been home to us for so long. Looking back, we are both in full agreement that there were moments during those tormenting hours of that very first night when we lay wide awake, silently debating a common thought: surely there were easier ways of making a living than by attempting this. But with the campfire blazing, and the gold of the hoisting sun swabbing the forest with colour, we both took a deep breath. Here we were and here we would stay. And here, if sweat and toil could do it, we'd give back to the land some of the wildlife and other natural wealth that it had when Lala was a child.

Chapter 4

"Timber!" Lillian yelled, but the stubborn tree wouldn't fall.

One had to be sort of careful about how he felled the trees. If you dropped them across a shallow gully, they broke in two, and that was one you lost. And we couldn't afford to lose any. Or if you didn't undercut them just so, they went back on you and then the saw pinched and you couldn't get it out. Or if there was no sign of a lean to them, and they were straight up and down like a plumb bob, you could saw clean through them and still they wouldn't go down.

As was the case now with the one we'd been working on. Back cut had met undercut but still the tree was upright. And Lillian stood off a few feet from the stump, puffing a little and gawking up at its top, wondering how it still stood there. And Veasy was several such tree lengths away, well clear of danger, also gawking at the tree that wouldn't go down. I had a ten-foot pry pole braced against the tree and was heaving and grunting, all the time watching the back cut, hoping it would open up a little so I could get the saw free.

The pry pole slipped off the bark, and I almost went flat on my face. Recovering, I got the end of the pole under a limb higher up the tree, and taking a deep breath I pushed with all that was in me.

"Timber!" Lillian yelled again. And I saw that at last the cut was

34

opening, and I jerked the saw out and watched the tree crash to earth right where we wanted it to be.

Lillian came over and squatted down on the tree, and rubbing a pitchy hand across her forehead asked, "How many more do we need?"

I laid the six-foot crosscut saw on the ground and sat down beside her. "According to my count, that one makes us forty-five." Then I scratched my head and went on, "Figuring on twelve for each wall, and the two ridge logs, fifty should do the trick. They're good logs too, straight as an arrow, sound as a silver dollar, and hold their size, and don't taper off at the tops as do the logs in some cabins I've seen."

"My, but I'll be glad when the last one is felled," breathed Lillian.

"So will I," I grinned. "Then maybe you'll throw those old overalls away and get into a skirt again. Overalls were made for men, not women. Didn't you know that?"

She pouted. "Not until the logs are up, and a roof above them, and at least one window in, will I discard the overalls and think about skirt and blouse again." Then she laughed outright. "I sure must look a sight!"

"Apart from that pitch all over your forehead and the smears on your cheeks and chin where you squashed a mosquito, you don't look too bad at all. In fact," I assured her, "pitch or no pitch, mosquito or no mosquito, you look okay to me."

"Pitch!" Lillian grimaced. "I sure don't like that pitch. It's all over the saw and axe handle too. You can't squat down on a log a minute to rest without getting that pitch all over yourself." She suddenly jumped up, glanced around and cried, "Veasy! Now where's that boy hidden himself?"

"He's all right." I'd been keeping an eye on Veasy. "He's over there behind that rotten windfall. Chased a squirrel down its hole and is trying to make the hole big enough to crawl down after it. That should keep him out of mischief for a while."

If I'd had my way about things, the logs for the cabin would have been felled with the axe, not the heavy crosscut saw. The saw was a two-man affair, at least where felling trees with it was concerned. Its makers never intended that it would be used unless there were two men pulling and pushing on its handles. Certainly no woman, and especially one that weighed only around a hundred and fifteen pounds fully clothed, was expected to have any part in its use. But where Lillian was concerned I didn't always have my own way about things, and she very often had hers.

We weren't lacking in material for the building of a home, for the forest held almost everything that was needed. It was simply a case of going into it and helping ourselves to what was there. I judged that I could make far better time chopping the trees down with the axe than by cutting them alone with the crosscut. But Lillian said, "Use the saw, and I'm going to help too. It will be quicker for the two of us to saw them down together," was the stubborn logic she used.

"Of course it would," I agreed. "But helping to fell trees with a six-foot crosscut is no job for a woman."

"Why isn't it?"

"Well, pulling on the saw handles wouldn't do your back any good, would it?"

She said flatly, "I want a roof over my head and the quicker the better."

So together we felled the trees, and sawed them into the proper lengths. And after I had snaked them out of the woods with the team and piled them on the flat, we shucked them of their bark.

Veasy—the name is a family one on my side—was determined that he too should assist in the peeling of the logs, so we outfitted him with a dull butcher knife that would hardly cut grease and told him go to it. He scraped and peeled away with vigour and ambition for a minute or two, then, wearying of it all, walked over to an anthill and began worrying its occupants with a stick.

Indifferent to all else but getting the cabin up as quickly as possible, our only clock was the sun. We began work shortly after it rose and didn't lay our tools down again until after it was gone. We heaved and we panted and sweated, and laid the heavy green timbers on top of each other, notching each snugly into place so that it rested tightly against the one below it.

That first cabin was perhaps a crude sort of a dwelling as some modern homes go, but after the dust and the smoke of the tent, and everlasting insults from the mosquitoes, it was good enough for us. Six days after we began cutting the logs, its four walls stood white and pitchy to the sun. Now came the laying of the ridge logs and roofing. That done, I hauled dirt in the wagon and spread an eight-inch layer of it over the split timbers of the roof, thus ensuring the cabin a maximum of coolness in summer, plus equal warmth in winter. While Lillian cut and peeled slim straight pine poles, I nailed them between the logs. Together we sawed out the gaps for two windows and a door, fitted these in, cemented the cracks with mud and stepped back, surveying our creation with pride. All of ten days had gone by since the first night of the mosquitoes, and now we had a home to live in. It was eighteen feet wide by twenty-four long, and even though its floor was the packed earth, now, when we closed the door and windows, we were shut away from the attention of the insects. No matter how sharp might be the lash of the winter storm outside, within these four stout walls all would be protected and warm.

"Someday," I promised, "when there's a bit more money in the kitty, I'll haul lumber in from Riske Creek and put down a proper floor." But "someday" was a few miles off yet.

The cabin built and moved into, another necessary chore stared us in the eye before we could enjoy any real peace of mind; we had to build some sort of fence where we could hold the horses and stop them from wandering off. The horses had been a problem since the very first day. They were born and bred to the open range country to the south, and seemed to have little liking for this timbered country with its mosquitoes, deer flies and, far greater torment, the black bulldog flies, almost as big as hornets and which, according to competent authority on the subject, got away with two ounces of flesh every time one settled on the skin.

Since their first attempt at a getaway, the horses had tried to quit the country on two other occasions. At their second attempt, I finally hauled up to them seven miles south of the cabin, but then they had followed the track out to Riske Creek, and I didn't have too much trouble in locating them. But at their last bid for desertion they got nigh clean out of the country before, almost bankrupt of wind and limb myself, I finally ran them to earth.

That morning at daybreak, there wasn't a sound from the bells. It had become ritual with me, even before starting a fire, to step out of the cabin at daybreak and locate the whereabouts of the horses from the bells. But this morning I could hear nothing but the pert chatter of squirrels, or the less frequent cry of an osprey circling high above Meldrum Lake, a telescopic eye wide awake and watching for movement of squawfish in the water below.

Going back into the cabin, I kindled a fire, put the coffeepot on the stove and told Lillian, who was just rubbing the sleep from her eyes, "They've hit the trail again. But they can't have gone very far. I'll light out now and maybe be back with them by the time coffee is brewed."

I followed the wagon track southward, first at a fast walk, then at a faster jogtrot. Three halters were wound around my waist, and my eyes were glued to the ground, looking for a horse track. Three miles from the cabin it slowly and uncomfortably dawned on me that this time they hadn't headed back down the track, but instead must have started out in another direction altogether. "But what direction?" A chipmunk, tailed back on a rock three feet away, cheeks cupped meditatively in its paws, glanced quickly toward me, but had nothing to say at all.

I jogtrotted all the way back to the cabin, shaking my head as Lillian came to the door, eyes firing a question. "They're gone." And dully I added, "We're afoot."

Lillian always looked on the brighter side of life. "They must be somewhere close by or you'd have surely seen their tracks down the road." She stepped outside and stood there, listening. "Maybe they're only a little ways off, standing still. If we both listen real hard we'll maybe hear the bells."

So I listened real hard, and Lillian listened real hard, and sensing that something important was afoot, Veasy came out of the cabin, stark naked, for Lillian hadn't yet dressed him, and listened real hard too. But we couldn't hear the bells.

Carelessly, trying to conceal my concern, I said, "Horses can't fly. Wherever they've gone, they've left tracks behind them." The smell of the coffee on the stove made me aware of the fact that I was hungry. "Make us a batch of hotcakes, about two dozen of them. And fix half a dozen rashers of bacon too. I'm that hungry I guess I could eat a parboiled pack rat."

Breakfast over with, I again cinched the halters around my waist and struck off into the woods to make a wide circle of the whole area within a mile's radius of the cabin. I'd almost completed the circle before finding the tracks. They were, I judged, made quite some time before daylight. The horses were travelling one behind the other, as horses usually will when they are heading for faraway places. Now that I had the tracks to guide me I had to slacken pace and stick to them like a leech. If ever I lost those tracks I might have to cast about for an hour or longer before finding them again.

They were lining due east, through thick lodgepole pine, and the fact that if they kept travelling thus they'd eventually come up against the barrier of the Fraser River gave me no comfort at all. To anything with wings, the river was at least forty miles away, half as far again to anything without them.

Ahead of me now was a fringe of cottonwood surrounding a pool of water. I paused, listening, hoping that maybe the horses had taken time out to drink at the puddle, and then gone to grazing. But there wasn't a horse bell within miles of me, at least none that I could hear. There was only the shiver of cottonwood leaves, and the rustling of the leaves kept telling me, "You're afoot, you and the woman and child you left alone at your cabin. The horses have more sense than you. They want no part of this country."

The horses had passed within fifty yards of the water but hadn't gone down to it to drink. That merely confirmed what I already suspected was fact: they'd pulled out sometime in the night, and maybe passed the water before dawn, and their bellies were full, and they weren't thirsty, and only the Almighty knew where they were at right this very minute, and He wasn't telling me.

I quit the tracks, plunged through the cottonwoods and made a full circle of the lake, eyes riveted on its alkaline shoreline. If there were no horse tracks in the mud, there were others, left by a cloven hoof. First I thought that a half-dozen deer had been down at the pond watering, and within the last hour too. But no, the tracks had been made by a single deer, a buck, too, I guessed, maybe a three- or four-year-old. Maybe the buck was ranging in the surrounding woods and twice daily, morning and evening, he came down to the water to drink. I frowned, wondering if I would ever be able to find the puddle again. Well, I could at least try, so filing the buck tracks away in my mind for future reference, I struck up into the timber and again latched onto the horse tracks.

About a mile east of the water they veered slightly southwest, then a mile farther on they struck due south. Now I knew that they had set their minds upon getting back to the open range, and that eventually, unless I caught up to them, they'd reach it.

In the lodgepole pine, where the timber grass was lush, I was able to follow along at a fast walk, making perhaps three miles an hour. The crushed stems of grass were all the tracks I needed. But through scrub patches of aspen, or thickets of second-growth pine, where the soil was sandy and barren, I had difficulty seeing a track at all. Here my pace slackened, for I dared not lose those tracks.

How many miles now was I from the cabin? A hard question to answer, but a squint at the sun, now well over in the west, told me perhaps all of a dozen. And what of Lillian and Veasy? Well, Veasy was far too young to worry about truant horses and whether or not his father would get turned around in the woods and become hopelessly lost hunting them. But with Lillian it was different. Now there was a girl who understood how tricky the everlasting forest can sometimes

40

be. She knew how easy it is, when the sun goes down and night changes everything, for a body to get off course and turned around, and perhaps start travelling in circles, not knowing east from west, north from south, and not caring either. When one is badly turned around in the deep woods, and getting more so all the time, it is only a short step from cool sanity to a state of feverish panic. And a madness of sorts besets you, and now running, now tripping over the windfalls and falling headlong to the ground, you go on and on, indifferent to direction, until finally physical and mental exhaustion is complete, and you lack either will or strength to go a step farther.

Lillian was aware of all such things as these, and at sundown she'd be standing at the cabin door, very still, listening real hard for the sound of the horse bells coming, or my step snapping a twig or knocking on a windfall. And worry of it all would linger in her eyes for many a day to come.

I climbed a rock-studded hogback and dropped down the other side, freezing suddenly in my tracks as a large, dark form took shape in a clump of spruces fifty yards beyond. One of the work horses was a dark brown, almost black, in fact, and the thing there in the spruces too was dark, and stood as high as any horse of ours.

"There they are," I cried aloud in relief. But it wasn't a horse at all; it was only an old cow moose without a calf at her heels. The cow stood there for all of ten seconds, then her head turned away from me and her ears dropped, and she took off through the spruces, with only the occasional rattle of hoof against windfall to tell me where she was going.

The sun was close to setting when at last I heard the faraway ring of the bells. I stopped, listening to make sure that the woods weren't fooling me, that instead of horse bells it was only the "belling" of some flying squirrel. The shrill bark of a flying squirrel sometimes sounds like the ring of a distant bell.

Satisfied that it was the horse bells, I broke into a run. The horses were out on a bit of meadow, grazing, and while they threw up their heads at my approach, they quickly lowered them again when they saw who it was. One of the horses had broken its hobble straps, and no doubt he was the leader who'd taken the others so far away. Unbuckling all the hobbles and strapping the lot to the neck of one horse, I caught three of the others and tied two of them, head to tail, to the tail of the one I was going to ride. Then, jumping on it bareback, I shot a glance at what was left of the sun, which was really nothing but an aftermath. It would be dark in another hour, so I started off at a sharp trot, aiming northwest, figuring that if I held that course I would eventually come to the creek.

It was inky dark when I got back to the cabin. Veasy had been in bed for three or more hours, but Lillian stood outside, a few yards from the door, and as I slid from the back of the horse, almost at her feet, I heard her murmur, "Thank God you're back."

"You weren't worrying, were you?" I scoffed, giving her a hug and a kiss. For if there are moments when such is warranted between any man and woman, this was surely one.

"A little," she confessed.

"There was nothing to worry about. I was just getting acquainted with some of these woods. Found a water hole too." Then, in a more serious tone, I promised, "Come hell or high water we'll start on a fence in the morning."

The matter of a horse pasture was soon solved. Two hundred yards downstream from the cabin, the creek dumped into a two-hundred-acre lake. The ever-present decayed beaver dam stood at the mouth of the lake, and the creek crept through the dam to meet yet another lake a few hundred yards farther on. This lake, Meldrum by name, lies north to south, and a half-mile from where the creek tips into it makes a decided bulge eastward. By erecting a pole fence from the lake by the cabin across country to this bulge in Meldrum, we shut in a hundred and fifty acres of good horse pasture. Once again it was a case of helping ourselves to what we needed, unruffled by any thought about our lawful rights in doing so. Now, the fence has been there for twenty-seven years, and in summer the horses we now have still pasture within it.

With the fence up we were able to take the hobbles from the horses and

42

turn them loose, and go to sleep at night without having nasty dreams over where they might be in the morning.

～

If eaten once a day, say for breakfast, with an egg or two to keep it company on the plate, a lean rasher of bacon is one product of the pig very easily digested. But if bacon, fried, boiled, baked or otherwise, is on one's plate three times a day, you soon lose all respect for a pig. For over two weeks there had been no other meat but bacon for Lillian to cook. Not even a ruffed grouse or snowshoe rabbit. Work had claimed almost every minute of our time and there had been none left over for hunting. But now we had a home, and the horses had a pasture. And I was tired of bacon, and Lillian was tired of bacon, and even Veasy pushed the rasher aside when it was put on his plate.

Having made up my mind to do something about the situation, I said to Lillian, "You'd like a roast of real meat, wouldn't you?"

Lillian aimed a glance at a half slab of bacon sitting on a shelf, wrinkled her nose and said, "Anything but bacon."

"How about a deer?"

"I'd sure like to smell a deer steak frying in a good hot pan. We could keep one quarter fresh and salt the rest down in my crocks. That is, if we had the deer."

"I know where to find tracks," I confided, remembering the watering hole in the lodgepole pine.

Lillian wasn't too impressed. "I can't fry tracks."

"Maybe I can't find that puddle again, but I'm sure going to try," I said after telling her of the water hole. "I'll go out on one of the horses this evening, and if I can locate the place again I'll squat down in the cottonwoods and maybe shoot us a deer."

"Can I come too?"

I let on I was thinking that over, though all the time I wanted her to go with me. "I guess so. But you'll have to sit mighty still."

She pouted. "I can sit just as quiet as you. Quieter perhaps, because

43

you can't sit down for the wink of a cat's eye without starting to fidget."

"Can when I'm hunting." Then, looking toward the other member of the family, I asked, "But how about Veasy?"

"Good a time as any for him to learn," she said practically.

We left the cabin at five in the afternoon, I on my chestnut gelding and Lillian on one of the work horses. Behind her on the horse's rump rode Veasy, arms around her waist, feet stirruped in the knotted saddle strings. Every once in a while his legs swung forward and he kicked the horse in the belly and chortled, "Giddup!"

"Shush!" admonished Lillian. "You'll scare all the deer."

There had been no rain to obliterate the horse tracks that I'd followed five days ago, and I had no trouble finding my way back to the watering hole. I tied the horses to a couple of pines a hundred yards from the water, then. slipping five shells into the magazine of the rifle, I inched cautiously toward the puddle, Lillian, holding Veasy firmly by the hand, inching along behind me.

A drake teal had the puddle all to itself. Maybe the hen bird wasn't far away, sitting on her eggs. I sat down behind a bush, and Lillian dropped alongside me. The teal paddled off to the opposite shore, stretched its wings and then, inquisitively and in half-circles, began swimming toward us. It came almost to water's edge, and was so close to us that Veasy struggled to free himself from Lillian's iron grip to run into the water and catch it.

"Keep still," Lillian warned. "Daddy's going to shoot a deer."

From somewhere off in the woods a ruffed grouse started to drum. It was late in the season for grouse to be drumming, for nearly all the hen birds were sitting now. But the cock bird had probably been there on the same log, morning and evening since the snow went off, drumming away for a hen bird to come along and accept him for a mate.

"Sit still." Lillian was having her troubles with Veasy, for where he was concerned there was neither work nor play to sitting behind a willow bush watching the sun go down. Far more fun to be tearing an anthill down or romping in the water trying to catch a teal.

We'd been there for over an hour when the buck finally came. Lillian heard it seconds before I saw it. She suddenly stiffened and whispered, "I heard a stick crack."

With scarce a movement I picked up the rifle and slid a shell into the breech. "Whereabouts?"

She gestured across the pond. "Somewhere over there."

The buck stepped mincingly away from the cottonwoods, out into the water. The gun eased into my shoulder. But I didn't touch off the trigger, not while he was knee-deep in water. Having satisfied his thirst the buck stood there, staring off into space and thinking about things buck deer usually think about when they're standing out in the water. It seemed a pity to shoot such a harmless and graceful fellow as he, but if I didn't shoot him, who knows, maybe tomorrow night a timber wolf or coyote might snuff out his life. And we needed the meat mortal bad.

I shot him through the base of the skull as he turned away from the water to go back into the woods. And Lillian helped me skin back the hide from his belly and gut him. Then, putting liver, kidneys and heart in a clean flour sack, we heaved the carcass onto my saddle, lashed it down and backtracked to the cabin.

By the time the deer was skinned out and quartered, and the meat hung in the spruce behind the cabin to cool off, Lillian had to light the coal-oil lamp to see to undress Veasy and tuck him away in his bed. Within seconds the child was fast asleep, maybe dreaming of buck deer treading the game paths, or of willow grouse drumming on their logs.

Then Lillian made a pot of coffee and we sat together at the table, slowly sipping it down. "Tomorrow," she said, "I'll salt three of the quarters down in my crocks." She fixed a thoughtful eye on me. "Then what?"

"The trapline," I promptly replied. "Day after tomorrow we'll load a camp outfit on a pack horse and strike out through the woods and find out just what that one hundred and fifty thousand acres of creek, muskeg and forest contains in the way of worldly wealth."

Chapter 5

"They don't smell very nice, do they?" said Lillian of the marshes, when the wind carried their stench into camp.

I wasn't so choosey about words. Wrinkling my nose, I scowled, "They stink like hell."

The whole watershed, at least what we had so far seen of it, stank of aquatic vegetation in various stages of death and decomposition, of mud and, here and there, of the putrid flesh of cattle that had bogged down and perished in the muck while trying to slake their thirst at a puddle of slimy water that was beyond possible reach. Though not too heavily grazed as yet, a few cattle wandered back from the open range, cropping the pea vines and vetches that grew lush in the forests about the creek.

And that, I figured, was how such a deplorable state of affairs would continue unless every stinking decadent acre of marshland was again inundated by sweet, cool water.

"How in the devil do we go about reflooding all these marshes, filling up the lakes?" I had acquired the habit of asking Lillian's advice on a great many things, and often she had it to give. But this time she only shook her head and said, "I don't know."

For the last twenty minutes Lillian's attention had been given to her needle and thread, and the job of repairing Veasy's shoes. The boy was forever getting his feet wet, what with paddling in the lakes or the shallow water of the creek. The shoes weren't built to take that sort of treatment, and now their stitching was rotting, the soles parting company from the uppers. After a little while she replaced needle and thread in her holdall and, glancing disapprovingly at the footwear, commented, "I'll have to try my hand at tanning the deer hide and make him some moccasins."

Skirt had again given way to overalls. Slacks, Lillian called them, but to me overalls are overalls by no other name. Overalls—or slacks—didn't suit Lillian; she looked far more feminine in a skirt as of course she properly should. But still, I had to admit that skirts aren't very handy to ride in, or comfortable either, perhaps, so whenever she went places on horseback I figured yes, she could wear the overalls—or slacks—if she wished.

For five days we'd been wandering like gypsies, merely to ascertain what assets we possessed on our wilderness trapline. The game trails were our only paths, the horses our only mode of transport, and the tent our only roof. Every game trail we came to presented a challenge of sorts, since we didn't have the faintest idea where it came from or where it went. So we'd turn and follow it, and maybe after a while emerge at some pothole meadow or small lake. And if the day was about spent, we'd stake the horses in the swamp grass and fix a camp for the night. Or if the sun said it was only two or three o'clock, we'd file the meadow or lake away in our minds and then cast about like a hound dog for scent, for another trail to explore. There was no lack of game trails.

But we'd covered a lot of ground in the last four days and seen a lot of country that not too many whites had seen. And at first sight nothing that we saw seemed to offer much promise of better things to come. "We're not going to get rich in a hurry anyway," I confided to Lillian.

There were the remnants of two score beaver dams without any beavers. There were several hundred acres—or was it several thousand?—of stinking, semidry marshland, which, if giving vague promise of a muskrat left here and there, lacked the water necessary for the production of muskrats in numbers that warranted their trapping. And we had an assortment of landlocked lakes (there had been beavers in them too once upon a time) woefully in need of water with which to raise their levels to their original banks. This then, apart from the limitless forest itself, was all that we had on which to build some measure of security and prosperity. If there have been less modest starts in life, I want no part of them.

If the marshes and lakes had their water back, there'd soon be an increase in muskrats and other fur-bearers. If we both held to the conviction that some day we were going to bring beavers back to Meldrum Creek, neither of us had the least idea how this was to be done. You don't go to an auction sale and purchase live beavers as you would a horse or a cow. And as far as we knew there wasn't a single beaver left anywhere in the Chilcotin, and mighty few in all of British Columbia, for that matter. But for the moment we shoved the matter of beavers aside and gave our immediate thoughts to the problem of how we ourselves might go about the reflooding of at least one or two of the marshes through which the creek pursued its unambitious way.

For provision and maintenance of habitat is the only real key to the increase and perpetuation of any wildlife resource. If the environment is provided, and if treated to the most rudimentary principles of conservation, nature can be relied upon to take over from there.

In 1931 the pelt of a muskrat was worth from eighty cents to a dollar. Hundreds of muskrats could be raised on the marshes once they had their water back, but in their present arid state they were of no economic value to us or anyone else.

One species of wildlife must nourish and perpetuate itself by preying upon another. If the marshes of Meldrum Creek were again inundated, the aquatic seeds and tubers that were still rooted in their soil would provide food for muskrats, waterfowl and fish. To prey upon these would come the mink, the otter and other carnivorous fur-bearers. If the pelt of the lowly muskrat was worth but eighty cents, that of the mink was worth from fifteen to twenty dollars. It was simply a matter of creating a habitat for the one so that there would be food for the other. Putting theory into practice was not quite so simple.

The solution to it all glared us in the face. With the beaver dams, there lay the answer. At the mouth of every tract of marsh, large or small, was a beaver dam. In many of the landlocked lakes, beaver lodges, long disused, could still be seen in the water. Though no beavers had been in Meldrum Creek for a half-century or more, the remnants of their dams and lodges remained to mark the once-upon-a-time presence of a rodent weighing about sixty pounds at full maturity, whose appetite for work and ingenious feats of engineering had not only bent the flow of the creek to his will but also the freshets that fed it.

Repair those beaver dams then, and let these wastelands produce! Close the gate in their breach, harness the creek as the beavers had once upon a time harnessed it. Throw the water back upon the marshes, allow none of it to dribble away and be swallowed up by the river. But we weren't the only ones trying to snatch a living from the creek. Those others in the valley below us were as badly in need of water as we were ourselves. And had far greater claim to what little there was.

∴

Asians first tapped Meldrum Creek of its water. Toward the middle of the nineteenth century, some two score Chinese swung their picks and plied their shovels, and so ditched water from the creek to the gravelly benchlands lying slightly above the Fraser River and six miles south of the mouth of the creek. When sinking their prospect holes in the gravel, they had dug up placer gold, and a plentiful supply of water was needed to sluice the pay dirt and separate dirt from gold. The closest available supply lay with the creek to the north, which yet lacked a name.

For a half-dozen years the Chinese diverted the whole flow of the creek into their ditch and brought the water to their mining operations downriver. And the water frothed through their sluice boxes, carrying the dirt with it, but leaving the precious yellow metal in the boxes. And the Chinese scooped it up in wooden spoons, ladled it into buckskin pokes and buried the pokes in the ground so that no thieving white man or Indian could steal it from them. And folks there are who say that to this very day some of the pokes are still buried in the ground, because some of the Chinese miners died of the smallpox and the secret of where they had buried their gold died with them.

Eventually the gravel was mined of its treasure, and the Chinese that the pox didn't want went digging for gold elsewhere. But now white men had found the creek and cast appraising eyes at the narrow, fertile valley lying about its mouth. The soil washed down from the hills above was rich and would grow vegetables and fruit, as well as hay and grain if you turned the soil with a plow. Upstream a few miles, where the land levelled off to form a large plateau, were thousands of acres of uncropped grass. The land could be had for the taking, and the ample year-round flow of the creek could be relied upon to fill the irrigation ditches that must bring water to the crops. So once again was Meldrum tapped of its flow, and around the year 1860 a livestock industry was born on the creek that still flourishes today.

In a land that is covered with three or more feet of snow for at least four months out of the twelve, an ample supply of hay in stack or shed is as essential to a healthy cattle industry as spring, summer and fall range. The carrying capacity of the range can be no greater than that of the stackyards that must furnish hay in winter when cattle cannot fend for themselves.

The soil in the valley was rich, and there was enough of it to provide winter feed for as many horses and cows as the summer ranges could support without their being overgrazed. But Meldrum Creek lies in the "dry" belt of British Columbia, where irrigation is as necessary to the growing of crops as the very soil itself. In 1860, and during the early part of the nineteenth century, that water was there, in the creek. It was there because for ages long gone one generation of beavers following another had been dedicated to the purpose of ensuring that it would be there. Though the whole water table of the creek began to lower when the last of the beavers was taken from it, not for a few years yet was that

50

gradual shrinkage noticeably observed and felt by the ranchers who had come to live in the valley. When the creek did become visibly sick, and there was scarce sufficient water with its summer flow to irrigate one acre of ground where before there was sufficient for a half-dozen, no one seemed to be able to diagnose the true nature of the ailment, still less suggest a remedy.

The root of the disease lay in the lowering lakes and drying marshlands above. They were the original source and supply of all the water that moved down the creek to make rendezvous with the river. Upon any glacial watershed, it is the eternal ice fields at its source that nourish the stream in summer, but if those ice fields were to be taken away and dumped into an ocean, the stream itself must dry up.

There are no glaciers at the headwaters of Meldrum Creek, but once upon a time the creek had its beavers, and as long as they were there the creek was always healthy. Not until the very last colony of beavers was taken from it did the creek begin to sicken.

In competitive haste to get the last few beavers, both white trapper and Indian cut their dams and set their traps in the breach, knowing that the most trap-shy beaver must move in at nightfall to repair the damage and prevent the loss of that precious water impounded by the dam. No other fur-bearer is quite so vulnerable to the steel trap as the beaver. He cannot conceal his presence, for it is instantly revealed by the evidence of his work. The prime function in the life cycle of a beaver is the conservation of water, and he cannot fulfill that function without leaving a sign behind him. The stumps of his cuttings always remain to reveal his presence to all who look for him. In the last decade or so of the nineteenth century there were many abroad upon the watershed with their traps, keenly seeking just such a telltale sign.

Upon Meldrum Creek the extermination of the beavers was both simple and decisive. Large tribes of Indians lived on their reservations within a day or so's journey of the watershed. Egged on by the greed of the white fur buyers, these Indians hunted the creek from source to mouth seeking freshly cut trees, which warned of a beaver's whereabouts. Indians were not the only vultures to squat down at the remnants of the feast. White men, too, passed up the pelt of no fur-bearer that could readily be turned into cash or trade. But soon no Indians and no whites came to the creek looking for fur. The beavers had ceased to exist.

Besides the many beaver ponds, the headwaters of Meldrum Creek were sprinkled with natural lakes, which when full to their banks contributed greatly to the healthy annual flow of the creek. After the passing of the beavers and loss of water in their dams, the flow of the creek dwindled to such a state that now there was an alarming shortage of water for the irrigation ditches. It was now that the ranchers gazed speculatively at these many lakes straddling the creek above. Speculation bred action, and in short order the lakes were ditched and lowered of their content. Thus was Peter robbed to settle accounts with Paul.

But now the beaver marshes were dry. There was no slow but assured seepage of water through the dams to maintain an even flow into the lakes at a time of the year when evaporation is at its highest pitch. Yet it was during that time that the irrigation ditches needed water most to bring moisture to the crops. The lakes were ditched to obtain this water, and to such an extent that the annual precipitation could not begin to repay the borrowings of the previous summer. Now real trouble stared the cattlemen bleakly in the eye.

In the fall of 1926 when I first saw the valley, the flow of the creek was such that of the six or seven cattle ranches there that had to have water in their ditches if they were to have winter feed for their stock, only the owner of the original water right on the creek had any at all. And that ranch had scarcely enough to irrigate a first crop of alfalfa, let alone a second.

Government, in the form of the Water Rights Branch, Department of Lands and Forests, moved in to appraise the melancholy situation, ran transits over the lakes, jotted down figures in their notebooks, shook their heads and departed—but continued to extract fees from the ranchers entitling them to use water that wasn't there to use. There was certainly no lack of dam sites behind which water might be stored and conserved.

What was lacking was concrete action whereby at least some of the major beaver dams above might be closed and their breastworks raised. But the cattlemen were so busy squabbling with each other over the nonexistent water that they apparently had no time to explore the means of providing it.

This then was the situation on Meldrum Creek that day in late June when we explored its marshes, seeing what they had to offer us, insidious doubt creeping into our minds that they could ever again support even a small measure of the wildlife that had been there when Lala was a child.

"We'll have to repair the dams before anything else can be done," said Lillian, "and turn the marshes into lakes."

"And just how do you figure on going about that unless we have the go-ahead from the Water Rights Branch or the ranchers themselves?" I replied.

Lillian kept silent. She knew as well as I that we couldn't tamper with or shut off the flow of the creek when there wasn't enough water there to meet the needs of the ranchers below. If we did we'd be hitched up to trouble.

Now, and after having spent five long days in the saddle, skirting the edges of the marshes and following the deer paths through the forest, and in all that time glimpsing no other fur-bearer's track except those of the coyotes (their tracks were everywhere), I summed it all up by declaring, "It's hopeless."

Lillian was staring into the flames of the campfire. With a sudden impulse, she looked up at my face and said quietly, "Eric, I never want to hear you say that word hopeless again. We may not have much of anything here in this wilderness. But the one thing that we'll always have plenty of is hope."

Chapter 6

It was so hot that sweat drenched our skin when we were just stretched out in the shade of the cottonwoods, busy with nothing but our thoughts. It wasn't a sticky heat so often dispelled by a thunderstorm, but an arid, molten heat that withered the pea vines and timber vetch, sucked the sap from the slough grass, turning its green a jaundiced yellow, and shrivelled the blueberries on their bushes as quickly as they formed. To Lillian, the loss of the blueberries was a tragedy indeed. They'd flowered out nicely in June, promising a bumper crop, and given a shower or two of rain in July, their bushes would be loaded with plump purple berries that she looked forward to picking and preserving as fruit and jam for the winter. But there was no rain in July, and not a drop in August. There was day after endless day, and week after endless week, of pitiless, searing sun, which meant we'd have no fruit or jam for the winter unless it came in tins from the trading post.

But the loss of the blueberries was only one of the calamities to strike Meldrum Creek in that summer of 1931, when prairie became desert, alfalfa fields rusted before they were in bloom, and when even the pines and spruces seemed unable to find enough moisture in the ground to freshen their needles.

From source to mouth Meldrum Creek's bed was as parched and

dry as the game trails leading to it, as were most of the lesser lakes about it too. And in the oozing black mud that soon crusted hard we saw the webbed track of many a duck or goose too young to fly, too clumsy to run and without wisdom enough to strike out overland and seek water elsewhere. For them there was no hope at all. Taking full advantage of a profitable situation when they saw it, the coyotes moved down on the watershed in packs to hunt where the hunting was easy. Many a scattering of duck and goose feathers littered the creek bed during that summer of frightening drought.

Waterfowl was not the only form of life to be snuffed out in the mud. With the creek channel and all lesser lakes in the timber dry, cattle wandered along the banks with their tongues hanging from their jaws, all seeking water. In front of the old beaver dams there was an inch or two of foul water that was as much mud as liquid, but between this and dry ground were several yards of deep and sticky bog. Goaded on by their thirst, the cattle wallowed out through the mud, trying to reach the puddles beyond. Many never got there but instead mired to the belly, unable to go back, unable to go on. And there in the mud they died, though the process of dying might take all of four or five days.

And come roundup time in the fall, many a rancher would be shaking his head at the wasteful loss of it all, and thinking that if things didn't change, the day wasn't far off when maybe his cattle would have to go all the way to the river to find themselves a drink.

But the stinking slime of Meldrum Creek was not the only mire laying claim to a victim. Other creeks were in like condition, and on open rangeland where water supply consisted mostly of shallow depressions in the ground that collected and held the spring runoff of the snows, the situation became so hazardous to livestock that the Grazing Rights Branch, Department of Lands and Forests, built fences around many of the potholes so that cattle could not try to get out to what little water might be left in them and so bog down.

If fencing was a temporary safeguard, it was not a permanent cure. In time, posts supporting wire or rail would rot in the ground and have to

Meldrum Creek in 1931, before the Colliers had repaired the beaver dams. Thirsty cattle seeking water were drawn to the puddles in front of the old dams, only to be mired in the mud along the banks of the creek, where they died.

be reset. And of what use to stock was the surrounding range if their only available water supply was fenced off and denied them?

The only permanent solution to the trouble was to conserve enough water in the kind years so that there would be plenty in the lean. That's what had to be done, and maybe it could be, too. Anyway, an idea began shaping in my mind, vague at first but becoming clearer the longer I thought it over. And when all was crystal clear, I told Lillian about it.

"The Water Rights Branch," I suddenly announced. "We'll write to them about it."

"About what, the blueberries?" With a laugh Lillian said, "I've got blueberries on the brain."

"It's a good thing you've got some somewhere, 'cause there's not a one in the woods." And after she'd wrinkled her nose up at me for this, I went on, "About Meldrum Creek and the beaver dams."

Lillian's face showed her skepticism. "What would the Water Rights Branch know about beavers?"

"Darned little, maybe. But they should know something about dams."

"Such as?"

"Well," I replied, "the more dams there are on a creek, the more water there'll be in it."

Lillian sniffed, and the sniff spoke for itself. "Then why don't they build some dams on our creek?"

"Haven't the time or inclination."

"Then why bother writing them?" Lillian was in a mood for arguing.

"Because," I began to explain slowly, "we'll do the job ourselves if they'll give us the go-ahead."

"I see." Lillian sat very quiet and still for a moment, hands folded in her lap. Then: "Sit down and write them about it," she said. "But I think it will only be a waste of time."

And so to the Water Rights Branch, Department of Lands and Forests, I penned a lengthy letter, explaining the situation as I saw it on Meldrum Creek, and emphasizing my belief that the only permanent solution to the water problem lay in repairing the beaver dams scattered over the upper reaches of the watershed, and reflooding the marshes. We were willing to do that work ourselves without asking help or payment from anyone. Would the Water Rights Branch give the project their official blessing and provide us with some protection for the dams after they were repaired? It would be silly of us to begin the job if before it had been given a fair trial the dams were tapped of their water by the ranchers below.

And the letter went off and in due time was answered. "We are of the opinion that your plan would be of no benefit whatsoever to the annual flow of Meldrum Creek—" There it was, polite, concise, chilly, the drab phraseology of officialdom wherever it might be encountered. There it was, the encouragement given us by the Water Rights Branch; but if it dampened our spirits for the moment, it couldn't douse them altogether. There was still another source we could turn to for encouragement, and it was Lillian who reminded me of it.

"Why don't you put the whole project before Mr. Moon?" she suggested, after the opinion of Water Rights had been digested and forgotten.

"Charlie Moon?" I lifted my eyebrows. "Darn it, yes, Charlie Moon." Then, heaving up from the chair and walking to the door and back again: "Why not?"

Charles Moon was the largest landowner in the valley. His Meldrum Creek ranch was only one of a half-dozen other such holdings scattered about the cattle ranges of the lower Chilcotin. He walked with a slight stoop as men nearing the three score years and ten mark are likely to walk, especially when fifty of those years have been given to hard but honest labour. An Englishman by birth, Moon came to the Chilcotin near the close of the nineteenth century and went to work for one of the cattle outfits of the day for a wage of thirty dollars a month and board. From such modest beginnings he lived to carve himself a miniature cattle empire that in 1931 ran some three thousand head of Hereford cattle, and had thousands of acres of deeded land under fence. This achievement was not a matter of luck at all, but of hard work, sound reasoning and good management.

His Meldrum Creek irrigation licence had first right on the creek for water and until its requirements were met all others must go without. It was to the rancher Moon, then, that we now turned for the encouragement that the Water Rights Branch would not or could not give us.

And with vastly different results. "Anything you do up there," wrote Moon in reply, "can't make matters much worse down here. I always have believed that the extermination of Meldrum Creek's beavers is largely responsible for the fix we are all in now. As far as I am concerned, go ahead with what you have in mind and let's see how it works."

This reply was all we wanted at the moment. If the largest landowner on the creek gave our plan his blessing, what more could we ask? Nothing, save that perhaps the Almighty Himself would send us a winter of heavy snows or a summer or two of prolonged rainfall. We were to get all the snows we wanted before many more winters had gone. In the meantime, we had to live. We had to live off the woods, and if they hadn't much to offer they were generous with what they had. Improvisation became the keynote of existence itself. Nothing was wasted that could be put to any use. Deer were not only to furnish us meat, but clothing too of sorts. The hide of the buck I'd shot at the water hole was still hanging on the limb of the tree where I'd thrown it, well out of reach of the coyotes. It was a bedraggled and smelly hide, too, what with the blood caked on it and the maggots crawling over it. But the maggots wouldn't hurt it any; there'd been precious little meat left on the hide when Lillian and I got through skinning the deer out. Anyway, not enough to keep a maggot healthy.

Lillian had been eyeing the hide for quite some time, in a contemplative sort of a way, before reminding me that "Veasy needs some footwear." And guessing that there was more to come I said nothing, just studying her face.

It wasn't slow in coming. "I'm going to try my hand at tanning the deer hide." The way Lillian said it, tanning a deer hide was simple. "And make Veasy a pair of buckskin moccasins." That sounded simple too.

Skeptically I asked, "You ever tan a deer hide before?" guessing that she hadn't.

"No, but I've watched Lala tan them."

"Oh yes, Lala." And the way I said that fetched a glint of stubbornness into her eyes and thrust her jaw out a little.

I half closed my eyes and ruminated, "Lala set out snares for blue grouse and caught them too. And she dug up wild sunflower roots with a sharpened stick, and roasted them in the campfire ashes like we'd roast a spud." An eyelid lifted. "Think you could snare a blue grouse?"

"Could if I had to," she snapped.

So I called a truce by saying, "Of course you could, but there aren't

59

any blue grouse around here. Just willow grouse and fool hens. And I can shoot them with the .22 rifle."

"Lala never had a .22, all she had was snares." After firing that one at me, Lillian softened a little and smiled. And to keep things that way, I said, "We'll start tanning the hide tomorrow, just like Lala tanned them. But you'll have to tell me what to do because I wasn't around when Lala was fixing buckskin."

It wasn't so hard after all. First we soaked the hide in a tub of lukewarm water for all of three days, then threw it over a peeled cottonwood pole and, with a drawknife made from the blade of an old scythe, scraped it of all hair, flesh and grime until it was almost snow-white. Following this, the hide was soaked for another two days in a solution of heavy soapsuds, and then wrung dry. Now the skin was ready for the greasing. Lala had always used the rendered grease of a bear for this, but we had no bear grease just then and had to use precious lard instead.

After another immersion in soapsuds to rid it of all grease, the skin was now ready to be stretched. Lacing the hide to a stout pole frame and taking up the slack in the laces until they were as taut as a fiddle string, we next devoted an entire day to probing the skin methodically with a flat, U-shaped, bevel-edged stone inserted and bound into a cleft stick. Following this mauling, the hide was now as soft and as pliable as the finest velvet, and ready for the final operation of smoking. To obtain just the right amount and quality of smoke, I dug a shallow pit, kindled a fire in it and then smothered the fire with fir cones. Over the pit we built a teepeelike structure, and wrapped the skin around its poles and covered it with saddle blankets. After several hours of smoking, the hide took on a golden brownish hue and was ready for processing into gloves, moccasins or a coat.

It took Lillian a couple of days to make Veasy his moccasins, but they were a success from the very first stitch. "My turn next," I said. "When are you going to make me a pair?" Lillian took careful appraisal of what was left of the buckskin.

"I want to make him a pair of gauntlet gloves too," she explained, "and after that there won't be enough left to make any more moccasins."

"I'll go shoot another buck."

Her eyes went to her stone meat crocks and she shook her head. "There's plenty of meat left in them yet. We don't need a buck now. Wait a while until we really need meat. Then you can hunt a deer, and I'll fix you some moccasins too."

It was Lillian's scheming mind that found profitable use for the squawfish. The three of us were sitting at the shore of the lake, watching them turn flip-flops in the water. It seemed as though there was a squawfish around for every square foot of space on top of the water.

"'We must grow all our own vegetables," she suddenly decided.

"Vegetables?" I scuffed the ground with the toe of my boot. "In that, and without fertilizer? Maybe it will grow hay of sorts, but vegetables, never."

"I'm going to have a flower garden too," she blithely rattled on. "No home is home without a flower garden."

At that I burst out laughing. "Sure, we'll have roses and orchids, and gladiolas and every other whatnot. See here, apart from the matter of altitude—we're somewhere around the thirty-five-hundred-foot level here, and it freezes almost every month of the year—this soil is so shallow that I doubt you'd even grow a spud in it; at least, it wouldn't be much bigger than a marble if you did."

She stamped her foot. "We'll grow potatoes and good ones too. And carrots and beets, and peas and cabbages. Don't you see, it's just a matter of fertilizer."

"Just a matter of fertilizer," I mimicked. Then went on: "In the first place, we're a long way from any commercial fertilizer, and in the second, it would come sort of high for our pocketbook even if there was any around to be bought. Of course there'll be some horse manure from the barn next spring, but—"

"Not nearly enough," she cut in. Then, pointing to the lake: "There's all the fertilizer we need, and the very best too."

"Lake—fertilizer?" It all sounded crazy to me.

But Lillian just nodded. "The squawfish."

"Squawfish!" It wasn't at all crazy now. "Well I'll be damned. Who'd ever think of that. Maybe you've got something."

Lillian said nothing for a moment, but just sat there, as if savouring her triumph. But after a bit she went on, "In the spring, when they leave the lake and begin moving up the creek to spawn, we can dip them out by the sackful. And spread them in layers on the ground and plow them under. Now can we grow 'most all of our own vegetables?"

I'd never thought of the squawfish as a possible source of fertilizer. Lillian had already tried her hand at frying them, but the experiment was a dismal culinary failure. There was nothing wrong about their taste, but they had so many little barb-shaped bones you'd starve to death separating bone from meat.

The following spring Lillian made a large dip net out of twine, and when the squawfish began moving up the creek to spawn we built rock dams in the channel, leaving a gap in their middle. Lillian held the net in the gap while Veasy and I went upstream a short distance, then waded down toward her, beating the water with sticks, shouting, falling over the slippery rocks, but forever driving swarms of fish into the mouth of the net. When piles of them flapped and squirmed on the bank, we loaded them into gunny sacks, toted them on our backs to the quarter-acre of ground already cleared of its brush, plastered it with fish and then plowed them under. Though that patch of ground stank to high heaven for three weeks after the sowing of the seed, by the time the smell was gone, young plants began thrusting up through the warm, gravelly soil, and by mid-summer we had a vegetable garden that might have evoked the admiration and envy of any professional market gardener.

Lala never had mentioned the squawfish, perhaps because in her day on the creek there had been few if any there. But then there were plenty of trout. She explained to me how the Indians laid their gill nets across the narrow waist of Meldrum Lake and hauled them in next morning heavy with plump, red-fleshed trout. At a later date, when exploring the shoreline ourselves looking for mink or other signs, we discovered the water-logged remains of many a pole raft used by those earlier Indians in their fishing. But all that lay with the heyday of the beaver, when every lake was kept at a constant level, and a swift cold stream of water flowed over the dams all summer, ensuring a continuous supply of well-oxygenated water from source to mouth of the creek.

With the extermination of the beavers and subsequent loss of precious water impounded by their dams, the creek became shallow, and in the summer much of its bed was dry. There was no longer a clear, cool flow moving between its banks, and without that flow, no trout could survive for very long. And as the trout perished, squawfish began multiplying, no doubt to fill a vacuum that was caused by the passing of the trout.

One evening, when squatted upon a block of wood at the cabin door, turning such matters over in my mind, I absent-mindedly re-marked to Lillian, "Think we'll ever see the day when you and I will be able to sneak down to the creek, sink a baited hook into the water and catch us a mess of trout?"

Lillian was brushing her hair, fixing it tidy-like for the night. Not until that chore was done to her complete satisfaction did she give me any reply. Then: "If the beavers come back, yes." And there was something in her voice that made me glance sharply at her and say, "You really think there will be beavers here again, someday?"

Her face was deadly serious as she retorted, "Of course I do. Don't you?"

Chapter 7

It was noon of a hot cloudless day in late July. Veasy was a hundred yards from the cabin by a dead cottonwood, watching a woodpecker fly in and out of a hole in the tree, feeding grubs and other morsels to the fledglings in the nest. Suddenly he turned away from the tree and ran helter-skelter for the cabin. He reached the door, puffing and panting, eyes agape. Then, looking back over his shoulder, he panted, "Someone come."

A horse and rider emerged from the timber, hesitated a few seconds at the edge of the clearing, as if undecided whether to keep coming or turn back into the forest. I solved the problem for him by waving a hand and shouting, "Hello there!" And speaking low and soothingly to his horse, which reared up on its hind legs at the sudden sight of me, the rider neck reined the animal toward the cabin.

Our visitor was a full-blooded Indian, one whom I didn't remember ever seeing around Riske Creek. Later we found out that he belonged to the Aniham reservation, which lay a good many miles west of Meldrum Lake. He was wearing heavy mooseskin chaps and a buckskin coat with long fringes at the shoulders and sleeves. The coat was spotlessly clean except for a smear or two of blood on the right sleeve. And since the carcass of a freshly killed deer was tied behind the saddle, the blood no doubt had a legitimate excuse for being there. The Indian was short and blocky and his face betrayed nothing of what was taking place within his mind.

Smiling a welcome, I pointed to a tree and said, "Pretty quick we eat. More better you tie your horse up and come eat too."

Then the Indian's sphinx-like face relaxed in an easy grin.

"T'ank you," he grunted, coming down from the saddle.

Our visitor didn't seem to have very much to say for himself. When forced to converse in a primitive form of English, the true Chilcotin Indian is frugal with his words. Such little talk as did take place centred on game in one form or another.

"Lots coyote tracks up in creek bottom," I began in an effort to un-limber his tongue.

"You betcha! Coyote him bugger to kill young duck and goose now no more water stop in creek." Although the Indian lacked proper under-standing of the word bugger, which the white man had introduced to his vocabulary, he guessed that it meant something bad.

After a moment or two of deep contemplation the Indian asked, "How much you t'ink fur buyer pay one good coyote skin bimeby he get prime?"

I grinned. "Fur buyer he cheat trapper to beat hell. S'pose one pale silky pelt worth ten dollars cash, fur buyer at store give you seven dollars' worth trade goods for it."

It was the Indian's turn to laugh now. "Ey ya! Fur buyer he bugger to cheat."

The deer on his saddle prompted me to ask, "You see much *mowitch* (deer) sign in timber where you ride?"

He nodded. "Lots. Him up an' down creek, try to find water. Fly give 'um hell now, and deer lie down in water with just his head stick out. That way fly can't hurt him."

In discussing wildlife of any kind, even with an Indian, it is hard to avoid the word "water." In summer water offers the mule deer their only means of escape from the persecution of the flies. There in the water of creek or lake the deer will lie for most of the day with just its nose and ears protruding above the surface. Not until shadows begin to lengthen and the cooling winds of night take over from the ardent heat of day will the deer leave water's edge and return to the timber to feed.

After filling his belly and belching, the Indian grunted a "T'ank you" to the tobacco and cigarette papers I shoved across the table, and rolled himself a smoke. Between long and thoughtful puffs at the cigarette there was more small talk of deer, moose and other meat animals of the forest. Meat was the prime essential of any Chilcotin Indian's life. Money he could get along without for weeks at a time, but meat he and his family must have wherever they made an overnight camp. Consequently, little of anything else ever occupied their thoughts. We were slowly acquiring much of the Indians' philosophy ourselves. It had its points at that.

The Indian was in no hurry to go now that he'd got acquainted. After finishing his cigarette he went outside and squatted on a block of wood, firing quick glances at the cabin, the wagon, at me and at Lillian and Veasy. If deep within his mind he was wondering why we were here and what we were doing, he didn't bother to ask.

Finally he got up and said, "Me go my camp now."

The inquisitiveness of the white man now asserted itself. "Whereabouts your camp?" I asked with curiosity.

With a jerk of the thumb into the north, he mumbled, "There." And since "there" was surrounded by several hundred thousand acres of timber, muskeg and pothole meadow, I was none the wiser for the question.

But we couldn't altogether shut ourselves off from the remainder of the world—that wouldn't be fair to Veasy. He had to learn that there were other people in the world besides his mother and father. So once a month anyway I wrangled the work team from the pasture and hitched them to the wagon and we drove out to Riske Creek.

These rare trips to the post office were events of huge delight to Veasy since they held certain promise of candy. It was a promise never denied him, even though its fulfillment did entail the serious economic matter of filching another precious two bits from the pocketbook. But youth must be served. Even the Indian children knew all about the large wooden

66

candy buckets that the trader kept under the counter. Their method of making trade consisted of poking a finger into their mouths and banging a five- or ten-cent piece down on the counter. In winter, a weasel pelt was apt to suffice for the coinage.

After attending to Veasy's trade, and purchasing another pound of tea or a couple of tins of tobacco, I gave my attention to the mail. Any letters smacking of importance—there were few of these—I dealt with then and there, availing myself of the trader's noisy typewriter to do so. Then, perched on the counter, I glanced through the papers. There was little of good cheer to be found there. The activities of an Austrian named Hitler seemed worthy of a little space in the large provincial dailies. But who in the hell was Hitler?

"A house painter," snorted Becher in reply. "Yes, sir, a goddam Austrian house painter who reckons he's another Bismarck."

The trader had a radio in his office that, between prolonged fits of static, gave forth with some music or news commentaries. Possession of the radio made the trader a veritable prince of learning. Indians consulted him on whether it was a good hunting moon or a bad one. If a rancher was out nine yearling steers on the fall roundup, he sought advice from the trader as to their possible whereabouts. And a homesteader's wife from up the crick a piece, who'd begat six sturdy sons in seven years of effort and was now bloated for the seventh time, consulted Becher as to whether this time it would be a girl or a boy. And the radio told all.

No, there was little of good cheer in the papers. Several thousand unemployed rioting in the streets of Vancouver, several millions without work in those United States of America. If that was the world of civilized man, the sooner we got back to our trapline the better.

The matter of when to start back was usually left to Lillian. It would be at least three or four weeks before we came out to Riske Creek again, and now that we were here I didn't want to hurry her about getting back. But after a couple of days of drinking tea and eating fruitcake with Mrs. Becher, and talking about all the mysterious things that women generally

67

talk about when two of them are together, Lillian stated bluntly, "I'd like to go home." And as if that wasn't maybe quite enough, she added, "There's hay to think about." I swear that no sooner had Lillian gotten one job off her mind than she began thinking about another. And perhaps it is just as well that this was so. I was sometimes slightly inclined to put things off, for a day or two anyway.

But she was right. Before September's shortening days brought the first really heavy frosts of fall we had to have winter feed for our horses. The horses were our only means of contact with the Outside unless we cared to make the fifty-odd-mile return trip on snowshoes or afoot.

Hay of a kind, like so much else, was there for the taking. On a small beaver meadow a step or so upstream from the cabin, we could cut a half-dozen tons of slough grass hay, which, if lacking the quality of timothy or clover, would keep flesh upon an animal's ribs until the backbone of a winter was broken and new grass in sight.

We had no horse mower and rake and didn't know where we could borrow them, for now every mower and rake in the land was busy piling up hay against the hungry months ahead. But we had outfitted ourselves with a scythe, a large and clumsy hand rake, and pitchfork. And of course we had fourteen hours of light each day in which to use them. I wielded the scythe, and if this was one mowing machine with which I'd had no previous experience, the compelling needs of the moment soon taught me how. After a couple of days of wracking backache I began to attain a sort of proficiency with the scythe, and each time the blade whished through the air, a swath of bright green hay lay wilting in its backtrail. As the hay cured, Lillian came behind with the rake and a pitchfork, piling it up in cocks. And as often as not, as soon as a cock was built, Veasy turned somersaults on it, knocking it to pieces.

Between the two of us we made a rack out of dried poles and pegged it to wooden runners, then hitched the team to the primitive, though very efficient, vehicle and hauled the hay and stacked it by the house.

The summer waned; fall stalked down upon us. The aspen and willow leaves traded their green for rusty gold.

September gave us a few days of light rain and once more a trickle of water slithered down the creek.

October's raw winds brought flocks of sandhill cranes and Canada geese to the scene, noisy as noisy can be as they circled the lake by the house. Southward bound were the cranes and the geese, and if the former seldom stopped to visit a while, the geese were more neighbourly. They squatted down on the lakes in large, gossiping flocks and stayed a week or two, resting their wings and gorging on the short alkali grass at water's edge.

On our trapline, any meat killed after the middle of October will soon freeze solid and stay frozen until late in the following March. If the wilderness was unable to supply us a turkey for the nearing Christmas, it could give us a goose. Taking the ten-gauge shotgun down from its pegs on the cabin wall, I saddled up a couple of horses, and with Veasy on the rump of Lillian's mare, we went about the job of hanging us up some geese.

This demanded teamwork between Lillian and me, as well as the need to curb Veasy's exuberant spirits for a few minutes so that he wouldn't flush the geese before everything was ready. First we must check on the wind, for when leaving the water Canada geese always take off against the wind, never with it. Satisfied on that score, I spent several minutes sizing the situation up, deciding what course the geese would take when they became airborne. Then I whispered to Lillian, "I'll snake around and hide myself in that patch of timber at the south end of the lake. Allow me ten minutes to get into position and then you bust out of the woods at a gallop. That should put them off the water right."

"How am I going to tell when the ten minutes are up when neither of us has a watch?" she objected.

But now a few of the geese were impatiently chattering to one another as resting geese often will when they are thinking about flying off. I had to get off and into my hiding place. "You'll just have to guess," was the only advice I could give her as I sneaked away through the trees.

But Lillian always played it safe. It was more like half an hour than any ten minutes before she moved out of the timber to flush the geese, although how she managed to keep Veasy quiet that long is something I'll never know. But anyway she came, sometimes at a trot, often at a gallop, confusing the geese and pushing them out low over my head, a perfect shot for any gunner.

"Bang-bang and goosey falls down!" chirruped the palefaced Hiawatha behind her as the ten-gauge dropped two of the geese. After a few hunts like this, and when a dozen geese were hanging under the spruce behind the cabin, where they froze solid overnight, we bothered the geese no more that fall. I had long ago divorced my mind from the principle of killing just for the sport of killing. The hunting and killing of any species of game, feathered or otherwise, was no longer the sport I had known it to be in England's far-off days. Hunting was now a part of our effort for survival, and when the need no longer existed, my guns went back to their peg on the cabin wall.

October's last day went like the final flicker of a candle. Lakes were belching and grumbling as thickening ice froze them tight. With the freezing of the lakes went the last straggling flocks of geese. A loneliness of sorts bore down on us with the passing of the geese, for there was ever something cheering about their chatter. With their departure we could now expect but a moment or two of respite before winter sank its claws upon the wilderness with grim reality.

But there were far more important things to do than contemplate the drab months ahead. There were traps to be steamed in a brew of fir needles, to rid them of all suspicious scent clinging to their steel. There was snow-shoe harness and webbing to check and oil, stovepipes to clean so as to lessen the danger of their catching fire when the stoves were banked with wood against the bite of the cold outside. Seldom a winter went by in the Chilcotin but that some two or three homes did not go up in smoke, taking with them almost all they possessed. Few of their owners could afford insurance, if indeed they had been able to get any on a building of sun-bleached logs, sod roof and with rusty stovepipes for chimneys. The only fire protection we had was keeping the stovepipes clean.

It required all of a week to set out and bait the traps, and by the time the last set was made, six inches of powdery snow had fallen. The coming of the snow reminded me of another job that must be done before we could give all our attention to the traps. It was a job as hazardous as it was urgent, and one that neither of us looked forward to. But due to the now almost-empty pocketbook, it was one we could not forego.

Chapter 8

Tossing a lighted torch into a bear den may seem a rather risky way to get a winter's grease supply, but we had no other choice. We lacked a year's supply of grease and we lacked even a small supply of money and had no intention of purchasing grease from any trading post if we could obtain it free elsewhere.

Late in September I had busied myself for all of three days prowling the woods in search of an "active" bear den. An active den in this case was one that had been cleaned out by a bear in late summer and made ready for winter hibernation. Finally I located one and blazed a trail from it back to the cabin, so that there would be no question of our being able to return to the spot when the den had a tenant.

Now that winter had come to stay, that tenant should be in residence. Hoping that this was so, we followed the blazes back to the den and cautiously approached its mouth. One quick glance told me yes, the den is occupied. The bear had crawled down its funnel and covered the mouth of the hole behind it with sticks and moss.

Gingerly I removed the plug from the mouth. Veasy sat on the rump of the horse, eyes popping with excitement. "Bang-bang and the bear falls down." Now I could wind the fetid stink of the bear, hear its slow breathing.

I straightened up and tossed Lillian an assuring grin. "Think you can go ahead with your share of the business?" I asked, as if she really had nothing to do at all.

I guessed that her heart was pounding furiously and that there was probably a knot at the pit of her stomach. For Lillian's share of the business was expecting a lot of any woman. But she stepped toward me, biting her lip. "I can try."

There was just a hint of doubt in her voice, which compelled me to stand very still, watching the mouth of the den. Was it really worth it? Weren't we taking desperate chances? What if I missed? What if the bear took a notion right now to come out of the den, with Lillian and I afoot, a couple of feet from the den? But the .303 rifle seemed to say it was all right. But what if the rifle missed? Shucks, I thought, it can't. It seldom did at a deer, so why at a bear, a few feet from its muzzle? And anyway, we needed the grease.

I said, "Let's fix the horses." And we led them off a ways and tied them to trees. Lillian lifted Veasy from the rump of her horse into the saddle proper. "Sit still," she warned him, "and don't you dare wiggle an eyebrow."

Returning to the den, I bolted a shell into the barrel of the .303. Then I touched a match to a long sliver of pitchwood. The torch spluttered and flared. I handed it to Lillian, at the same time giving her instructions that were terse but to the point. "When I shout 'let 'er go,' shove it down the den and scram for the horses." And in afterthought: "And don't miss the saddle."

I stepped behind a tree a half-dozen yards from the mouth of the den. I wiped a speck of snow from my right eyelash. My heart raced a little. But the rifle said, "Nothing to get skittish about." I made a final inspection of the gun, especially its sights. The front one was iced up a little, but I soon fixed that. I gulped air into my lungs, hanging onto it for a second or two. Then it whooshed out of me in one strident roar: "Let 'er go!"

Without a falter Lillian stepped almost into the jaws of the den.

I couldn't see her head and shoulders; they were in its mouth as she thrust the torch home. Then she raced for the horses and flung herself into the saddle.

For a moment that seemed like ten years I stood very still at the tree, resting the gun barrel against its trunk and lining the sights on the mouth of the den. And in a flash it happened. A huge bear scrambled out of the den, just as I figured it would, muttering angrily to itself, dense fur rippling along its spine. It was black as polished coal, fat as a grain-fed porker, and about as big as black bears come.

Crack! The bear somersaulted as the bullet whacked home. "Shoot again!" cried Veasy, who was enjoying it all immensely. The bear was down in the snow, flailing at imaginary enemies with a right front paw. Now it was upright, head rocking from side to side. There was neither nervousness nor excitement in me now. As of course rightly there shouldn't be with a gun like that in my hand. I sighted in again. Crack! And that one was through the forehead, and the bear reared backward and was dead when it hit the ground. .

Together Lillian and I skinned the animal out, while Veasy went into the den to see what things looked like there. We stripped the flesh and innards of their thick layers of fat and loaded it into gunny sacks. By the time the job was finished, the sacks contained enough bear fat to keep us in lard for a year when rendered out and mixed with moose tallow. Veasy crawled back out of the den. "Warm in there," he said.

I lashed the sacks on the pack horse and was about to hoist into my own saddle when a sudden thought occurred to me. I said, "Coyotes like bear meat too." A couple of heavy spruce trees stood a hundred yards off. Placing a hitch around the bear's head and taking a turn with the rope on my saddle horn, I snaked the carcass to within a few feet of the spruces. Lillian watched with puzzled eyes, so I told her, "Coyotes will clean the carcass up after a while. I'll come back tomorrow and set some traps under the trees." Nothing went to waste that could be put to any use.

A needling north wind flicked at our faces as we returned home with the spoils. While I unloaded the pack horse, and watered the horses and forked them some hay, Lillian banked the heater stove with wood until its sides were cherry red. Let it blow, let it snow! Now that we had our grease we could devote most all of our time to the traps.

By the end of the third week in December, twenty-five coyote pelts hung at the outer walls of the cabin. A line of small traps that Lillian herself had set out in the spruces paralleling the creek a few steps from the cabin door caught her fifteen weasels and a mink. The mink was treasure trove, for it was an extra-large male mink with silky charcoal fur, maybe worth all of fifteen dollars.

"Capitalist," I mocked, watching her skin out the mink. "What are you going to do with all that money?"

"There's a set of matched dinnerware in the catalogue," she began. Then with a shake of the head: "No, not that yet. We'll spend it on lumber so's I can have a floor." During the first winter of trapping, that was the only mink that left its track in the snow.

"It's time," I was thinking, "that we thought about trading off the catch."

With Christmas only four more shopping days away and our stock of groceries lacking much in the way of Yuletide treats, Lillian quickly agreed yes, we'd better sell the furs. So we hitched the team to the sleigh and headed south for the trading post.

The matter of trading the pelts off at the store was one that demanded infinite time and patience. "What are you paying for good coyote pelts?" I asked Becher by way of a feeler, dumping the skins on the counter.

He sniffed, then sighed, then sniffed once more. With almost tired indifference, he shook and examined the skins. He bit off the end of a cigar and lighted it. He squinted at me from beneath his heavy gray eyebrows and began palming his chin. He puffed steadily away at the cigar, looking out of the heavy plate-glass windows, as if maybe his thoughts were on England, or India, any place but Chilcotin, B.C. But finally his eyes came back to the fur. "Cash or trade?" he asked.

"Both."

Swinging up on the counter, heels gently drumming its side, the trader fingered a cigar a long moment, then tossed it to me. I too swung up on

A shot in early winter of Lillian, Veasy and Eric, ready to head out to Riske Creek to get the mail.

the counter, heels drumming its side. I bit the end off the cigar, took a firm grip on it with my teeth and asked, "Match?"

He sighed. "You just got the habit, eh?" But handed me his match-box.

An Indian woman entered the store, maybe twenty, maybe fifty, for who was I to judge her age rightly? The trader nicked a disapproving eye at her. "She hasn't a red cent piece," he complained. "Not a damned cent." But I'd worked for the trader long enough myself to know that whenever the Indians were flat broke, Becher would always give them a certain amount of credit and take a chance on their paying him later with either labour or furs.

"You want something, Sally?" Becher shot a quick glance at the woman and then his eyes returned to the window.

A blood-red silk handkerchief covered her head, an old woollen sweater her teats. She was almost as broad as she was long, and the cheap calico skirt from the hips on down barely covered her knees. Her teeth were yellow with tobacco juice, her nose was flat, her mouth was big, and she had eyes like a squawfish just hauled from the water. But I had to admit that apart from these minor deficiencies in facial character, she wasn't bad looking at all.

Now she giggled and said, "Tobacco."

The trader seemed suddenly to tire. "Not a damned cent." It was addressed to the window, not me or the woman. But after a while he looked at me and said, "They've got five papooses and they're broke flatter than a pancake. The buck has been sick, and can't hunt. They're living off dried salmon." And with that he flipped open the ledger and took a sack of tobacco from a shelf. "How you pay s'pose I let you have tobacco?" he wanted to know of the woman.

She had a quick answer to that one. "Yesterday I trap two muskrats. Bimeby when skin dry I bring you."

So the trader gave her tobacco, a two-pound tin of syrup, two books of cigarette papers, a box of soda biscuits and a small bag of candy. "When he ready you bring me your muskrat and pay your jawbone (credit)," he warned, and then gave his attention to my furs.

He complained, "Depression sure has thrown the monkey wrench into the fur business. Take coyotes, for instance." And he began fingering mine. "Can't hardly give a good coyote pelt away."

I remained mute, studying the end of the cigar. Becher shook and examined the skins, slowly this time. He picked up a pencil and began figuring on a scrap of paper. Then he braced himself and said, "Tell you what I'll do. I'll allow you two hundred dollars for the lot, half cash, half trade."

I began gathering up the skins. "Too cheap. Those furs are worth every penny of two hundred forty dollars if I ship them away to the auction sales."

"Auction sales!" The trader snorted. "They'll rob you blind, those auctions will. Commission, royalty, shipping charges—" And after allowing time for that to sink in, he went on, "They'll just steal that mink from you, will the auctions. Not a bad one, either." And he picked up the mink and blew into its fur. "Tell you what I'll do. I'll make it two hundred twenty dollars, all in trade."

But we needed cash as well as goods. "Make it two hundred twenty-five, half cash, half trade."

And with a "I'm losing good money on the whole damned transaction" complaint, the trader nodded and began sweeping up the skins in his arms.

So the furs were sold, and back through the snow, butt chains jingling, sleigh runners screeching, over a hundred dollars in the pocketbook, and enough of almost everything in the sleigh to last until spring. "Damn it, we're rich," I told the horses, flicking their rumps with the whip.

Also in the sleigh box, concealed in a gunny sack from Veasy's inquisitive eyes, were one or two small and mysterious boxes for the Christmas tree we aimed on cutting on the way home. Not until a few years later did Veasy solve the riddle of how Santa Claus managed to squeeze his little round belly down our six-inch stovepipe. But squeeze it down he did.

Christmas Day came in clear and bright, the thermometer at ten below zero, the spruces and willows along the creek a-glitter with spangles of frost. Breakfast eaten, we gave our attention to the tree. For Veasy, Santa had left a toy violin, a stocking of candy, nuts and oranges, and a popgun. For Lillian there was a fur-lined pair of bedroom slippers, and a musical sewing box that gave off with a little tune whenever its lid was raised. And for me there was a watch, the very same kind of a pocket watch that the trader displayed on his shelves with a price tag of two dollars and fifty cents. I wound the watch to make sure that it really would tick, and then glanced suspiciously at Lillian. Her face betrayed nothing, but somehow or other I immediately coupled my Christmas present with what she had received for the mink skin.

Small gifts these, but gifts just the same. It wasn't their value in dollars and cents that counted, and dollars and cents counted an awful lot to us then, but the thoughts that were a part of the giving. Gifts which, if soon to be broken or forgotten, knitted the three of us a little tighter to one another.

By nine A.M. the violin had lost two of its strings, the popgun its cork. The mercury stood at an even zero, so pulling on my mackinaw coat and fur hat, I bundled Veasy up in a heavy woollen sweater, pulled the parka down over his cheeks and ears and said, "Let's you and me go down the creek and set ourselves some rabbit snares." It wasn't that we needed the rabbits—we had moose and deer meat, as well as ducks and geese all frozen stiff under the spruce tree—but because right this very minute I knew that Lillian didn't want either of us in her way while she went about preparing the dinner. For the past month, since she had begun making the puddings and cakes, Lillian had had her mind fixed on the Christmas dinner. She loved to cook anyway—that is, when she had what she wanted to cook with. And this was Christmas morning, one morning in the year when I knew she'd like the cabin all to herself, for an hour or so anyway.

With Veasy plodding along behind me, I followed the ice of the creek, pausing where a rabbit path crossed it and setting a snare in the willows. So we came to the lake that had flooded when the first heavy snowfall straddled it. But now the flood water was frozen solid again and we could walk down the centre of the lake as if the smooth ice were hard cement. We investigated a couple of muskrat houses, stared long, hard and thoughtfully at the track of a timber wolf that had crossed the ice in the night. Then we moved over to the timber, sat on a fallen spruce and watched a squirrel shucking a cone on the limb of a nearby tree. "Wonder if the squirrel knows it's Christmas Day?" I thought. Probably not. The squirrel didn't give a hoot what day it was so long as there was no shortage of cones to twiddle around in his paws.

Lillian's face was deeply flushed when I led Veasy back to the cabin. Flushed from leaning over the hot stove, basting the goose, from lifting the lid of the kettle and peeking at the plum pudding, and from opening the door of her oven just to see if the mince pies were the colour mince pies should be when they're baked to a turn.

Although the Colliers usually had an abundance of moose, deer, duck and goose meat, they sometimes set rabbit snares. Veasy is pictured here with snowshoe rabbits taken from his snares.

"I'm that hungry I could eat a parboiled owl," I declared as the aroma of her cooking reached me.

"The goose won't be ready for another twenty minutes," she grumbled. "Why don't you set another couple of rabbit snares?"

Taking the hint I told Veasy, "Let's you and me go feed the horses some more hay. They're hungry too."

In England, the morning service in church was as much a part of Christmas as turkey and plum pudding. But there are no churches in the wilderness, not in our part of the world. But just the same, the wilderness need not be altogether devoid of religion. Though there is no hassock to kneel upon, no choir to sing "O Little Town of Bethlehem," no parson, pastor or priest to preach a sermon from the pulpit, one has but to stand

amid the calm, deep quiet of the forest for only a few moments to understand that there is indeed a Creator of all things bright and beautiful, and
that His presence is everywhere at the same time.

There in our one-roomed cabin on the headwaters of Meldrum Creek
this late Christmas afternoon in 1931, the sun about gone, night closing
in, I knew, and Lillian knew, as indeed Veasy was soon to know, that we
were as near to Almighty God as we'd be were we kneeling in some pew,
faces in the palms of our hands.

Chapter 9

Bitter January! Eight hours of daylight, sixteen hours of night. Thirty inches of powdery snow concealing every game trail, weighting down the branches of the larger trees, bending, crushing and stifling the seedlings. Wind keening down from the north, sharp as porcupine needles, not enough to blow the snow from the trees but more than enough to worry and prick at the skin when you faced it head on. Chestnut saddle horse fretting outside the cabin, hitched to the snubbing post, waiting, ears flat on mane, right front foot pawing uneasily at the snow. Me pulling into heavy woollen sweater and equally heavy sheepskin coat, buckling my high-top overshoes, working my legs into a mangy pair of bearskin chaps. But at least they'll keep the snow off my legs, will the chaps. Lillian busy fixing me up a lunch, then wrapping it in a square of waterproof canvas, handing it to me, trying all the time to make out she's not worrying a bit, but making a very poor job of it. "For God's sake be careful." The tone of her words themselves is sure enough proof that she's fretting. And maybe with some justification, for the chore ahead of me today is as bitter as the wind.

Since New Year's not a single coyote had got tangled up in the traps. Of course, there was reason for this. In northern climes the trapping of any coyote after Christmas is a questionable matter indeed. In January the annual rut or breeding season begins, and now all coyotes, male or female, steer sharply away from any meat that they haven't just killed for themselves. And of course they'll have nothing to do with any artificial scent or lure. Some there are who say that the fox is the smartest animal in the north woods, but the fox is plain stupid when ranked with the coyote. If the coyote is one predatory animal that man has so far been unable to wipe from the face of the American continent, this may be because the coyote is wiser than man himself.

I know quite a lot about the coyote. During those first few years at the head of the creek our economic security hinged entirely upon my ability somehow to keep coyote pelts on the stretcher boards as long as their fur was prime. There was little other fur to rely on. During spring, summer and early fall, it was a matter of paying out with nothing coming in. We lacked a good many things. We needed lumber to floor the cabin. We needed a horse-drawn mower and rake, and I had an idea where they could be bought secondhand for an outlay of sixty dollars. Sixty dollars! A modest fortune, that. I also needed a great many more traps, and Lillian more pots and pans, and linoleum to cover the floor when we finally got a floor. And the coyote must pay the score for all.

Shortly after Christmas I had pulled the coyote traps and hung them up in the spruce trees beneath which they had been set. The pulling of the traps was the cue for me to double up on Mr. Binks's daily ration of oats. Now that the traps were of no further use, a lot depended upon Mr. Binks. Mr. Binks was a chestnut gelding, standing fifteen hands, weighing about twelve hundred pounds. Out of a half-breed Arabian mare, by a wild unbranded stallion, he ranged with a band of wild horses until seven years old. When a wild-horse chaser corralled the bunch, the chestnut suffered the dual indignities of castration and branding, both at the same time. Shortly thereafter, in exchange for four prime coyote skins, he became mine, and I began gentling him to the feel of cinch and bit.

Since Christmas there had been a period of intermittent snowfall. So long as the snow continued to fall the coyotes would stay close to their dens, teasing a ravenous appetite with meatless scraps of skin and bone cached nearby. And so long as that snow continued to fall I too stayed fairly close to my own den, for on any wilderness trapline, only matters of life and death will coax any man far from the cabin to face the whip of an arctic blizzard without.

For three days and nights the snow slanted in from the north, a dry, sanded snow. Then abruptly, the gray overcast began to lighten and a silver-pale moon grinned down at the white world beneath. I measured the depth of the snow against the handle of a double-bitted axe and reckoned it at thirty inches. In that depth of virgin snow, any coyote out for a kill must follow a rabbit's padded path through second-growth thickets if he wants to stoke his gut. If crowded out of the thickets and into more scattered timber where there were no rabbit paths, his every yard of travel is one of maximum effort. Now that the skies had cleared, the joint task of myself and Mr. Binks was to crowd the coyote off the rabbit trails, away from the thickets, into the scattering timber. And then stay doggedly on his tracks until sheer physical exhaustion undid him. It was cruel and tiring work for both hunter and hunted alike. Yet it was work that had to be done if we were to survive in the wilderness.

Often the evasive tactics of the coyote played me or Mr. Binks out, and so he lived to save his brush for some other day. But sometimes he blundered, and then it fared him ill.

There was a hump in the chestnut's back as the cinch tightened on his girth. He squaw-hopped a time or two as I eased myself gingerly into the cold saddle, but as I reined him away from the cabin, the playfulness went out of him and he pricked up his ears and settled down to the grim business ahead.

When hunting coyotes upon a saddle horse in snow almost to the animal's chest, unnecessary haste is a poor sort of an ally. For fruitful victory or barren defeat hinges a lot upon having a final spark of strength and speed in the horse at a moment when most needed. I allowed Mr. Binks to pick his own slow way through the scattering of fir timber as we moved toward the thickets of second-growth higher up the hillside. Here and there the smooth surface of the snow was plowed by a moose

Eric with two of the coyotes that "had to pay." The pelts were traded for goods needed to survive in the wilderness, but Eric considered the business of getting the coyotes cruel and tiring work for both the hunter and the hunted.

track. Once, but for a swift second only, I saw a cow and a calf silhouetted against the skyline, then they were gone. I came to the first of the thickets—copses, we called them in the old country—only to find that it held nothing but rabbits and a couple of weasel. So I reined the chestnut away from it toward a larger acreage of brush ahead.

The brush was from five to seven feet high, dense as an uncut oat field, and every branch bowing beneath its weight of snow. I had almost circled the thicket when I found myself staring down at the track of a lone coyote, made, I judged, shortly after daylight. I sighed, buttoned the collar of my sheepskin coat tighter around my neck and turned Mr. Binks into the brush. Lumps of frigid snow fell into the saddle when we brushed the branches, and as I lifted in the stirrups to brush it away I found myself thinking what a hell of a way this was for a man to earn an honest dollar.

It was impossible to keep the saddle seat dry when forcing through the thicket, and soon the leather was groaning and squeaking with the frost and the cold that was in it. My coat and fur chaps became sodden with water as my body heat melted the snow on them. Soon the water would become ice.

In the deep heart of the thicket, close to a well-packed rabbit trail, I saw where the coyote had killed. I leaned over the side of the saddle and poked speculatively at the rabbit blood with a short stick carried expressly for that purpose. While the blood was frozen, there was a certain freshness about it that labelled the kill as very recent. Daybreak that morning, probably, for the coyote usually hunts with the dawn and dusk and beds during the brighter hours of the short winter day.

The size of the pad marks told me that I was dealing with no adolescent animal but a coyote that was old in years and wisdom. "Yo ho," I warned Mr. Binks, "we're in for a run this time." Coming down from the saddle and taking a reef or two on the latigo so there'd be no danger of the saddle turning when we began jumping windfalls, I heaved back into the seat and moved off on the track.

A half-mile later, under the boughs of a stunted spruce, I squinted down at the coyote's fresh bed. And then nodded; the tracks leading away from it were not those of a coyote taking his own sweet and leisurely time getting from one point to another; in fact, there were no pad marks at all. There were lunging pits in the snow, ten feet apart, deep and loose, the telltale sign left by a coyote who, in two or more feet of snow, is running to save his hide.

"Ay ya!" As the challenge spilled from my throat, Mr. Binks broke into a trot. "Ay ya!" All bedlam was called for now to keep the coyote at full run, to addle his nimble wits and herd him away from any convenient thicket.

The tracks took me back into the heart of that snow-laden thicket, and now the coyote was on the packed surface of a rabbit trail with nothing to hinder his stride. Mr. Binks's ears were tilted slightly forward, his mouth champing the bit. But I curbed his wild impatience, husbanding his wind and strength against the moment when I hoped to come to grips with the coyote on ground of my own choosing.

For the next several minutes there was no let-up to the relentless game of hide-and-seek going on in the thicket. At a slow but persistent trot, the chestnut crowded the coyote from one rabbit path to another. The coyote veered north, south, east and west, yet whenever I crowded him within sight of thinning timber he doubled back on his tracks and found yet another trail that would hold his weight.

Looking back on it all now, when it is no longer an economic necessity for me to indulge in such outlandish means of earning a livelihood—and when sheer weight of years would restrain me if indeed it still were—I have dismal recollections of occasions when more than one coyote out-witted my every effort to crowd him out of the underbrush to which he so stubbornly clung. For the finest horseflesh bred can take only so much punishment, and in bitter contest such as this, once the horse is spent victory is claimed by the coyote, as it might well have gone to this one had he not blundered and given me the chance I desperately needed.

At the western marge of the thicket a slim finger of seedling pine snaked out into more mature growth, and a well-travelled rabbit path branched off at an angle and came to an abrupt terminus at the far end of the seedlings. Perhaps I was too close to his tail, or perhaps my shouts were at least beginning to fluster him; anyway, the coyote tracks told me he'd made a beeline for the finger.

"Mr. Binks!" It was a plea rather than a command, and one the chest-nut understood. He hurled forward, and with gentle but compelling pres-sure of the rein I headed him into the pines.

The bushes ahead of me, still swaying and shedding snow after being brushed by the running coyote, were ample signal that I was only a few horse lengths behind. But when I emerged from the end of the thicket, with thinning stands of mature pine and unbroken snow ahead, the lengths of the coyote's jumps were sure indication that the animal still had a reserve of wind and strength sufficient to fortify him for another mile or two of chase.

"Ay ya!" At a slight pressure from my knees Mr. Binks let out his stride. The urge was strong in me now to give the chestnut his head and try to finish the job before the coyote beat me to another thicket. But experience whispered, "No." I must conserve my horse's staying power until the length of the coyote's jumps showed signs of shortening. I had not only to weigh the coyote's every strategy—and hope that I weighed rightly—but also to gauge to the very last ounce how much run was left in the chestnut.

I looked around for landmarks that might tell me just where in the devil I was. A blaze here and there on the trees recalled to mind where I had packed out a yearling bull moose from an acre or two of fire-killed timber three months ago. The old burn would be a mile or two away to my right. This knowledge of exactly where I was bred within me the uneasy realization that if the coyote held fast to his present course for another fifteen minutes he'd be down at Meldrum Lake.

The lake was in the process of flooding. I knew that. And until the flood water beneath the snow froze down to the old ice, I dare not put Mr. Binks out on the lake. But that flood water would not deter the coyote, for the frozen snow above it would hold his weight. Once he gained the lake he'd be across it and in the timber on the other side long before the chestnut could circle around the lake and take up the tracks again.

I leaned low over the saddle and gave Mr. Binks his head. Now there was neither sense nor policy in following the tracks of the coyote. Instead, I must beat him to the ice, keep him away from the lake and force him back on top.

The chestnut's hoofs were plowing snow within sight of the lake. I turned and ran parallel to the ice, hugging its edge for almost a mile without cutting the coyote's tracks. Breaking Mr. Binks into a trot, I left the ice and reined the horse back up the hill, for, balked in his plan to get to the lake, the coyote must now gamble his very all on regaining the upper rabbit pastures where dense brush would again slow up the hunt.

Going back up the hill I thought of the cabin, and Lillian and Veasy. Veasy of course had no proper idea of what the gruelling danger-ous business now taking place on the timbered slope west of Meldrum

Lake entailed. In a few years' time, when he himself tried his hand at the game, he quickly learned about it. But if Lillian had never chased a coyote, she was aware of the hazards involved. No horse was altogether infallible, and galloping over windfalls, often hidden by snow, any horse might stumble and go head over heels, pinning its rider beneath it. In dense lodgepole pine there was always the danger of breaking a leg when crowding the horse through the trees. Or of a snag gouging you in the eye, or an overhanging limb tumbling you clean out of the saddle. Of these things Lillian knew. But if she fretted about them she also knew that, now that the traps were of no avail, if coyote pelts were to go on the stretcher boards, this was the way I must get them.

When again I cut the track I saw that the coyote had almost beaten me to the ice, only to be headed off and turned back up the hill when he knew I was below him. His jumps were now visibly shortening, and where possible he was travelling under or on top of the blowdowns, taking full advantage of any break in the snow that would make for easier travel. At last he was beginning to tire.

Under circumstances such as these a mature coyote will sometimes display uncanny intelligence in a bid to save his skin. If able to throw his pursuer off his tracks in a thicket, he'll deliberately bed down in the snow and lie there regaining his wind and conserving his strength until the horse is almost on top of him. Once, when trying to wean an almost exhausted coyote away from the thicket of spruces in which he was hiding, I glimpsed him a few yards away stretched out on a flat rock, eyeing my every move. Yet before I could line the sights of my .22 rifle on him he was down off the rock and had melted away in the spruces.

I was tolerably certain that at long last this coyote was buckling under the pressure. Now it was entirely a matter of timing, of calculating just when and where to call on my horse for that final burst of speed that would draw him alongside the coyote. And the timing had to be right.

The trees ahead were thickening, the inevitable clumps of seedlings reaching out from gully and ridge. We were hauling back to the rabbit country. The jumps of the coyote were now only inches apart and their freshness said yes, the coyote's only a stone's throw ahead. A feel of the horseflesh between my knees told me of how much run there was left in the chestnut. He was good for about another half-mile.

"Mr. Binks!" The quirt flicked the gelding's quarters and the chestnut catapulted. I swung low over the saddle to dodge the reaching limbs. We twisted here, twisted there, like couples in a square dance as the chestnut pounded down on the ever-shortening jump marks in the snow.

At last the view halloo. Twenty-five pounds of almost exhausted coyote bobbed up and down in the snow like a scrap of driftwood rising and falling on the wavelets of a lake. Perhaps there should have been pity in me as my hand snaked down to the scabbard and I drew out the .22 and bolted a shell home. And maybe the pity was there, yet it was one I could not heed. How often in February and March, when the crusted snow will support a loping coyote but give to the weight of a deer, have I stared down at gruesome evidence in the timber indicating where coyotes had chased an animal down and then slowly killed it. No matter how many I might run down thus in the deepening snows, coyotes will still be killing deer when I am gone from the woods.

"Mr. Binks!" A mere whisper now. And the chestnut gave me generously of his final spark of speed. No need for sight or aim as we drew abreast the loser. I leaned away from the saddle, poked the cold snout of the .22 against the coyote's ear and quickly squeezed the trigger.

This business of pitting one form of life—the horse—against that other—the coyote—lacked justice to either one. Never for a moment did I look upon it as sport. It was a necessity of the moment, as eating and drinking are a necessity. In my time I have snuffed out the lives of many, many coyotes thus, yet it was not a task to my liking. And it was one I abandoned altogether when the need no longer existed.

The wick of the coal-oil lamp had been burning for two hours or longer when I got back to the cabin. Its pale light in the window acted as a tonic to my aching body, and I dug my heels into the chestnut's flanks, telling the almost spent horse, "Another hundred yards and we'll both know what it is to be warm again!"

The chestnut was gray with frosted sweat. Icicles were matted to its tail, making a harsh swishing sound at each stride the animal took. I leaned well forward in the saddle, mittened hands pressed against the horse's withers, as if trying to steal a little of the animal's body heat to comfort my own tortured flesh. For the past hour it seemed that that flesh was sheer ice.

That's how it always was when I got through chasing a coyote in the snow, whether I killed the animal or not. The excitement and furious tempo of the chase seemed to heat my blood, often brought perspiration to the skin. But with the chase and excitement of it all over, the bitter cold again became almost unbearable, especially on the way home.

The cabin door was open; I could see that when I was fifty yards from it. I thought, "She's out there, watching and waiting, and listening."

I heard her little cry of joy and relief when her body was just a vague form in the night. I reined the chestnut up to her, turned in the saddle and began fumbling with numbed fingers at the knots in the strings binding the limp, lifeless coyote to the skirts of the saddle.

"Here, let me." Quickly, Lillian untied the knots and lifted the coyote down.

I eased gingerly out of the saddle and pressed my cold lips against the warm ones she offered me, then she slipped the bridle from the chestnut's head, took the halter shank and bade me, "You go in and thaw out. I'll stable and feed the horse."

I reached for the halter shank. "I'll tend to the—"

"You'll go inside at once," she cut in. It was an order, not a suggestion. "You've had enough cold for one day." And she started with the horse for the barn, leaving me gawking stupidly after her.

I lugged the coyote into the cabin and began unbuckling my overshoes. Veasy inspected the "kill," then piped, "Daddy, when will I be old enough to chase coyotes?"

"By the time you're old enough for that," I solemnly told him, "I hope beyond anything that neither of us ever *has* to chase coyotes down in the snow." And fervently hoped I was right.

Chapter 10

I had been staring thoughtfully at the saucer for all of five minutes. It wasn't even a clean saucer, it was the one we fed the cat in. It was lying on the ground outside the cabin, upside down. Whether Veasy's feet or the antics of the cat had propelled the saucer to its present undignified stance was hard to say. Anyway, it didn't matter. It seemed to sort of blend into my thoughts as the colour of a deer blends with the background of the forest.

Winter was almost spent, although there was still the odd patch of snow here and there. Yesterday the creek had awakened as freshets commenced moving down it. And yesterday an advance echelon of Canada geese had passed over the cabin, high up, true, but there just the same. And the geese never fooled either themselves or anyone else. When they passed over the cabin, heads north, tails south, spring was here to stay.

Veasy was over by the hay corral, hunting fictitious deer with the bow and arrow I'd made him. He was stalking one right this very second. Suddenly he crouched down, placed the notch of the arrow against the string, then straightening, sped it toward the target. Then he whooped. Of course he'd killed himself a four-point buck because he never killed lesser fry, like two points or spikes. And of course he never shot at does or fawns.

Lillian and I were seated outside the cabin on blocks of wood, busy with nothing at all, just thankful the winter was over, just as right this very minute all over the Chilcotin, ranchers and trappers, stump farmers and wild-horse chasers, and squaws and papooses were all seated on blocks of wood outside their homes, busy with nothing at all, thankful the winter was over.

By and large the winter hadn't treated us too badly. Through January and up to mid-February I'd chased and killed thirteen coyotes. According to my recollection, five others had outguessed or outrun me. It wasn't a bad percentage in my favour. And thirteen coyotes in terms of ten-dollar bills added up to maybe one hundred thirty dollars. But in mid-February a twenty-four-hour chinook wind followed by deep-freeze temperatures had put an iron crust on the snow, and then the coyotes could gleefully thumb their noses at me. Only a fool or a greenhorn would match horseflesh against coyote when the snow was crusted like that.

For the next six weeks there was little else to do but get still further acquainted with the handles of the crosscut saw. Stove wood, like money, was something one just could not have too much of, for when the thermometer glares at you with a reading of minus fifty, wood, like money at any temperature, just seems to evaporate.

But now the geese were back, and the creek was in flood, and the lake ice rotting, and the saucer lying upside down in the dirt. And thinking about all that water going down the creek made me think of the saucer. Water and saucer—they blended perfectly.

I went over and picked it up, returned to the block of wood and began twiddling the saucer around in my fingers. Veasy was through hunting for a while, for of course any hunter gets tired. He stalked over to the cabin and began watching the saucer.

"Did you get it?" I asked.

He nodded.

"Was it fat?" Another nod.

"Did it have a liver?"

He frowned. "All deer have livers."

I said, "Good. I'm sure starved for a feed of fresh deer liver. After a while you and me'll go skin it out."

My thoughts went back to the saucer. It made me think of something else. So: "Blotting paper," I suddenly sang out. "I want a piece of blotting paper."

Lillian's eyebrows tilted. "What on earth for?"

I said impatiently, "Go find me some blotting paper, there's a good woman. And bring me a dipper of water too."

"Pen and ink?" she suggested as she stepped into the cabin.

"Of course not," I answered. "Just blotting paper and water." What foolish questions women sometimes ask, I thought to myself.

On her return I tore off a piece of the blotting paper and placed it at the bottom of the saucer. Then, a drop at a time, I tipped a little water into the saucer. Then I turned the saucer upside down.

"Where water go?" Veasy wanted to know on seeing that none left the saucer even though upside down. Veasy was not yet acquainted with the full properties of blotting paper.

Again I dribbled water into the saucer, a drop at a time. Following a good many drops a little water was now visible in the saucer. Still I continued dribbling water into it until it was half full. Gradually the saucer filled until water began running over its brim.

I squinted at Lillian over the top of the saucer, much as a schoolmaster glances at his class, and explained, "Every dry marsh along the creek is like that saucer with its blotting paper. The marshes themselves are so much blotting paper, absorbing all rain or snow as quickly as it falls or melts. But if we could just soak up their blotting paper as I did, in the saucer, the rain and melting snows would gradually fill them until they too overflowed and again fed the creek. Simple, isn't it?"

"To hear you talk about it, yes. But—" Lillian shook her head as if it wasn't that simple after all.

"Never mind the buts. Let's figure out how we can start filling one or two of the saucers." And getting up and feeling for my pocket knife, I said to Veasy, "Now, let's skin that deer and get at his liver." But Veasy

wasn't interested in any deer. He was pouring water into the saucer and
holding it upside down.

~

From source to mouth, Meldrum Creek follows a leisurely and at times
somewhat aimless path. On leaving the lake of its origin the creek travels
northeast with many a twist and turn until arriving at Meldrum Lake,
ten miles downstream. There it takes an easterly course for another ten
miles to spill into a chain of lakes lying roughly north to south. These
were the lakes that had earlier been tapped by the ranchers for water for
their irrigation ditches.

After passing through them, and as if now in impatience to reach
journey's end by the shortest possible route, the creek flows due east for
another nine miles and so comes to the river.

But not until it is almost within sight of the Fraser is there any noticeable fall to its grade, for above the trench of the river the land slopes but
slightly, and here the gentle flow of the creek offers numerous sites where
the beavers of old were able to build and maintain their dams. In a few
days' time, as soon as the frost was gone from the ground, we too were to
become beavers of sorts.

Fortified by the moral encouragement of the rancher Moon, we were
now ready to take the first hesitant step in our grand design of eventually reflooding every acre of marsh upon the creek that could be flooded
without doing harm to anyone else. To me, the principle of the saucer
and its blotting paper was beyond all dispute, but there were so many
saucers, so much blotting paper, and if for the time being we could do
nothing about the larger ones, we might do something with the lesser.

The success—or otherwise—of the plan hinged upon our being able
to shut off the tap without robbing the irrigation ditches of what little
water they had. At first thought it seemed a sheer impossibility, and well
might have been were it not for all the "saucers" and their blotting paper.
If we inundated one or two of the lesser saucers at the head of the creek,
might we not be merely impounding water that would only soak away

on some larger marsh below before getting anywhere near the irrigation ditches? And would not the filling of even one small saucer to a point where the water spilled out of it result in just that much more water in the creek channel below? Here were questions that we were now about to try to answer.

In rebuilding the first dam we employed the tactics of a beaver itself. An examination of what was still left of their dams showed us that their concrete had mostly been sticks and other trash. Good enough for us. We felled spruces and other conifers and toted their limbs to the dam site, where they were laid out on the surface in network design, tops upstream.

Again, although against my will, Lillian insisted that she too should help at the handles of the crosscut saw in felling the timber. As soon as the trees crashed to earth she dropped the saw, hefted her short-handled, single-bitted axe and began hacking at the limbs. Originally the dam had been some three hundred forty feet long, and the task of rebuilding it without even a plow or scraper seemed one that had no end.

After arranging a mat of boughs along the dam, we then wheeled dirt from a nearby pit and dumped it on the boughs. First a layer of boughs, then a layer of dirt, boughs and dirt, dirt and boughs, hour after hour, day after day, until it seemed that we'd logged off all of the forest and moved a hilltop besides. But finally the job was done and when the dam filled there would be five or more feet of water where now there was stagnant marsh. The boughs comprising perhaps half the bulk in the dam served two useful purposes: in the first place they saved us some of the drudgery of shovelling and wheeling dirt and gravel, and in the second, now that the job was finished, water could cascade over its top without danger of the whole structure washing out. That was the principle upon which the beavers built their dams, and if it was good enough for beavers it was good enough for us.

The reflooding of a mere ten acres of marsh to a depth of five feet is a slow and tedious process when the flow of water coming into it is only a mere trickle. It seemed that the saucer was never going to fill. But eventually its blotting paper was soaked, and water began inching up the face of the dam, until, three weeks after its completion, the water licked at the top and began spilling over.

And then the weather pattern itself decided to give us a hand. Shortly after the dam was finished, the skies clouded over, the wind rushed in from the south, and rain began to fall. It fell intermittently for forty-eight hours, sometimes a drizzle, sometimes a deluge that kept us in the cabin. But we didn't mind that. Lillian had her sewing—she never did seem to catch up on that and I doubt that she ever will—I had Darwin's *On the Origin of Species* and *The Descent of Man*, a book well calculated to keep any thoughtful man occupied for many a rainy night, and Veasy had the canoe he was whittling from a piece of cottonwood split. Let it rain! The more it rained, the better the canoe would float when it came time to run the rapids.

The rain was surely hint enough for us to begin work now on another beaver dam a half-mile below the first. The job took all of a week, for it had originally been two hundred feet long and eight feet high in the creek channel. But we hacked down more spruces and we trundled another hill or two away on the wheelbarrow and finally that job was done and another few acres of marsh was lake.

Now came a few days of dread and gnawing anxiety. For over two weeks the "tap" had been shut off at the head of the creek. Had the irrigation ditches, miles below us, gone without water as consequence? If so, we'd know about it before long. All now hinged upon whether or not one of the ranchers, or his hired help, moved in on the scene to investigate a sudden shortage of water in an irrigation ditch.

"Heck of a note if all of a sudden we hear boom-boom-boom, and find that they've blown our dams to Kingdom Come," I cheerfully summed up this period of dark and hideous uncertainty. But there wasn't a single boom. No one came near the dams. The irrigation ditches hadn't been affected.

As soon as they had their water back, the marshes again began producing crops of aquatic grasses and tubers. The root systems, of course, had been there all the time, and only water was needed to induce them to show life. By late July a half-dozen different varieties of aquatic weeds and grasses pushed their stems above water, and the ponds took on a vivid greenish hue. Three hen mallards suddenly appeared on the scene, warily piloting their broods of half-fledged youngsters among the waving grasses. A mink left its catlike track in the soft dirt of the dams, and muskrats began building feed beds in the flooded willows.

One evening in early August, nine Canada geese winged low over the cabin, heading upstream. Watching them, I saw them set their wings and a few seconds later I heard the thrash of their wings as they braked down on the water.

"They're down in our first dam," I decided. "Let's go see if we can spot them."

In single file we trooped up the creek. Nearing the dam we went down on hands and knees, and cautiously peered over the top. The geese were fifteen yards away, splashing the water and punctuating each splash with a subdued honk. The geese themselves were no novelty at all. What was a novelty was the fact that not for a half-century or more had Canada geese been able to wet their breasts on that marsh. Our wastelands were beginning to produce.

Chapter 11

Crack! Crack! Crack! Faint and far off though the shots were, the message they bore compelled me to stiffen in the saddle, jerk the chestnut to a stop and stare anxiously into the north—that's where the reports had come from, somewhere off to the north.

"Rifle fire!" I muttered uneasily. "Those three shots came from a 30-30 carbine." As their echo rolled away, Lillian and I gazed questioningly and maybe a little fearfully at one another. No doubt they'd been fired at a moose or a deer, but who would be out on our trapline this early in the spring, hunting meat for the camps?

The morning sun was still riding the treetops. The young timber grass had a sad and forlorn look about it, wilted as it was by the overnight frost, but within a half-hour the rising sun would bring each blade to life. A robin trilled reveille from the top of an old snag, and a half-dozen cock willow grouse strutted onto their logs and began drumming love lyrics to the nearby hens.

A moment ago I was relaxed in the saddle, ears keenly tuned to the natural sounds of the everlasting forest, eyes penetrating the timber ahead for a glimpse of some startled buck—but now the sound of those rapidly fired shots was like a needle pricking my skin, giving birth within me to a sharp pang of consternation.

"Indians!" I jerked out. "But they wouldn't come this far from their reservation just to hunt meat. They're out after fur!"

In theory it's as simple as ABC. You have a hundred and fifty thousand acres of wilderness, ninety-eight percent of which will never—either today or tomorrow or one hundred years from now—be scratched by the share of a plow, since its soil is so stony and barren it is incapable of producing any other crop but the shrubbery and grasses and twisted scrubby timber that God put there in the beginning; one hundred and fifty thousand acres, at which man, in his wide search for new lands to plow and cultivate, took one disinterested glance and then passed on. Its creeks and its lakes and its forests did contain wealth of a sort, but it was a wealth that was soon spent. The name of that wealth was wildlife.

But in theory it seems simple. Since all life is conceived at water's edge, you begin by conserving the water in order to establish an environment necessary to the production of almost any wildlife population. That's how we saw it from the start. What others before had torn down, perhaps we might rebuild. It was that simple. But cluttering the orderly path of Theory are the bothersome blowdowns of Fact. It was one thing for us to provide habitat for and conserve a wildlife crop until sheer preponderance of numbers warranted a sensible harvesting of the crop, but another altogether to prevent others stepping in to reap what our efforts had sown.

If under the game regulations of British Columbia it is unlawful for anyone to trap or otherwise take fur-bearers beyond the confines of his own registered trapline, enforcement of that edict is a different matter indeed, especially so in a land where a single game warden must bleakly try to enforce game regulations over an area such as the Chilcotin Plateau, some two hundred miles from east to west, a hundred-odd from north to south.

And the whole added up to a seemingly limitless wilderness through which one could travel for week after endless week with but dim prospects of bidding a fellow being "good day," pathed mostly by only the game trails. In a land such as this most any written game regulation was one easily broken.

It is a simple matter to prove ownership of a cow or horse with a registered brand upon its hide, but a sheer impossibility to do so with fur-bearing animals that cannot be branded in the first place and so become the lawful property of the first trapper to tack their pelt to a stretcher board. The game warden did his best, but the odds against his ever catching an offender in the act of stealing—or poaching—furs was a million to one. And the poaching of furs, where furs were there to be poached, was a profitable occupation. We were forced to the decision that from now on, within the confines of our own registered trapline, we ourselves must make our own game regulations and enforce them as God saw fit to direct us.

We expected trouble from our Indian neighbours—to start with, any-way. For that pinprick upon a map of the Chilcotin that might indicate the whereabouts of our trapline is flanked by three Indian reservations: Aniham to the west, Soda Creek to the north and Riske Creek to the south. The Indians of these reservations were accustomed to wandering far and wide from their own barren traplines to other parts where furs might be more plentiful. Perhaps they had a plausible excuse for doing so. Theirs was the right to trap and hunt at will long before they were moved onto reservations. Game was their only road to survival, and if that road were denied them, they and their kind must vanish from the face of the earth.

The Indians were almost totally illiterate. They had their own names for the valleys, mountains and watersheds, but such names often differed from those printed upon the white man's maps of the Chilcotin. Each Indian family in a reservation had its own individual trapline and well they knew its boundaries. They were not quite so familiar with those of a white man's trapline.

For those first half-dozen years on our trapline, in early spring any-way, we assumed the habits if not the hue of the Indians themselves. As soon as the snow was gone we bade a temporary "so long" to our cabin and began patrolling the watershed, reasoning that here was a far more efficient method of protecting our slowly increasing stock of fur than by wishfully expecting any game warden to do it for us. That God helps those who help themselves was good enough for us.

I led the way, trailing along behind me the pack horse that toted much of our worldly belongings. Lillian followed in my tracks on an old pot-bellied mare so good-natured and satisfied with life in general that she cared not a jot for the additional burden—Veasy—who rode behind on her rump. And at close of day, to the symphony of drake mallards grumbling to one another in the bulrushes, or Canada geese talking overhead, we pitched our tiny tent at the edge of some unnamed lake and while Lillian got the meal and laid a mattress of fir boughs, I began circling the water, looking for tracks that rightly shouldn't be there. Or if the sun went down on a field of gold we did not bother with the formality of stretching tent. Instead we spread our bedding beneath the branches of some friendly tree and fell asleep with the pitchy tang of the needles pungent in our nostrils.

∾

The sun heaved higher, the robin was out of breath, and each blade of timber grass had long since sprung to life. In single file we neck reined our horses through the timber, heading due south. Later I turned into the west, then north, making a wide circle, eyes to the ground. Lillian and I seldom had anything to say to each other when riding thus through the woods. Talk was something best kept for the campfire, when the chores of the day were over and we could stretch out by the coals and relax. Prolonged silence when in the saddle was becoming habit with Veasy too, for the young quickly learn to mimic the habits of their elders, good or bad as the case may be. This morning, sensing that something important was afoot, he held a still tongue even when a deer jumped up and bounced off in weaving flight.

The task of locating the whereabouts of one, two or possibly more Indian hunters in such limitless tract of forest might at first consideration seem as hopeless as finding a minnow in the ocean. But it wasn't quite that hopeless. The Chilcotin Indians never travelled afoot. Wherever they went their horses went too. And horses leave their sign behind them. And that's why my eyes never left the ground. Maybe if I stared at it long enough I'd be rewarded by cutting sign.

I'd just turned to the south again, and was following a game trail, when I hauled in sharply on the lines and breathed a tense "Whoa." I leaned out of the saddle, eyes to the ground. Then slowly straightening, I glanced at Lillian and inclined my head. "Horse tracks. They cut the trail right here, and they seem to be heading south. Two of the horses are shod, the others barefoot. I reckon there are four riders altogether."

Lillian drew up alongside me. Veasy's tongue suddenly came to life. "Poachers?" he piped up.

I said, "They're not government surveyors."

The tracks of the four horses did not follow the game trail as loose horses might, but momentarily cut it at that single spot. A born tracker himself, the Chilcotin Indian is too shrewd to follow the path of a game trail when abroad over the traplines, intent on poaching fur.

Turning with the tracks, eyes on the crushed grass stems, I urged the chestnut slowly under the trees. For the next couple of miles my eyes never deviated from their fix on the ground ahead. Then, abruptly halting the horse, I shot a glance back over my shoulder and said crisply, "At Rawhide Lake, that's where we'll haul up to them. They're out after muskrats."

It was the spring of 1934. On the creek itself a half-dozen minor saucers had again been dammed and reflooded. As soon as a marsh over-flowed, life, furred and feathered, came back to it. But we'd also dammed some of the landlocked lakes, and Rawhide was one. We ourselves gave it the name on finding a scrap of rawhide at an old Indian camping ground close to the shoreline. In the summer of 1932 we repaired an old beaver dam at the outlet of the lake and by thus holding back the spring freshets of snow water that drained away from the lake to lose themselves in the gravelly soil beyond, we succeeded in raising its level to a point where the dry marsh around it lay under eighteen inches of water. Now the lake was beginning to produce a crop of muskrats, but a night or two of indiscriminate trapping could quickly destroy much of the foundation of breeding stock that we had been almost two years in establishing.

There was no need now to bother about any tracks. I was certain the horses were being reined toward the lake, and there was a huge impatience in me to get there ourselves as quickly as possible. I booted the chestnut into a trot, then a gallop. The nose of the pot-bellied mare was at Mr. Binks's tail, Lillian crouched forward on its withers, face almost touching the mane. She'd been wearing an old straw hat when last I looked back at her, but now the hat was gone, and the wind was playing with her hair as if it wanted to carry it off too.

"Where's your hat?" I shouted back at her.

"Don't ask silly questions." Lillian's face lifted long enough to toss that at me, then went back to the mane.

The horses plowed through thickets of second-growth, cleared windfalls without breaking stride, responded instantly to pressure of bridle line against neck as we piloted them through the rocks. And so we came to Rawhide Lake.

There, all seemed as innocent as innocence could possibly be. Surely there was no one but ourselves within miles and miles of the lake. But fifty yards back from the shoreline, in a grove of young aspen, were horse droppings, and trampled ground where the horses had been tied to trees. Moving away from the aspens we hitched our own horses well out of sight among the jack pine. Leaving Lillian and Veasy squatting at timber's edge where they could see without being seen, I began circling the lake, knee-deep in water. Now and then I splashed out through the bulrushes and picked up a trap. Occasionally the limp body of a muskrat dangled at the end of the chain. The Indians had set thirty-six traps in Rawhide Lake, and eleven of them held muskrats.

Yet there was neither dismay nor anger in me when I dumped the traps at Lillian's feet and took their catch from their jaws. This was all part of the game, and if we couldn't play it through we had no business starting.

Though five of the muskrats were females, heavy bellied with young, I felt no rancour toward the Indians responsible for their destruction.

Any more than I would hold a grudge against a little child who climbs up on a stool and helps himself to the cookies. In fact, I smiled as I dropped down at Lillian's side. "Bimeby I t'ink we see a leetle fun," I said, aping the pidgin talk of the Indians themselves.

For a half-hour or more we lay flat on our stomachs under the trees, chins in our hands, not a word to say to one another. Then I came up on my elbows. Out of the timber came a coyote, running hard, tail stiffened. It stopped for a split second at timber's edge and glanced back over its shoulders. Then, wheeling sharply right, it entered a copse of willow, not to be seen again.

Carefully I hoisted to one knee. "They're coming now," I said in muted tones.

The four of them came noiselessly out of the woods a little down lake from us. They reined their horses into the aspens and there tied them up. Then they split into pairs, two going around the lake clockwise, two counterclockwise. At that time, three dozen No. 1 traps, the size used for the trapping of muskrats, would cost about fourteen dollars at any trading post. Those I had picked up had seen little use, which indicated that the Indians had but recently purchased them. To me it seemed foolish for the Indians to wade all around the lake when on finding their first few sets gone they must surely realize that someone else was there ahead of them. But circle the lake they did, completely, then they joined forces and after a moment or two of consultation they came around the water and hurried toward the horses. But before they reached the aspens I was standing there, between the trees and their ponies.

They dragged to a halt a few yards away from me, eyes on the ground, soggy moccasins nervously scuffing the dirt. There was neither hostility nor fear in their faces, just an indifferent apathy. They had been caught red-handed in the act of poaching furs and, like a coyote caught stealing the bait from a trap, were now resigned to whatever the consequences might be.

Two of the Indians were middle-aged, the others not yet out of their teens. All wore faded blue denim overalls and threadbare flannel shirts.

Their caps were "store" caps, ill-fitting and shoddy. Only their buckskin footwear bore any resemblance to the clothing their forebears had worn before cloth and button supplanted skins and sinew. The moccasins came halfway up their legs and were decorated with multicoloured beads. Both eyes of one of the youngsters were disfigured by a cataract of sorts, and I guessed that he'd be stone blind before reaching middle age unless the cataract was removed. Which of course it wouldn't be.

Holding Veasy by the hand, Lillian too moved away from the timber and was there by my side when I broke the awkward silence. "What place your home stop?" I mildly inquired of one of the older Indians.

After a strained silence the Indian falteringly replied, "Tingley Creek."

"He belongs to the Alexandria reservation," I thought.

My eyes flicked across to the other. "And you?"

Without looking up from the ground: "Pelican Lake," he informed me. Pelican Lake lay forty miles west of the western boundary of our own trapline.

I then scrutinized the two lads, who restlessly shifted from one foot to another as if not quite sure which was the safest to rest upon. Suddenly I asked. "Young feller, you ever see beaver?"

There was no movement of the lips, just a shake of the head. So turning to one of the oldsters, I went on, "Maybe one of you fellows see beaver some time?"

This brought a stony silence from the one, a jumble of words from the other. They poured out of his mouth like chatter from a magpie. "Me just leetle boy when one tam' my father find where one beaver stop in Chilcotin river. He set trap for that beaver and bimeby kill 'um. Then he take skin to store and make lots good trade, and we all eat beaver meat and he good meat too. That one only beaver me ever see."

I looked at Lillian. She was looking at me. And then I knew that her thoughts were my thoughts too.

Before us stood four Chilcotin Indians whose ancestors had known the land when its watersheds teemed with beavers, yet only one had seen a beaver himself and that was perhaps all of thirty years ago.

106

"Why," I suddenly wanted to know, but of no particular one, "you not stop your own trapline instead of coming to steal fur from me?"

A quick reply of "No damn fur stop" was the reply I sort of expected. "No damn fur stop," I echoed softly. "No, it was all trapped out before any of us were born."

My eyes kept shifting from one brown face to another. Veasy stared boldly at all four. Lillian was blankly watching the lake. A drake mallard rich in the plumage of the mating season paddled in off the water and began preening his feathers. From deep within the bulrushes came the subdued quacking of his mate.

My tongue was groping for words, the kind I had to use. Here was no occasion for long-winded rhetoric. What I must say must be brief and something the Indians would understand. A great deal hinged on what I said and did in the next minute or two. Indians, not only these four, but Indians in general, could cause us a great deal of harm unless we handled this situation right. Not bodily harm, for where their dealing with the whites were concerned the Chilcotin Indians were passive enough, and never went on the warpath. But harm to the fur-bearers we were trying so hard to conserve, harm to almost everything that had brought us to the creek in the first place. And suddenly my mind cleared and I knew just what I must say, just what I must do.

I took a deep breath. "Come here." It was more of an invitation than a command. With the toe of my boot I smoothed off a patch of ground, then, kneeling, began tracing lines in the dirt with the tip of my right index finger. Curiosity stamped on their faces, the Indians inched closer until they had formed a circle around me.

The lines in the dirt began taking definite pattern. A lake was mentioned here, a creek or muskeg there. The Indians perhaps knew more of such places than I did myself.

"Inside this line," I patiently began to explain, "my trapping country stop. Damn little fur stop here now, but once upon a time lots beavers, muskrats, mink, otter, fisher stop. But now no more beaver stop because no one leave any beaver in water to raise papoose 'nother year. And when beaver go, most all other fur go too."

I hefted a small pebble and, bracing back on my heels, hurled it out into the lake. "Look!" I said quietly. And the Indians turned on their heels and watched the spot where the pebble had splashed.

"You see how ripple spread out over water where rock falls?" I asked. And just to make certain, I threw another. "Bimeby, s'pose Indians not steal them from me that's how my beaver, mink and muskrat and other fur spread too. Until pretty soon so many stop my trapline some he got to move away to other place. That's the time he maybe move onto your trapline, and s'pose you leave alone just little while and let him get papooses, lots of fur stop your country again too."

I stepped back into the jack pines and returned with the traps and muskrats. I stared long and thoughtfully at the traps and fur. According to the unwritten law of the wilderness, any traps found upon a registered trapline automatically became the property of the owner of the line, as did, of course, any fur that was in them. No one, least of all those who had unlawfully set the traps, ever questioned that long-established principle. Mine was the right now to claim ownership of the fur and traps in my hand. The Indians were fully reconciled to the loss of both. But I knew that that wouldn't do. So I dropped both fur and traps and fumbled in my pocket for tobacco pouch and cigarette papers. After rolling myself a cigarette, I asked the Indians, "You smoke?"

The only talkative one of the four inclined his head. "S'pose tobacco stop."

I lit my cigarette and took a deep puff. "No tobacco stop now?" And receiving a negative gesture of the head in reply, I thought, "There's not a five-cent piece among the lot of them." So I passed over the makings and watched while each built himself a cigarette.

Slowly then, I began tossing the traps down at their feet. Muskrats followed the traps. "Take them and go back your own country," I told them. "And remember what I say to you: s'pose Indian leave me alone and not steal my fur, pretty soon lots fur come back his country too."

They picked up the fur and the traps and shuffled away to their horses. Suddenly one of the older ones halted and looked back across his shoulder. "T'ank you." His voice was barely audible. And then they swung up into their saddles and single-filed into the dark mass of the forest. Long after they were out of sight, I kept staring at the forest. Then, turning to Lillian, I commented, "Well?" as if asking her for her own thoughts.

She made a quick little gesture with her hands. "You gave them back their traps, and the fur that was in them too." She broke off, glanced at the lake, then exclaimed, "No other white man would have done that! Eric, I know the Indians a great deal better than you do—I should, since I am part Indian myself. You gave them their traps and the fur and they'll never forget it. And soon, in every reservation around us, all the Indians will hear how you gave them the traps and fur when you might have kept them yourself. Some people might say you were foolish, but you weren't. You did just what had to be done. I don't think we ever need worry anymore about Indians stealing our fur."

Chapter 12

There was no indication in the fall of 1934 that disaster was about to stare us in the face. The fall had been a mild one, and not until mid-October did any large flocks of geese move in on us from the north. And the geese knew a thing about weather, and their judgement could usually be relied upon.

With November's first snowfall we backtracked to a bear den and routed out its tenant. Then I shot a two-year-old bull moose and hung its quarters beneath the spruce tree. The mouse cycle was at its peak, so we looked forward to a profitable catch of weasels when their coats would be white and prime. The shifting moods of the cycles, which have such paramount bearing upon the affairs of the different wildlife communities, had become something of a study with us. They played a major role in our economic well-being, so it was essential that we should have some understanding of them. If the plentitude of muskrats, waterfowl and other aquatic life resulted in an increase in mink, so too was a plentitude of mice accountable for a similar increase in weasel. No form of life can be permitted to increase beyond the carrying capacity of its food supply. There must be a little "left in the bank." A wildlife community can increase just so long as there is a certain food supply in sight to warrant the increase. Beyond that point it cannot and will not go.

A conservative estimate made during the summer of 1934 told me that by investing a few dollars in additional traps we had good chance of taking at least two hundred dollars' worth of weasel when they primed out. So the traps were purchased and in mid-November set out and baited. The winter's work had begun.

We never had actually feared the winters, despite their snow and their wind and their savage bursts of colder than usual temperatures. A colder than usual temperature was when the mercury registered fifty below zero and the wind lanced down from the Arctic. In winter there were no flies to pester us, and almost every single day was one of enticing expectancy. Though a trap set for a mink might only catch a no-account flying squirrel or pack rat, it might catch a small dark fisher worth one hundred fifty dollars. Or a trap set for a coyote might, if luck blew from the right direction, catch a silver fox worth ten times as much as the coyote.

If once in a great while loneliness beset us, it was only for a moment. Of a fact there was scarcely a spare moment to take so much as even a quick thought of loneliness. Lillian had her chores around the house to do, as well as one or two outside. She had her own little trapline, a mile of it, up and down the creek. This she travelled every day, weather permitting, with Veasy slipping along on a pair of homemade skis at her heels. Seldom a day went by but what she didn't get at least a weasel or two in the traps. And of course she was ever buoyed up by the possibility that the very next trap she came to would hold a fine mink.

Veasy was already delving into the mysteries of spelling. He knew that D-O-G was dog and C-A-T was cat. He knew other things, too, though how he came to know them is a question without plausible answer. Once, when looking for coyote tracks in the snow, I cut what was obviously a fox track. After a run of a couple of miles I ran the animal down, shot it with the .22 and tied it behind the saddle. Veasy was skiing a little way from the cabin when I came in sight. As fast as skis and legs and wind could carry him, he shot straight for the cabin door, shouting, "Daddy's got a fox!" He'd never seen one before, but since it obviously wasn't a coyote his line of reasoning perhaps told him that it had to be a fox. Or maybe the knowledge just came naturally, as a newly weaned coyote pup learns that the hunting of porcupine is a pastime only indulged in by coyotes long in years and wisdom, and if attempted by an adolescent predator will only result in a mouthful of barbed quills.

~

Our first warning of an impending change in the weather pattern came to me in late November. When running a long line of traps I continually crossed the well-packed trails of deer travelling one behind the other. Apparently overnight, the deer had made sudden resolve to migrate to their wintering grounds proper along the Fraser River. "Now why," I wondered, "should they be pulling out for the river this early?" Usually the deer stayed with us until well along in January.

For the next three days the continual movement of deer toward the river showed itself wherever I was running the traps, but on the fourth day when making my rounds, I cut the tracks of only a few. The main herds had passed on; only the stragglers were left.

There is usually an explanation for much that takes place in the wilderness if one tries hard enough to find it. The ribbonlike paths of the mule deer, a hasty migration underway six weeks earlier than usual, pointed up one sure fact: a change in the weather was at hand, and a change that would be for the worse. Perhaps the deer could scent the change in the air, or perhaps their instinct for survival warned them of its advent. Anyway, they knew.

Forty-eight hours after the passing of the deer herd, the wind began moving down threateningly from the north. Tallowy clouds blotted out the sun, and a foreboding hush brooded over the forests. The chatter of red squirrels no longer scolded me when I passed beneath the trees. Spruce hen and willow grouse winged away from the scattering timber, seeking less exposed habitat elsewhere. Moose that were pasturing in the alder thickets higher up the hillsides began trailing down to the muskegs and beaver meadows below. And snowshoe rabbits stayed close to their holes, ready to bolt down into the bowels of the earth when the threat of an approaching blizzard became actual fact.

With December the first granulated kernels of snow commenced slanting in with the wind. I stepped out of the cabin one morning to face the wrath of a snow-laden wind that nigh crushed the breath from my lungs. Fourteen inches of snow had fallen during the night, and the trail from cabin to barn was buried. I glanced at the thermometer hanging on the outer logs of the cabin. The mercury was at eighteen degrees below zero. That would not have been too unpleasant if it hadn't been for the wind, and drive and thrust of the snow. In clear still weather one can run a line of traps in a temperature of thirty or more below at the cost of perhaps only a slightly frost-bitten cheek or nose, but when even a mere ten below is spiced by an arctic wind, no trapper in his right senses moves far from the shelter of his cabin.

For three weeks the snow continued to fall intermittently, reaching a depth of forty inches. Our hopes of a large catch of weasel lay buried beneath its mass. Even the coyotes had forsaken us to follow the deer to the river. From a short-term viewpoint, that December of the heavy snows was a catastrophe indeed, yet every inch that fell added to a total that decided our eventual plan.

Christmas sulked in on a quartering moon. The skies cleared temporarily and snow no longer rustled against the windowpanes. The wind from out of the Yukon blew sharp as splintered glass. The spruces along the creek cracked as the frost bit into them, and from higher up the hill a little red fox yapped and wailed its ravenous misery.

∻

Moose calves hoisted up from the snow at daybreak, legs stiff with frost. Chickadee birds dropped from their perches in the spruce trees, tiny feathered bodies frozen solid as they roosted. It was Christmas, the birthday of Our Lord. Christmas Day and the mercury reading exactly fifty-three degrees below zero.

Only the moose or occasional wandering timber wolf saw fit to wallow through the depths of snow now crushing the forests, for fifty above or fifty below, moose must continue to forage daily lest their body heat forever be extinguished within them.

For the first time since entrusting our destiny to the wilderness, we now had to forego our customary pre-Christmas journey to the trading post at Riske Creek. I had hoped somehow to breast the snow with team and sleigh and go out for supplies and mail a few days before Christmas, but in a temperature of zero minus fifty it is not fit that either man or horse should be out on any trail.

It was apparent that Santa Claus wouldn't pass himself down the six-inch stovepipe this Christmas, and somehow I had to break the sad news to Veasy. But how? Then I had an inspiration. On Christmas Eve, just after sundown, I took him outside the cabin and stood studying the sky. The cold was so crisp and sharp that the very process of breathing compelled me to cough. A few drops of moisture coming from Veasy's eyes froze as they formed on his cheeks.

I shook my head and muttered, "Don't see how anyone can travel in weather like this." And after a timely pause, "Not even Santa Claus."

Veasy pondered over this a moment or two, then said, "He'd freeze, wouldn't he?"

I nodded. "He and his reindeer too."

Veasy said, "And then there'd never be any more Christmases, would there?"

"Well," I replied cautiously, "there'd be other Christmases, but maybe no more Santa Claus."

"I hope he stays in the warm," was Veasy's reaction to the melancholy news.

Fifteen inches of new snow fell between Christmas and New Year. Our pantry shelves were almost as bare as Mother Hubbard's, although we didn't lack meat and vegetables. And if a three-meal-per-day menu of moose or deer meat, with the occasional goose for variation, became monotonous, it at least kept flesh on our ribs.

We hadn't seen another human being for over two months, or received or sent off mail in the same length of time. We were Crusoes on the island, around us a sea of snow. Yet these were trivial matters, inconvenient but not serious. But there was one insidious thought of which we couldn't rid ourselves: what if serious illness suddenly stalked into our home? Although the healthy life that was ours was seldom disturbed by even a common cold, I had disturbing recollection of other trappers who, shut away from any possible medical help in the wintry isolation of their traplines had sickened and died alone in their cabins to rest there frozen, not to be found until spring or sometimes later.

The more Lillian and I brooded over the matter, the more urgent seemed the necessity of our somehow breaking out to Riske Creek with the team and sleigh. This was easier thought about than done, for apart perhaps from the occasional moose track, which would be of no help to horses at all, the track from Meldrum Lake to Riske Creek hadn't been travelled since the snow first began falling.

Lillian finally brought matters to a head. "We've just got to break a trail through to Riske Creek," she blurted out across the breakfast table.

"I've been thinking along those lines myself," I agreed. "It'll likely take me all of four days if I make the round trip on snowshoes—"

"Snowshoes!" she cried. "What good would a snowshoe track be to me if you broke a leg or Veasy came down with pneumonia or something? Eric, it must be done with the team and sleigh." And when this brought no immediate response from me, she furthered, "We can take a camp outfit along and fill the sleigh box with hay for the horses."

"We?" I shook my head and said, "Snowshoes or team and sleigh, this is one trip I'd best tackle alone."

"Veasy and I are going too." Lillian's voice had hardened. "Think I want to sit here not knowing whether you got through or not? Of course Veasy and I are going. It won't be the first time we've slept out under trees, and probably won't be the last for that matter."

"In over five feet of snow, maybe thirty or forty below zero?"

"Yes, in five feet of snow and fifty below if it likes." Lillian's voice sounded unnaturally firm, and her face was set with iron determination. Her eyes never flinched as she stared me in the face. Here was one facet of Lillian's character that had never before asserted itself, at least not since she was married to me. Usually she tried to make her point by diplomatic and gentle persuasion. Now, however, I knew that my wishes were of no avail whatsoever against the granite of her resolve.

"Okay," I sighed, "we'll all go."

On bare ground, with the horses hitched to the wagon, we could make the trip from the cabin to Riske Creek in eight or ten hours of slow but certain travel. Hitched to the sleigh, and with only a few inches of snow on the ground, the team could get us out in less time still. But with the snow at its present depth it was a highly debatable matter whether we could get through with the team at all. But by giving the horses their time, and making an overnight camp when they could pull us no farther that day, we at least stood some chance of getting through to Riske Creek. There was danger, to be sure, but after you've been snowbound for one or two months without a sign of a human being, it seemed to us that almost any chance was worth taking. We took it.

Chapter 13

We postponed the moment of harnessing and hitching the team to the sleigh in slender hope that there could be a sudden warm-up in the weather. The hope was slight, because Chilcotin winters had taught us that for every twenty-four hours that a snow-freighted wind blows down from the north, one can usually expect that there will be another twenty-four hours of silent, deadly cold when the wind and the snow cease.

Finally the skies shed their gray, but as gray gave way to blue and an argent sun again looked down on the woods, the mercury skidded to zero minus forty. But still, after almost a month without a glimpse of it, there was something cheerful, if not warming, to the bright stare of the sun. So, trying to forget the telltale evidence of the thermometer, we piled blankets, camping outfit and hay into the sleigh box, coupled the team to the neck yoke and struck out to the south.

At least there was no wind to pry at our clothing, and if the fur trim of our parkas was soon hoary with frost, and we were continually forced to rub a heavily mittened hand across our eyelashes to rid them of the ice, down in the depths of the sleigh box, head and hands just above the blankets, we managed to keep our bodies reasonably warm.

For the horses, every yard gained was a yard of cruel effort. The snow piled and pushed ahead of the neck yoke until such a solid mass of it was windrowed up in front of them the horses could not wiggle the sleigh another inch. Now I had to climb down from the sleigh, wallow around to the neck yoke and shovel the snow aside before the horses could get the sleigh runners squeaking again. The presence of any short pitch in the road called for a minute or two of rest for the team.

Two miles out from the cabin we came upon gruesome evidence of the toll that December's "bitter" moon was exacting from the wildlife of the forests. Square in the middle of what had once been the road before it was blanked out by snow lay a calf moose. Its head rested back upon its withers, and both hind and front legs were doubled beneath it. So natural did the calf look there in the snow, it seemed that surely this poor little waif of the wilderness was not dead but only sleeping. But that was the way it died. Unable to stay in the track of its mother, all will to live slowly but inexorably sapped by the relentless torture of the cold, there finally came a moment when the output of energy required to search for a mouthful of forage exceeded the input of energy gained by the consumption of the food. And so, tiring of such hard struggle for existence, the calf knelt down in the snow and lay there, breath crystallizing upon its lips, heart feebly ticking away the final moments of life.

I had to drop the neck yoke and fasten a chain to the doubletrees to pull the casualty off the right-of-way. After recoupling the horses I jumped back into the box and told Lillian, "There's no sign of any cow track around."

"Maybe the wolves got the mother," suggested Lillian with a sigh.

"Could be." I shook the lines and got the team moving again. When next we paused to give the horses their wind, I stated grimly, "There'll be more than one moose dead in the woods before this snow has melted."

∿

The watch that Lillian had given me for Christmas in 1931 still kept good time. I had wound it when leaving the cabin but hadn't looked at it since. The very thought of peeling a mitt and feeling for the watch was an unpleasant one, and one quickly discarded. The matter of keeping the fingers warm was far more urgent than just knowing the time.

As the sun went down, a patch or two of gray smeared the northern horizon. As near as I could reckon we'd now covered eight miles, in about the same number of hours. Icicles, twelve inches of them, hung from the noses of the horses. Their bodies were gray with sweat that had frozen to their hair almost as quickly as it came from the pores of their skin. Alongside the track stood a lone fir tree that had probably been a sturdy sapling when Columbus came to America. It had a girth of five feet, with limbs so stout that the snow on them scarcely bent them at all. As if sensing my own weariness, the team stopped alongside the tree and stood with drooping heads and heaving flanks, breaking their icicles against the neck yoke.

"They've had it," I reasoned aloud. "The team is beat."

Lillian pushed the blankets aside and peered around. "I'm that stiff I doubt that I ever will be able to walk again," she said. For the past hour Veasy had been buried beneath layers of blankets and hay. Now, with a sudden heave, he came to sight again, complaining, "I'm hungry."

The boughs of the fir tree had broken much of the snowfall, and beneath them it was only a couple of feet deep. "It's as good a place as any," I said, "and a great deal better than some. Here's our hotel. You and Veasy had better stay in the sleigh while I unhitch the horses."

I unhitched the team, blanketed them and fed them an armful of hay. There was no nearby lake or creek in which to cut a water hole, so for tonight anyway the horses would have to eat snow instead of drinking water.

The horses attended to, I shovelled a space some ten feet by twelve beneath the tree. Now Lillian and Veasy were able to crawl down from the sleigh box without miring in snow. It was darkening, with no prospect of a moon to give us any light, so I decided against wasting time or energy on pitching the tent; instead we spread it out beneath the tree and dumped blankets and cooking utensils on top of it.

Even in several feet of snow and at below-zero temperature, a camp without benefit of stove or tent can be made tolerably warm and comfortable if you know how. Inhospitable though the forest might seem to be in its frigid winter garb, the north woods hold an abundance of material that, with proper use, makes inhospitality thaw and a scowl become a smile.

Quick action was the answer to the cold that knifed our bodies as soon as we forsook the shelter of the sleigh box. We'd fetched dry kindling wood along from the cabin to meet the needs of just such a situation as this, and in seconds a campfire was spitting and blazing. Now both Lillian and I stepped onto our snowshoes and, with me breaking track, plowed a trail to a nearby thicket of young fir. It took but a single slash of my axe to topple a tree, and after a half-dozen were felled Lillian gathered them up in a bundle and packed them over to the campfire. To Veasy belonged the chore of pushing their butts down into the snow so that they stood erect once more. In the wilderness, the offspring of the wild creatures are not the only youngsters who must learn to fend for themselves.

In ten minutes' time the camp was protected by an almost solid wall of the "Christmas" trees. Not only would the brush act as a windbreak, but it would also serve as a sort of reflector to the campfire within, throwing its heat back against the girth of the tree. And providing we had enough dry wood stacked within the windbreak to keep a fire on all night, our camp should stay reasonably warm no matter what the weather said outside.

Leaving Lillian to her pots and pans, I axed down dry pines, chopped them into three-foot lengths and stacked them inside the windbreak. By that time moose steaks were done to a turn in the skillet, and a gallon of strong tea brewed in its pail by the coals. And so in Indian fashion, half kneeling, half sitting, we squatted by the fire and gave our attention to the food.

Not only does travel in sub-zero temperatures give one a ferocious appetite, but too much of it at one time also numbs the body and mind. Squat down by a heated stove after being exposed to such weather all day and within seconds the head starts to loll, and within a minute or two you are asleep. Here, the campfire was our stove, the fir tree and wind-break our cabin. And primitive though the shelter was, no sooner had we eaten supper and washed the dishes than our senses were befuddled and our heads started to loll. And we burrowed deep into the bedding that Lillian had arranged on a mattress of fir boughs and within seconds were sleeping, utterly exhausted.

It was only half light when I stoked the fire in the morning. Lillian stuck her head out of the blankets as I scooped up snow in a pail and placed it on the fire to melt. She coughed as the cold air bit her lungs. Wind bansheed through the treetops, and snow drove in against the windbreak.

"Better stay covered up until I've got the coffeepot boiling," I advised, shrugging into my sheepskin coat. It was a suggestion she wasn't hesitant about accepting.

I packed her a cup of coffee. "Snowing again," I grumbled. "Damn the snow anyway. Wind is getting up, smack out of the north. Yesterday was bad enough, but today will be a real heller."

And a heller it certainly was. We broke camp with the daylight, snow stinging our faces. The horses balked a moment or two when the pull of the cold collars came against their shoulders, then snorting and prancing they took up the slack in the traces and the sleigh began to move.

In between frequent pauses for rest, they hauled the outfit through another five miles of timber, and then the trees began thinning out. Dimly ahead loomed the drab monotony of a gently undulating stretch of prairie.

"Island Lake Flats," I grunted. I might have been announcing our arrival at the gates of hell itself.

A pleasant enough spot in summer is Island Lake Flats. Blessed with an adequate supply of drinking water in the form of several landlocked lakes, the Flats are also dotted with minor stands of aspen and pine, which provide plenty of shade spots for livestock grazing them. In early fall thousands of ducks and hundreds of Canada geese come quacking and honking to the ponds, and prairie chicken crouch low in the grass when the threshing of wings above warns of the approach of hawk or owl hunting an easy meal. And even on the hottest August afternoon a breeze ruffles the tops of the grasses, now from east, now from west, or south or north, but cooling just the same.

But in winter all is different. The ponds are cemented over by two or more feet of ice. The ducks and the geese have departed for points far to the south. The prairie chicken have fled to the deep woods; only the wind is left.

Though there might not seem to be a breath of wind in the forests, out on the open flats it always blows. It stirs the snow, lifts it up and bears it along several hundred feet or yards before relaxing its grip and dumping it in some gully or gulch, until finally there is no gully or gulch, just the seemingly innocent snow.

Out on the edge of the flats, the forest behind us, we braced ourselves to meet the onslaught of that wind. A scum of drifting snow careened across the prairie, cutting visibility to a scant fifty yards. The cold was deadly. There was no sign of any track, not even a boulder in sight to remind us where one had been. "Get going!" I shouted at the horses, who had suddenly started to flounder.

"You're driving them into a gulch!" cried Lillian.

But the warning was a second too late. What with the frost on my eyelashes and the snow driving in against my face, I hadn't noticed the gulch drifted over with snow. Neither had the horses, who sometimes have the knack of sensing, if not seeing, such traps.

The team broke through the snow, went down on their bellies, then rolled easily over on their sides as if to inform me, "We've had enough of this."

"Have to unhitch now," I mumbled, dreading the thought of getting out of the sleigh and wallowing around in the drift. "Must try and get the horses and doubletrees over to the other side and then pull the sleigh over on the end of the chain." I began throwing blankets and other gear around. "Logging chain—where the devil is that logging chain?" I asked impatiently.

"Here." Lillian knew just where the chain was because she ever made it a habit to know the whereabouts of such sometimes vital things.

"Good little woman." I grinned. I took the chain, got down on the sleigh tongue and pulled the pin from the doubletrees. Then I crawled precariously along the tongue and dropped the neck yoke. And standing aside, waist-deep in snow, I sang out, "Get going there."

The horses raised up and lunged forward, and relieved of the lug of the sleigh they got across the gully. Halting them, I again fastened the chain to the sleigh tongue. Again I shouted, "Get going!" this time emphasizing the words with a crack of the whip. And the sleigh runners screamed, and Lillian and Veasy hung on to the sleigh box for dear life, and the horses heaved and grunted, and pulled with all that was in them. And then that gully was behind us with heaven only knows how many more ahead.

We had got halfway across the Flats when the horses stopped dead in their tracks. "Get going there!" But it was no use. The team was at the point of utter exhaustion. They'd given us all they had, but it wasn't quite enough. I looked stupidly at Lillian and she looked blankly at me. "What now?" Lillian beat me to the words by a breath.

"Bareback, I guess," I said glumly. "We'll have to leave harness and sleigh here and try to get through to Riske Creek riding the horses bareback." It wasn't an enticing proposition, but it was the only choice we had.

Suddenly Lillian stood up in the sleigh box. She stared southward with an intensity that watered her eyes. "It's smoke," she sang out. "I believe I can smell smoke."

I had one foot on the doubletrees, the other in the sleigh box.

"Smoke!" I burst out. "Out here on these flats—in this? You're crazy."

"I'm not crazy," she snapped. "It *is* smoke. Can't you smell it?"

Then I could smell it myself. Yet couldn't believe my nostrils. Smoke, on Island Lake Flats—in *this*!

"There's a fire somewhere—" Lillian broke off and stood very stiff, staring ahead. "I can see it. It's a campfire. It's Indians!"

I too stared hard into the south. Rubbing my eyes to make sure they weren't fooling me, I gasped almost incredulously, "It *is* Indians!"

Ahead of us, some four hundred yards away, was a campfire, and beside the fire a team and sleigh. A half-dozen figures were grouped about the sleigh, and my eyes gradually discerned something large and dark also close to the sleigh. "It's a moose," I guessed. "Someone has killed a moose."

I shook the lines and cracked the whip. "Get up out of there, horses. Tighten those traces, lift that sleigh! There's company up ahead." And as if understanding just what I said, the horses wallowed up out of the snow, lifted their tired heads and inched the sleigh forward.

And Indians they all were. There was Redstone Johnny and his plump, giggling woman, Lizzie. There was old Azak, who squinted up at us through weakened eyes and muttered, "White man come." And there was Eagle Lake Johnny, who derived his name from the large lake a hundred miles to the north, where he was born. And there were four scantily clad papooses who seemed totally oblivious to the sting of a cold north wind that fairly chilled our own warmly clad bodies to the very marrow of our bones. Indians from the Riske Creek reservation, all of them, and we were informed with much gusto that Redstone Johnny had shot the moose late yesterday evening, and today all had come back to haul the meat home. Redstone Johnny had often dropped in at our cabin to share a meal or a cup of tea with us, and tell of his woes—as Indians ever will if they can strike a sympathetic audience. Now the carcass of the moose was axed up into quarters, and all were standing about the fire, roasting huge slabs of the rib meat on spits stuck in the snow.

No white man would ever hunt meat in weather such as we'd had for the last month. He'd live on straight beans before he'd get out and hunt in weather like that. Then again, white men usually killed enough game in fall to last all winter. But not the Indians. Living only for the present, they never thought or worried about the future. The menfolk were hunters born and could kill a moose or a deer in weather when a white man might tramp the woods for days without firing a shot. Once he cut fresh sign, the Indian stayed with that sign until he caught up to his quarry and shot it.

"More better you get out of sleigh and eat," Redstone Johnny now greeted us. Then, rolling with laughter, he asked, "Why in hell white man like you travel in this no good weather?"

The fire was warm and the smell of roasting moose ribs drew saliva to my lips. "I'm crazy, Johnny," I laughed back. "Crazy all same loon. S'pose me not crazy, me and my woman and kid never get out of cabin 'til spring come back again. More better s'pose white man all same bear: crawl down hole in fall and not come out until snow all gone." And borrowing Redstone's hunting knife, I carved three huge slabs of meat from the backstraps of the moose and set them on sticks before the fire to barbecue.

Our Indian hosts had a ten-pound syrup can of scalding tea by the fire, and Redstone's woman filled three tin cups and handed them to us. Never has tea tasted better, no matter what sort of a cup it was in.

Heeling back by the fire, we bit into our steaks before they were properly cooked, inwardly thanking a kindly fate that had enabled Redstone to shoot his moose so close to the road. Shamelessly belching as the fresh meat digested in their bellies, the Indians loaded the quarters onto the sleigh. The four papooses burrowed down under a mass of rabbitskin robes, chuckling and jabbering away at one another in their own gutteral tongue. Redstone gathered up the lines, then fired a question at me. "White man want to go ahead?"

"Not by a damn sight," I returned. "Indian horses more better than mine. Mine he just about played out. More better you go ahead and I follow behind." For the Indians would have to go past the trading post to get to their reservation three miles farther on.

The broken track ahead of us put new life into the horses. No longer was the neck yoke pushing snow, and if the footing was poor, the horses managed to move steadily along at between two and three miles an hour. By sundown we reached the trading post.

The Riske Creek Store and Post Office seethed with activity. A six-horse freight team had just pulled in with its load of trade goods destined for the trading posts farther upcountry. "Goddamnest trip I ever done made since I've been freighting on the roads," grumbled the teamster, as I led our team into the barn and found a couple of vacant stalls. "Nary a sign of a track back on Becher's Prairie, everything drifted over plumb to hell. Took the horses ten hours to pull the load in from the Bristol place where I stabled them last night." The Bristol place was another roadside stopping place ten miles east of Riske Creek.

"You had better luck than we did at that," I consoled him, stripping the harness from the horses. "We parked under a fir tree for the night." The freight-team skinner was tall and lean, and his eyes were red and swollen from staring too long at the snow.

"The hell you don't say!" he ejaculated. "Your woman and kid too?" And when I nodded, he put a finger against his nose, cleared a nostril and said, "That reminds me of the winter of '21–'22 when I was freighting a four-horse load of grain for one of the ranchers upcountry a piece. Well, sir, you know that piece of road between Harper's Meadow and Hance's Timber? Talk about drifts! Never have seen the likes of such drifts neither afore nor since. And damn me if one of the wheelers didn't go and cork itself and go lame on me. And there I was in the drift with close to four tons of grain, and it colder than billy be damned and—"

And he was still stuck in the drift when I left the barn and headed for the sitting room of the trading post.

An itinerant Roman Catholic priest, bearded, side-whiskered and fat, shook hands with Lillian and me as we dragged our chairs alongside the heater stove. Known throughout the Chilcotin as Father Thomas, and by no other name, the priest concerned himself mostly with the spiritual affairs of his Indian flocks. Here in the sitting room, all conversation pivoted on a single subject: the weather. A cowboy trying to warm his feet at the stove said, "Jesus Christ! My feet ain't been thawed out for a month." A wild-horse chaser, praying for a warm-up in the weather so's he could pitch camp over at Bald Mountain and start hunting up horse sign, chipped in with, "Goddamn country sure is going to hell." He was short and stooped, and his legs were slightly bowed from too much gripping of saddle leather. Deafening his ears to the blasphemous grumblings of the cowboy and horse chaser, the priest told Lillian and me of his own troubles. He'd been due at one of the reservations farther west a week ago, but the severe cold of the last several days had kept him holed up at Riske Creek, awaiting the arrival of the Indian-driven team and sleigh that was long overdue to haul him on another leg of his journey. Maybe the Indian teamster had arrived at the conclusion that his soul would be none the dirtier if he kept his team in the barn until more favourable weather came along.

A couple of roving fur buyers and a Chinese man were seated at the table, playing poker for sizable stakes. Three Indian trappers shuffled in from the store, watched the poker game for a few minutes, then produced a soiled deck of cards of their own and went to playing blackjack. I watched the gambling at the table for a while, long enough to arrive at the conclusion that the luck lay with the Chinese man. "Hope he cleans them right out," I muttered to myself, and then went to the store. I've never had much sympathy for fur buyers.

The trader was in his office juggling with Accounts Rendered. He glanced up at me, rubbing his hands, maybe in expectation of some profitable trade to come. "Thought maybe you'd all died," he greeted me cheerfully.

"There were moments back on Island Lake Flats when we pretty near did," I responded a bit sourly.

The trader thought a long moment, then said, "Heller of a winter, all right. Recalls to mind that winter that poor old Joe Isnardy froze to death. Guess that was a year or two before you left the old country. Before prohibition, and I ran a bar here then." He knit his brows as if trying real hard to recall events from the past. "It was forty-five below when Joe lit out of here with his team and sleigh, heading east. A couple of miles out the cold caught up to him. Joe had a case of Scotch in the sleigh, and to sort of counteract the cold he tapped a bottle. Seems like a couple of drinks wasn't enough to even warm his hands, let alone his innards, so he goes back at the bottle again. After a while he tied the team up, squatted down on a log and just sat there, pouring the whisky down his gullet. That's how they found him, a week later, sitting there on the log, frozen stiff as a board, two empty bottles in the snow, a half-emptied one in his hands."

"What happened to the horses?" I asked with curiosity.

"What do you think?" he snorted. "They died and went to heaven and lived happy ever after."

After a half-hour of obstinate haggling I peddled our scant catch of furs off for one hundred and seventy dollars' worth of supplies. There was no cash in the transaction this time; it took our every pelt to pay for all we needed.

We stayed at Riske Creek for three days, resting our horses, talking about the weather to whoever wanted to listen, poring over the mail and hoping real hard for a warm-up in the weather that would let us get back home without freezing to death on the way. And on the fourth day, with the temperature at a mild zero, we said "so long" to all at the trading post, and thirty hours and one overnight camp later, arrived back at the cabin. There to sit the winter out until the cry of a wild goose said sure enough it's spring.

We have spent more than two dozen Christmases now at Meldrum Creek. But when I look back over all of them, I think that that Christmas season spent on Island Lake Flats in a sleigh at forty degrees below zero, partaking of the open hospitality of Redstone Johnny and his plump woman Lizzie—roast moose and a roaring fire—stands out as one of the best of all.

Chapter 14

Moleese was a hunchback. He wasn't born a hunchback, but according to Indian history, his back was broken at four years of age, when a horse fell and rolled on him. Nature, not surgical skill, eventually, after a fashion, reknit the broken back bone, and Moleese was able to ride again. But Nature could not possibly hide the evidence of her handiwork: the hunch would still be there when Moleese set out for his last happy hunting ground. Besides being a hunchback, there was this about Moleese: he was the first man I'd hired. For despite his deformed back, it was Moleese who helped me tame and harness the floods that spewed down Meldrum Creek in that spring of 1935.

In early spring of 1935 a major flood threat lay over the Fraser River drainage system. Five feet of packed snow covered the three- and four-thousand-foot levels, nine to ten feet at six thousand feet, and still more above that. Whether there was to be cataclysmic disaster or not all depended upon when and how the snow melted. In normal springs, all snow at the lower levels had run off to the river at least three weeks before the snow at higher levels started to move. But if, because of an unseasonably late spring, the runoff at lower and higher levels coincided, then the Fraser River, where it spreads out and moves slowly through the reclaimed lands about its mouth, could not possibly digest the flow within its banks, and unless the man-made dikes about it were stout enough to contain the surplus, thousands of acres of farmland must again, momentarily anyway, go back to that river from which they had been filched in the first place.

Depth of snow was not the only factor contributing to the threat. The prolonged cold of last December and January presented still another, in the form of ice. Unless there is sufficient volume and depth of water moving along any watercourse, at a temperature of fifty below zero the flow becomes momentarily dammed by the action of the frost, and then the water backs up and forms a miniature ice field. Eventually the law of gravity exerts itself, and the water cuts another channel through the ice and starts moving downgrade again, but only to find itself once more shut off by frost a little farther downstream. By spring, such miniature ice fields are present at frequent intervals along the whole watershed, each awaiting a moment when the sun and the wind will melt them. Then, every such ice field melting and feeding the watershed when its banks are already filled to their carrying capacity contributes just that much more water to a drainage system that neither needs nor can properly digest it.

But in the spring of 1935 the province was spared major flooding. By early May the snow at the lower levels had melted and run off to the Pacific Ocean. The freshets from the mountains did not get underway until early June, and by that time the Fraser River could contain them. The dikes barricading the farmlands were never in serious threat of being breached, and contented farm folk tilled their reclaimed acres behind them, watching the broad sweep of the river pass innocently by. Not for half a century or more had those reclaimed lands been inundated, and in the meantime the dikes had been raised and strengthened, and thousands of acres of hay, grain, vegetables and other crops were being cultivated behind them. Never again would the Fraser breach those dikes—at least, so everyone thought.

To us, this sudden extravagance of water was as a gift from heaven. The snows that had so seriously upset our hopes where the winter trapping was concerned now gave us fleeting opportunity to proceed with the building of many more dams. Several winters might come and go before such opportunity came our way again.

In early May every gulley and fold ribbing the watershed was bursting its britches, spewing the melting snows into Meldrum Creek. There was no need now for us to worry about the ranchers and their irrigation ditches. The creek channel held more water than all the agriculture at its mouth could use. It rushed down the land in a muddy, turgid tide, through many a broken beaver dam, out of the ditched mouth of many a shrunken lake, tarrying nowhere, fired by a frantic urge to keep its tryst with the river in the briefest possible time.

Apart from the few dams we had built, there was nothing to check the flow and hold and conserve all this excess water. But if agriculture, river and ocean had no use for it, there were others on the creek who did: ourselves. For five years now we had been almost praying for a chance of this sort to come our way, and now it had come, bringing with it opportunity to close the gates upon the larger marshes, soak their blotting paper and fill their saucers until they overflowed.

In the five years that had gone by since we had come to the creek to live, we hadn't fared too badly. The cabin now had a board floor in it. The secondhand mowing machine and rake were there in the makeshift shed. We had been able to replace the blocks of wood that were our original chairs for more elegant furniture. And besides these indexes of accumulating wealth, we had managed to amass a bank roll totalling almost three hundred dollars. So, comforted by thoughts such as these and convinced that if we now smote while the iron was hot and allowed none of the water to go to waste, we would soon be able to start trapping large numbers of muskrats. I took a deep breath and arrived at a momentous decision: I would become an employer of labour.

In the opening up of a frontier or the taming of a wilderness, woman has often played equal part with man. Without Lillian at my side sharing the common life through good fortune or bad, giving to that life the many things that only a woman can give, I know that my hopes and aspirations to do with the waters of Meldrum Creek would never have been fulfilled.

But enough is enough. Though Lillian had helped me with every dam hitherto built, I could now hire an Indian for two dollars a day and board, and we had money enough to pay such a wage for maybe six weeks. Working from seven in the morning until six at night, I reckoned two men could move a pile of dirt in six weeks and rebuild several dams.

When I broached the matter with Lillian, she stamped a heel angrily down on the floor and scolded, "Six weeks wages and board to an Indian means parting with around eighty dollars in cash. With that much money," and her eyes darted around the cabin, "we could buy a little more furniture, or that set of matched dinner dishes I've been wanting so long."

"Why the dinnerware?" I asked mildly, grinning. "We've been eating off enamel plates and drinking out of enamel cups for a good many years now and don't seem to be any the worse off for it."

"You just don't understand," said Lillian flatly.

"Sure I understand." Then, in more serious tone, I said, "It's not right that you should be shovelling dirt now that we've money enough to pay someone else to do it. And then again there's another problem we'll soon have to tackle."

"Problem?" Lillian frowned. "What sort of a problem?"

"Veasy's education," I replied quietly, then waited for that to sink in.

Veasy would be six years old on the 28th of next July. The very thought of sending him away to school and boarding him with others was more than either Lillian or I cared to contemplate. We were miles from any school. The environment of the wilderness had made the three of us as a single unity, the one dependant upon the other. From one month's end to another we seldom saw anyone else. At five years of age Veasy could set a snare and catch a rabbit as professionally as I, for the woods themselves had been a school of sorts to him. And the process of setting the snare demanded a certain amount of patience, a concentration of thought and effort, which is why I taught him how to set them in the first place. The job sharpened his mind, gave him something constructive to think about, and so taught him how to make use of his brain.

He was already trailing along at my heels now and then when I went out in the woods to hunt, and often his keen eyes spotted a deer before I saw it myself. "Look, Daddy, deer!" And then I'd see the deer myself, lying very still, head and neck flush with the ground as deer often will lie and watch the hunter pass by.

Already the simple everyday chores of the woods were leaving their mark on his character. He never asked Lillian or me to do anything for him that he could possibly do himself. Lillian no longer had to fill the woodbox at night if I wasn't home in time to do it for her. Though he could only pack a few sticks of wood at a time, Veasy took care of the woodbox. If, when playing by the lake, he came running to the cabin with the news that he'd just seen a timber wolf or moose travelling the shoreline, then we knew that it *was* a moose or timber wolf he'd seen. He never lied, perhaps because he'd never known occasion when a lie was needed to cover up the truth.

Mostly at his own initiative, he was already spelling out simple words in a book, and making sense of them too. If so far he couldn't write or print the words, I judged that he was only a short step from being able to do so. I'd given considerable thought to the matter of somehow giving him a fair education and arrived at the conclusion that between Lillian and me we'd try to do the job at home and see what came of our efforts.

In England, I had gone from governess to kindergarten, kindergarten to grammar school. Along with other subjects, I'd delved into Latin and chemistry, algebra and trigonometry, and like matters usually taught in correct establishments of learning. But since my thoughts were so often leagues away from the book on my desk, no sooner had my mind mastered a verb or equation than the process of its mastering was promptly forgotten.

But Lillian never had been blessed with such opportunity for education. At eleven years of age she'd been shipped away to Soda Creek, forty miles from Riske Creek, to board with relatives, and walked three miles each morning to a one room log schoolhouse attended by nine other pupils. At fourteen she quit school, but in the three years at Soda Creek she had learned to read very well, write fairly well, to add and subtract, multiply and divide. And every lesson she learned was one she never forgot. So what with all that I'd forgotten, and all that she remembered, I saw no good reason why we should send Veasy away to school and so break up the unit.

∾

"We'll sit down right now," I said to Lillian, "and send away for pencils, scribblers and textbooks. And from now on you can do far more good keeping him anchored to his lessons than helping me build dams." Then, remembering the set of matched dinnerware, I promised, "Come next March I aim to trap around four hundred muskrats, and I know that I can do it. Out of the proceeds of the fur, I'm going to buy you the fanciest set of dinner dishes there is in the catalogue."

Moleese was no darker than any other Chilcotin Indian, no fairer either. As was the case with so many of the Indians, a white man had to guess at his age and claim top marks if he came within ten years of guessing right.

Moleese and his woman Cecelia occasionally came to the headwaters of Meldrum Creek in early spring to catch the squawfish moving upstream to spawn. Though the white man might turn up his nose at such bony fare, the true Chilcotin Indian, in the spring of the year when moose and deer were thin and tough, considered them a delicacy, bones and all.

In that early spring of 1935 Moleese and Cecelia again had an appetite for squawfish and came to the creek to net them. They pitched their tent a mile upstream from the cabin, and the ring of their horse bells told me of their presence. That evening I paid them a visit.

The layout of the camp was as familiar to me as the smell that pervaded the atmosphere around it. The tent, pitched under a pine tree, was small, maybe eight feet by ten. The canvas, once white, was now a dirty gray. It bore evidence of continual patching, but no doubt it shed rain after a fashion. The customary campfire smouldered in front of the flaps, and behind it was another fire, mostly smoke, burning beneath a rack of peeled pine poles. On the rack rested scores of squawfish, split and opened down the belly, flesh to the smoke. It was the smell of the curing fish that permeated the atmosphere. Cecelia was behind the tent too, methodically and stoically scraping hair from the hide of a recently killed deer. Deer hides were everywhere, though all but the one Cecelia laboured at had obviously been skinned from kills of long ago.

Moleese grinned at me as I approached and, twisting his distorted back, heeled down by the fire on a deerskin. The two saddles chucked carelessly under a tree had deerskin blankets beneath them too, as was the case with the two pack saddles a few feet away. I was quite certain that if I peeked into the tent there would be a deerskin flattened out— serving as a sheet to the mattress of boughs it covered. Just as there'd be a deerskin spread on the dusty floor of the tent on which food was served when it was too cold or wet to eat outside. I thought, "Take away their deer and what have they left?"

Bidding Moleese a gruff "Hello," I too heeled back by the campfire, as if absorbed in its flames. It was fatal to appear in a hurry when doing business with an Indian.

Then, after at least two minutes of silence: "You catch lots fish?" I inquired to open up proceedings.

"You betcha." Moleese patted his belly. "He damn good too."

"How long before your belly get all the fish he want?" I asked.

Moleese picked his teeth. "Two—three days and then me and my woman don't want to eat fish for a long time."

It was time to come to the point. "You want catch job for maybe five or six weeks?" I said it casually, as if I didn't care whether he replied yes or no.

The grin dropped from Moleese's face. His eyes took on a hard, crafty look. "What kind of job?" he asked suspiciously.

"Shovel job. You damn good man with a shovel. All you have to do is fill barrow with dirt."

"Goddamn hard work," complained Moleese. "That kind of work make my back sick."

That I didn't believe. In 1927 Moleese had dug a ditch for the trader at Riske Creek two hundred yards long and six feet deep, and in quick time too. My back wasn't broken when I was four years old, but I doubt that I could have dug it in less time.

After fifteen minutes of barren silence Moleese said cautiously, "How much you pay me?"

Knowing there would have to be a great deal of skirmishing before a wage was settled upon, I offered: "Dollar and a half a day and grub."

Moleese scowled. "Too cheap. Two dollars and fifty cents more better."

Not if I had my way. "One dollar and seventy-five cents."

Moleese waggled his head. "Two dollars and twenty-five cents more better."

I said, "Just fill shovel with dirt and then fill barrow. Easy job, that." And: "One dollar and ninety cents," I came up to.

But it wasn't quite enough. "Two dollars more better."

"Okay, you win. Two dollars a day it is." Though I intended to pay that much anyway, I scowled as we clinched the deal, letting on that an Indian's shrewd bargaining had bested that of a white man. And Moleese registered his satisfaction at the way things turned out with a gaping grin. "When we start work?" he asked.

Moleese was worth every cent of his hire. Sparing of words as so many Indians are, breath that might have been frittered away in small talk was given to loading the barrow. The work proceeded swiftly and efficiently. Six miles downcreek from the cabin were two of the largest marshes on the watershed, one containing some two hundred acres, the other slightly less. In two weeks the gates in the two dams were closed, and slowly the water in front of the first began spreading out over the marsh and creeping higher up the face of the dam. How very different now were aquatic conditions on the watershed than those that had existed when Lillian and I hesitantly began work on our very first dam. Then the creek was so anemic it seemed that only a miracle could succeed in restoring its health and vigour. Perhaps miracles had happened, and the winter of the heavy snows was one. Anyway, now we had water to work with, plenty of water, and not a drop of it was permitted to make its escape to the river. Our recently constructed dams upon these two larger marshes stopped it in its tracks, forcing it to drop its plunder of precious topsoil that was being carried toward the river and dump it on the marshes, where soon it would enrich the bottoms of the lakes, thus making sure all forms of life that moved into them to breed and multiply would always have plenty of food. So, with the help of the hunchback Indian Moleese, the freshets of 1935 were harnessed and put to use.

In the meantime, and for five hours every day excepting Saturdays and Sundays, the cabin became a classroom. The pencils, scribblers and textbooks travelled from Riske Creek to Meldrum Lake on the back of a pack horse. Promptly at 9:30 A.M. Veasy sat down at the table and applied his mind to the work Lillian set before him. Promptly at 11:30 he shoved away from the table and ran outdoors to stretch his legs and his lungs. Sharp at 1 P.M. he was again seated at the table, there to remain until 3:30, when Lillian sang out, "School's out for today."

One morning around 10 A.M., shortly after "school" had opened, I walked into the cabin to scrounge a cup of coffee. Veasy glanced up at me as I entered and then, without a word, his eyes went back to his books. I poked Lillian playfully in the ribs and told her, "You missed your true vocation in life. You should have been a school marm."

Lillian replied with a quick laugh, "I could teach you a thing or two," and she meant it.

Save for the patch of land we'd cleared for the vegetable garden, the three- or four-acre flat around the cabin was a jungle of aspen and willow. A few hundred feet upstream from the flat was the beaver meadow that so far had supplied us with winter feed for the horses. The remnant of the beaver dam was four hundred and sixty feet long, and shaped something like a horseshoe, as beaver dams often are. Either end of the dam tied into a steepish bank that would, I judged, provide an ample source of easy-shovelling dirt and gravel. If for the moment we hadn't the vaguest idea as to how or when a pair or two of beavers could be brought back to the creek, never for a moment did we waver from the firm conviction that someday, and in our time too, they would come back. I had already made a few inquiries as to how one went about purchasing live beavers, but with negative results. So thoroughly had the watersheds of British Columbia been ransacked of their beavers that in 1920 the B.C. Game Department prohibited any further trapping of beavers throughout most of the province. With a situation like this existent, what hope had we of ever getting a pair of beavers to begin the restocking of Meldrum Creek? If the question was without answer at the moment, we knew that somehow that pair would be found. And furthermore, we believed with all our hearts that someday the meadow that now supplied us our hay would again be occupied by beavers.

With one eye on the tangle of brush and the other on the beaver meadow, I decided that the aspens and willows must go, the tough sod be plowed and the flat seeded down to a permanent crop of hay. But any time spent in clearing and plowing the flat would be wasted unless water could be brought to the land to irrigate it.

With the use of a somewhat crude triangle and plumb bob, I surveyed the right-of-way for a ditch that would carry water from the dam to the projected hayfield. In order to raise the water high enough on the meadow so that it would flow of its own free will into the mouth of the ditch, the dam itself had to be raised almost four feet above its present level. I don't rightly recollect how many spruce trees were cut down for their branches, or how many hundreds of wheelbarrow loads of dirt and gravel were wheeled away from the pit and dumped on the boughs before at last the job was finished, and the entire length of the dam raised four feet. But finally, with the help not only of Moleese, but also that of Lillian and Veasy when the school day ended, we were able to lay down our axes and shovels and watch the water spread out of our hay meadow.

Then came the digging of the ditch, and it took most of a week. By that time the dam had filled and I was able to test the accuracy of our survey work. There was nothing wrong about that survey; the water flowed serenely along the ditch, and if some seeped away through the gravel, a sufficient amount reached the end of the ditch to ensure that as long as the dam held, our hay crop would not wilt for lack of irrigation.

Clearing the brush from the flat was the hardest task of all, for every aspen and willow had first to be chopped off well above the ground and the tops cut into lengths and packed away and windrowed up in piles, ready for burning. Then, with the help of our work team and cable and blocks, the stumps were lifted from the ground and hauled off too. Then all hands pitched in to grub out the network of roots, with only one mattock and bare hands for tools. With most of the roots removed, the ground was not too hard to plow, and when the very last furrow was turned I hitched the team to the wagon, journeyed out to Riske Creek and obtained temporary use of a set of spring-toothed harrows from the trader. By late June all was done. Except, that is, paying Moleese his wages.

One had to be careful about this when dealing with an Indian who was as primitive as he was independent. You didn't hand him a check or a roll of bills as you would a white man, and say, "I'll not need you any longer." At least, not if you wanted his respect. But between us, Lillian and I had all this figured out several days before the moment of parting. On the night of the pay-off, we'd ask Moleese and Cecelia down for supper and treat them like royalty if they came.

∼

Moleese wore a clean, unpatched pair of denim overalls and an equally plain, though badly faded, black silk shirt with the head of a horse embroidered in pink thread upon the flap of its breast pocket. Obviously the decoration hadn't been there when the shirt was purchased at a trading post. Cecelia's gnarled fingers were no doubt responsible for the artistic design. His face and hands were clean too, and his black coarse hair plastered straight back over his forehead. That was unusual; as a rule it was as dishevelled as a magpie's nest. Cecelia was dressed for the occasion in a snow-white cotton blouse and print calico skirt. The raven-wing, braided ropes of hair that trailed almost to the thin buckskin belt about her waist were at least partly corralled by a huge yellow handkerchief. Cecelia was obviously several years older than Moleese. You could tell that by the miniature gulleys that lined her face. Cecelia's face somehow reminded me of an eroded patch of dusty ground that has long lost hope of growing anything bright and beautiful.

Lillian had opened two jars of her precious willow grouse, canned the previous fall, and made a dandy stew of them, complete with feather-light dumplings. For dessert she had a deep blueberry pie. The berries too had been preserved the previous summer.

As Lillian and Cecelia were cleaning up the dishes, I handed Moleese a cigar—in mid-May the trader had given me a pack of five for a birthday present—and lit one myself. Then I spent two tedious hours teaching Moleese how to print his name with the stub of one of Veasy's pencils. He learned surprisingly fast, and at the end of the lesson could sign his name in crude but readable fashion. Then with a simple "Thanks Moleese," I paid him off.

The two Indians stepped out through the cabin door. There was yet light in the sky. Moleese hesitated. He scowled, as if he was thinking of something he couldn't put into words. The scowl evaporated, and he grinned from ear to ear. "Goddam, you one damn good white man" was his parting. Coming from an Indian, that was a compliment indeed!

Chapter 15

One night we had a visitor, one that didn't knock at the door as visitors properly should, but instead stepped silently up to the window and stood there surreptitiously peering in at us. We didn't hear its approach through the slightly crusted snow, which was strange since it weighed close to fifteen hundred pounds. And the face in the night might have been the face of a horse, or a mule, or a camel, or a likeness of all three.

Through December and January there was seldom a night that the cabin windows weren't frosted over. As one's breath came in contact with the glass, it moisturized and instantly froze. But on Monday nights the frost on the panes was thicker than on any other night of the week, maybe an eighth of an inch thick. And with the nail of the index finger you could write your name on the window, or draw a fine picture, or a map of the whole world if you had the urge and inclination. For Monday was washday, when steam billowed up from the large wooden tub in which Lillian did the weekly washing. As soon as the steam came in contact with the window, it became ice.

According to Lillian, packing boughs to the dam sites was far easier work than bending over the wooden tub, knuckling the sheets and shirts and other whatnots against the corrugated face of the washboard. "Makes my back ache," she complained.

"The mail-order catalogue lists a washing machine powered by a gasoline motor," I said somewhat vaguely. "One of these days when the fur business picks up, I'm going to buy you one of those machines. Then come Monday nights you'll have no sore back. The machine does everything for you."

"Washing machine indeed!" Lillian sniffed disdainfully. She was darning socks, had been for the last hour and, judging by the size of the pile with holes in them, would be for quite some time yet. Snowshoes and skis were hard on socks; the rub of the harness soon wore heels out. "There's lots of things to come before that. And anyway," she went on, "I wouldn't know how to wash with one if I had it."

"You could learn, couldn't you?"

She held the needle up to the light, threaded another length of wool through its eye and retorted, "I think I prefer my washboard. It keeps me trim."

It was Monday night, and tonight the frost on the glass was thicker than it usually was even on a wash night. A January moon was ripe and full, and the sky was built of stars, and there was no need for me to look at the thermometer outside to tell whether it was forty below or fifty; all I had to do was step outside and take a deep breath. If it was fifty below or colder, I couldn't drag air into my lungs without throwing violent fits of coughing. During the bitter winter of 1934–35 my lungs got touched with frost, not badly, but sufficiently to now start me coughing when I breathed air made brittle by a fifty-below cold snap. And tonight, when I went to the barn after supper to fork the horses some hay, I coughed all the way there and back.

I was sitting at the table, writing in my journal by the light of the coal-oil lamp. The lamp was all right in its way, but it was sparing with its light. Now, pen travelling over the foolscap, I wished that there was an electric light bulb over my head instead of the coal-oil lamp on the table.

The table was against the window, and on it, beside the paper and coal-oil lamp, was a houseplant that Lillian ever hoped would bloom in our wilderness in winters. She was a great one for messing around with houseplants, and I told her that someday, some winter, if she could only wait long enough, one of the plants would really bloom at a season of the year when no plant in its right senses should be blooming.

But it was frustrating work. Invariably, just as a bloom was about to be born, some exceptionally cold night it froze. But Lillian never gave up trying.

Veasy was stark naked in the washtub, taking a Monday-night bath. I'd pushed the plant quite close to the window, to make more room for the writing material. I dipped the nib into the ink, ready to start on another paragraph, when something dragged my eyes to the window. I stiffened, and dropped the pen. There on the glass, an inch or two from the plant, the frost was actually melting. It had never done that before, not on Monday nights. I leaned forward, catching at my breath. No mistake about it, the frost was melting, and on one pane anyway was almost all gone. And pressed tightly against the glass was a huge, ungainly nose, a thick, pink tongue touched the glass and then disappeared. I watched the nose for a second or so and then relaxed back in the chair. "If it breaks that glass, it'll be that houseplant of yours that's to blame," I growled.

Lillian put down her needle. Veasy dropped the soap with a noisy splash. They both looked at the window and Veasy sang out, "It's a moose!"

"And its breath has melted the frost," said Lillian.

"You'd better move that plant," I suggested, "or that darned moose will break the glass for sure and hike away into the woods with the plant dangling from its mouth, pot and all."

"If it does it'll have company," Lillian retorted. "No moose will munch on my plant."

"Where do all the moose come from, anyway?" Veasy wanted to know.

So I moved the plant from the window, out of temptation's way, rolled myself a cigarette and sat back in the chair and told him how the moose first came to the Chilcotin:

In late summer of 1916 an Indian of the Riske Creek reservation, hunting mule deer a few miles north of the trading post, suddenly riveted his eyes upon an animal the likes of which he'd never before seen. Almost jet black was the huge beast's body, and there were grayish stockings on its hind legs. At the high point of its withers it was taller than any saddle pony that the Indian had ever seen and would maybe equal the weight of any horse too. But it was the massive horns and grotesque head of the animal that compelled the Indian to catch at his breath and then expel it in a noisy belch of excitement and astonishment.

Instinct perhaps informed the hunter that the flesh of the thing must be edible, and he levered shells into the barrel of his 30-30 carbine, firing them as fast as he could pull the trigger. At his fourth shot, the animal turned slowly around in its tracks; at the fifth, it dropped dead in the timber grass.

The Indian whacked off the lips and tongue of his kill with his hunting knife, tied them behind his saddle, galloped his horse every ell of the way back to the reservation and in excited gutteral grunts told the others of his tribe what had taken place. And they sucked at their breath and saucered their eyes as they beheld the size and weight of the lips and tongue.

Then, throwing riding and pack saddles on their horses, a dozen of the menfolk returned to the scene of the kill and loaded meat, hide and head, as well as parts of the intestines that are choice tidbits in the diet of any well-bred Chilcotin Indian, on the pack horses and trooped back to the reservation with their spoils.

Every son and daughter of the tribe, ancients and youngsters alike, spilled out of their log huts when the cavalcade came in sight. They darted among the pack horses like crows around carrion, getting in one another's way in their hurry to unlash the pack ropes and rid the horses of their weight of bloody meat. Stropping their hunting knives on the soles of their moccasins, they hacked off pieces of the meat, eating it raw and blinking questioningly at one another. Never had any of them seen such a huge deer as this.

Presently a withered crone, blind in one eye and drooling tobacco juice, clapped her hands and cried, "Ask Tenasstyee, the Old One! Let him feel of the horns and smell of the skin that perhaps he might tell us what kind of a deer is this that has come to live in our forests."

144

So they toted the hide and the horns over to the doorway of a hut where Tenasstyee, the Old One, blind now for fifteen years gone, sat plucking whiskers from his chin with a homemade pair of tweezers. And they dumped them at the Old One's feet and then stepped back, waiting in tense and respectful silence for him to render his verdict.

First the old hunter ran his bony fingers over every tine of the horns. Then hefted part of the hide, plucking the hair and smelling the skin. For all of five minutes the Old One stared vacantly off into the empty distance, muttering inaudibly to himself. Finally he spoke aloud.

"The big deer white man call elk me kill lots of long, long tam' ago, before white man come this country. This one," tapping the horns, "he no that kind meat."

Here the venerable hunter paused for a few seconds, as if his brief recital had sapped him of both energy and inclination for further talk. But after a moment of rest he gathered his wits and breath and continued, "Lots more deer stop this country then all same lots that kind stop now. This one white man call mule deer. Before my eyes go *mamaluse* (dead) me kill more that kind of deer than leaf stop tree in springtime."

Again his tongue was mute while his hands probed doubtfully at the hide. Then wearily, and with a bewildered shake of the head, he informed his tense audience, "But this kind, the biggest deer of them all, I never before see."

And if Tenasstyee, the Old One (reckoned to be 106 years old when he died), who could look back to a day when the only clothes he knew were stitched from the skins of wild animals, and when a white face in the Chilcotin country was as rare as an albino porcupine, was unable properly to identify this biggest deer of them all, who else was there abroad hunting and trapping in the forests qualified to do so?

Eventually it was Becher, the Englishman at the trading post, who solved the riddle. Around the turn of the century Becher was a factor of the Hudson's Bay Company, trading with the Indians of the Peace in northeastern British Columbia. Moose were beginning to migrate into the northerly regions of the province at that time, and Becher had bartered with the Indians of the Peace for their meat and hides. So when the Indians of the Riske Creek reservation brought the horns and the hide to the store to find out if they had any trade value, he gave them a dollar's worth of tea for the hide, sixty cents worth of chaw tobacco for the horns, and tossed in the true biological name of the species to boot.

Almost four years passed before a moose was again killed in the Chilcotin, and when I arrived on the scene few of the Indians and almost none of the whites had laid eyes upon the track of a moose, still less one in the actual flesh.

In the fall of 1925, while on a brief hunting trip of my own at the headwaters of Riske Creek, I too came into almost head-on collision with an animal the likes of which I'd never before seen. If instinct too told me that the flesh of the thing was edible, it also informed me that only some twenty-five paces lay between the ambitious snout of my rifle and the neck of a trophy bull moose. And I chucked the gun against my shoulder, lined its sights on the rut-swollen neck and hopefully pressed the trigger. And got both the thrill and surprise of my life when the bull went down as dead as dead can be.

There was no shortage of moose along Meldrum Creek when we invaded its headwaters, and the killing of a bull at any time of the year seldom called for more than a few hours of hunting. Their sunken paths crossed every muskeg and meadow, and every salt lick in the forests was churned to a deep mud by the countless moose that came to them to lick the saline soil.

In winter every moose that had been ranging the higher elevations through spring, summer and fall moved down into the valley to browse in the aspens and willows along the creek. Then there was seldom a morning or evening but what there weren't at least six or eight moose within a stone's throw of the cabin, bickering and fighting with one another over which had the most right to browse in this willow patch or that. And the more moose there were in sight, the bigger the nuisance they became.

If when first they made our acquaintance the moose were somewhat distrustful of us, they had good reason for it. Since the earliest moments of the fur trade, the wildlife of the North American continent has been waging a losing battle against a mankind that is not only encroaching upon and destroying its habitat, but generally meddling with the orderly pattern of its life.

But familiarity was ever the breeder of contempt. On discovering that they had nothing to fear of us, our winter guests soon became as tame as our horses, and when coming face to face with one on the packed trail leading from cabin to barn, the moose often stood stubbornly in its track,

On any given day in winter, six to eight moose were within a stone's throw of the cabin. Lillian eventually decided to feed hay to the hungry visitors.

eyeing me belligerently and compelling me to leave the trail and flounder through unpacked snow to the barn. It was easier and safer to go around than to try and remove the moose from the trail.

The idea of feeding the moose hay originated with Lillian, whose scheming little head was always full of ideas.

"If," she began quietly and serenely across the breakfast table one bitterly cold morning when the feuding of the moose outside the windows was assuming disorderly proportions, "we were able to feed them a little hay now and then—"

"Hay!" I exploded, "Feed moose hay!"

"Why not? We've got chunks of fat hanging out for the birds, haven't we?" And the way she put it, feeding moose was no harder than feeding the chickadees.

Just then my eyes happened to fix on a scrawny-necked cow whose every rib stuck out like curved fork tines through her hide. She had a still scrawnier calf trailing along at her heels. "That old lady out there looks as though she could do with a forkful of something," I observed thoughtfully. "But where's the hay coming from? It's about all we can do to grow enough for the horses without taking on moose."

Already Lillian had that figured out. "We've just got to clear a bit more ground. And this time we'll grow alfalfa instead of timothy and clover. I have an idea the moose would really like alfalfa."

"Alfalfa!" I spluttered, half to myself. As if we didn't already have enough on our hands to do with wildlife propagation, here was Lillian placidly suggesting that we saddle ourselves with the job of winter feeding a herd of moose.

Of course she had it her way. Whenever Lillian got an idea into her head, action soon followed. We cleared another acre of ground of its brush, grubbed out the roots and seeded it down with alfalfa. Once the roots became firmly established, this added bit of farmland hacked out of the wilderness produced a crop of alfalfa yielding three tons of hay to the acre.

And the moose took to the hay as a hog takes to corn. Since its original planting, we have fed scores of moose at the cabin. A calf that had been there all winter with its mother could be reckoned upon to be there next winter as a yearling if disease, predators or other natural calamity did not snuff out its life in the meantime. And it would perhaps be back again as a two-year-old, now with a calf of its own. A number of winter snows have come and gone since Lillian's head first hatched the idea of feeding the moose hay, and since then we have witnessed both the birth and the death of many a moose that at one time or another moved in on us in December or January, bumming a forkful of hay.

When one is able to approach almost within hand touch of any wild animal, a photo of the subject becomes an absolute must. Now stored away among the litter and confusion of my desk are hundreds of snapshots of moose that we have known through the years. Photos of bulls with massive horns, bulls that have shed their horns, cows with calf at heel, and cows without calf at all. And somewhere among the lot is a photograph of one of the largest bull moose I've seen, and it is not a pretty photo by any standards. The ears of the bull are flat on the nape of the neck, and its mane stands on end. And there is rage and animal hate in its eyes as it hurls forward through three feet of virgin snow, and the object of that rage and target for the hate is Lillian, who stands there, helpless, on her snowshoes, only a few feet away.

Chapter 16

It was all my fault in the first place. One foot more and Lillian would have been killed. It started when I was hunting mule deer in a tongue of lodgepole pine and fir that licks almost at the long walls of our home. A November moon was dying, and three inches of snow covered the kinnikinnick and blueberry bushes. The wind was faintly from the north, the air tangy and crisp with a loaded hint of more snow shortly to come.

Now was the time when I must go to work and stock up with meat against the needs of hungry months ahead. I found my buck, a three-pointer, bedded on the rim of a gulch, staring languidly into the westering sun, as bucks have been doing on late November afternoons ever since there were bucks. I shot him in his bed, dragged him away from the gulch a bit and gutted him. Then I laid him on his back beneath a fir tree to cool out. In the morning I'd come back with a pack horse and haul him home.

Standing beside the steaming carcass, thirty yards from the rim of the gulch, I could neither see nor hear any movement below. Yet I had the sudden intuition that life was abroad down in the bowels of the gulch, though why I do not know. It was like the intuition that abruptly came to Lillian and me when we were once pitching an overnight camp in the woods. We were about to stretch the tent between two green and sturdy pines when some little voice started to whisper, "No, not between those two trees." It was just like that; we ready to pitch the tent, the voice saying, "No, not there." So we rolled the tent up, moved on a quarter of a mile, picked out another spot for the camp and then set up the tent.

Along toward midnight, wind began worrying the treetops, and within seconds a mild hurricane was footloose through the forest. Several trees around our camp died that night, and at daybreak I strolled down to the spot where we had first intended pitching the tent. One of the trees to which our ridgepole would have been fastened had blown down in the night, and had the three of us been asleep in the tent we'd have been crushed as a rolling wagon wheel crushes a grasshopper.

Now, standing very still by the deer, the selfsame voice said, "Watch that gulch"—just like that. So I bolted a cartridge into the barrel of my .303 and crouched back on my heels, eyes and ears working overtime.

At full maturity, a bull moose weighs around fourteen hundred pounds on the hoof, and many carry a set of antlers spreading sixty inches or more. It does not seem possible that an animal so large can move through the timber as silently as a foraging lynx cat. But it can and does. A bull moose in heavy timber is nearly always seen before being heard.

As was the case now. The horns came up out of the gulch first, a spread of some forty-five inches, I judged. Then I saw the grotesque Roman nose, followed by the rest of the head and neck.

It was a couple or so seconds before horns, head and all four legs were clear of the gulch, and if I have often seen moose carrying a larger spread of horns, never have I seen one with a heavier frame of body.

Head up, nostrils feeling the air, the bull moved stiffly toward me. That seemed odd too, for he could well see me crouching tensely by the body of the deer. By all ordinary rules of the game, he should have wheeled and gone back into the gulch far more quickly than he came out of it. But he moved up to within twenty yards of me before he stopped and gazed at me intently, obviously unafraid of me. And if ever I've seen mayhem in the eyes of any bull moose, it was there in his.

I fingered the trigger of my rifle, watching the bull with both caution and curiosity. Of one thing I was sure: I had never laid eyes on him before. He appeared to me to be a strange moose, travelling through a strange country. Never a forkful of our alfalfa had he ever eaten.

When a bull or cow moose has fight on its mind—and quite often they have—there is much in its expression that isn't exactly pleasant. The ears flatten against the neck, the mane comes erect, and the whites of the eyes show. Usually there's but a soft grunt of warning before the animal lunges forward. And they come exceedingly fast.

One does not work and live among moose for winter after winter without coming into contact with the occasional bad-mannered rogue. Certainly I've encountered my share in my time, yet never have I been forced to use the rifle in self-defence. When moving among them at home, feeding them hay, I've often beaten some truculent bull or cow across the nose with a pitchfork to teach it better manners, but never harmed them worse, or they me.

But there was something about the actions of the bull in front of me that warned me here was one moose who would never be turned aside by any pitchfork once he made up his mind to charge. Looking back on it all now, I think I was actually afraid of the bull from the moment of first setting eyes on him, and afraid with a fear that had never been in me before. Which perhaps explains why I slowly brought the gun in to my shoulder and lined its sights on that broad massive head. And maybe I should have touched off the shot and settled the business for good in that single split second. Had I done just that, Lillian would have been spared the ordeal that came later.

I know now that I'd have been forced to shoot if a yearling bull had not suddenly got into the act, because here was one moose that would kill or be killed himself. But the yearling temporarily solved the problem for me, paying a harsh price for involuntarily doing so. My first warning that there was a third party in the act was when the big bull suddenly jerked his eyes from me to stare questioningly and angrily at something off in the timber.

I lowered my rifle and followed the line of his stare. At first I could see nothing but timber, but after another searching look I made out the form of a yearling bull moving slowly toward the gulch. The little fellow wasn't doing any harm that I could see. He was just nipping off the shoot of a red willow here, rubbing his poor sprout of horns against a seedling fir there. Feeding slowly toward us, he apparently didn't notice the big bull until he was within thirty yards of him. Somehow I wanted to yell, "Get the blazes out of there, you fool, while the getting is good." But it wouldn't have done any good to toss him a warning like that, and so I held my tongue and stood tense and expectant in my tracks, rifle at the ready.

The yearling was oozing good nature, and it was as clear as the air I was breathing that he just wanted to heave up alongside the big bull and pass the time of day. As he started forward again I heard the big bull grunt. There was a weight of warning in that grunt to anyone familiar with moose talk. Again some intuition prompted me to shoot, but I hesitated about squeezing the trigger. The old bull charged before I could decide—not at me, but at the yearling.

Contrary to widespread belief, a bull moose does far more fighting with its front feet than with its horns. True, the antlers are used extensively and sometimes with fatal effect when the heat of the annual rut is on, but at any other time of the year it is the front quarters that throw most of the lethal blows.

The unfortunate yearling was in far more luckless plight than any babe in the woods. By the time he came awake to what it was all about, the big bull was almost within striking range. Then the youngster did something I've not often seen any moose do: he wheeled and broke into a gallop. At their customary gait when in flight—a swift trot—a moose moves easily and gracefully. But a galloping moose is as graceful as a knock-kneed man in a sack race.

The first blow flicked out so fast that I didn't even see it. Crack! It was a sickening crack, too, one that might have been heard from one end of the gulch to the other. Crack! I saw as well as heard it this time. It was like the flick of a swamp adder's head. And the little fellow went down in the snow.

That's when I roared the anger that had been coming to a head within me. The right front foot of the big bull was poised for another blow, but at the sudden clamour of my voice it went stiffly down again. Thus the yearling got his one chance for a getaway, and he lost no time in grabbing it. Limping badly—I think his hip had been dislocated—he came up from the snow and lurched away into the sanctuary of the gulch.

The big bull continued his hostile appraisal of me for a moment. Then he cleared his nostrils, scratched at his right ear with a hind foot, shook himself and moved slowly away.

"You cantankerous old bum!" I yelled after him, just to let him know what I thought. Old Cantankerous was as good a name as any, and he was certainly to live up to its every syllable.

Almost six weeks were to pass before I laid eyes on the bull again, weeks during which the snow inched deeper every day and that saw a constant dribble of moose coming down off the hilltops to browse the willows along the creek bottom.

Shortly after New Year's I was kneeling down, placing a mink set in the overflow of one of the beaver dams, when I heard the threshing of willows a short distance upstream. I froze tight on one knee, eyes fixed on the willows. A moose took on vague shape in the bushes, then the outline of the animal became more pronounced as it stepped clear of the willows and paused on the edge of the ice, forty yards away from me.

I was about to give my attention to the mink trap again when the head of the animal slowly turned. and its eyes fixed on the beaver dam. Then I recognized him: it was Old Cantankerous, though a different-looking gentleman from the Old Cantankerous who had crippled the yearling at the gulch. Now both horns were shed, and that made a difference.

Since the wind was blowing upstream, I knew he hadn't winded me. And since the eyesight of any moose is poor in the bright of day, I doubted very much that he could see me either, and he probably wouldn't provided I stayed still.

A beaver dam covered with sodden snow provides exceedingly treacherous footing, and my snowshoes were on the far side of it, three hundred feet or so away. When finally I recognized the bull I cursed myself, because my rifle was with the snowshoes. I began scheming how I could get over to the rifle without drawing the bull's attention but came to the conclusion that it was hopeless. And without the rifle I was a sitting duck if the bull should suddenly become aware of my presence and display that same spirit of belligerence that was in him when first we met. Somehow I smothered the urge to make a quick dash for the gun, and instead inched down behind the dam, trying to make myself as small and inconspicuous as possible. I certainly wasn't looking for trouble and hoped that he wasn't either. After about fifteen minutes of indecision—minutes during which the cold began numbing my body—he smelled the snow, belched and veered up the pond and back into the willows.

From that moment on, the big bull was a perpetual menace to the peace of Meldrum Lake. Having once tasted a mouthful of the hay we were feeding others of his kind, he was constantly in sight of the stackyard, moving in on it at a brisk trot whenever his sensitive ears picked up the sound of fork against hay. No other moose was able to approach within a hundred yards of the stack when Old Cantankerous was in the vicinity. His strength was so massive, and he used it so brutally, that he could give any moose a twenty-five-yard start, overtake it before it got another fifty and rain punches at its body. There was more than one crippled moose in the vicinity of Meldrum Lake that winter.

The ears of the big bull flattened if I approached too close to him, and often I was forced to jump on one of the horses bareback and ride up the trail from stackyard to house if he was between me and the house. For strangely enough, though he had nothing but arrogant disdain for either a human being or another moose, he became an abject coward when faced by an oncoming horse. "A horse," I remarked to Lillian, "is his Achilles' heel."

"I'm glad he's got one somewhere," she replied tartly. Lillian had little love for Old Cantankerous on account of the way he bullied the other moose.

The more I saw of that bull, the greater became the temptation to get a photo of him somehow, at really close range as I had with so many others of his kind. And the longer I put the matter off, the greater became the temptation. But to appease it would be a somewhat tricky and difficult matter, one that raised the problem of how to handle camera and rifle at the same time. For to attempt any such piece of photography without the rifle in my hands as life insurance would be an act of irresponsible foolishness. No matter how quick I might be, it would take a second or two to drop the camera, unsling the gun, slip the safety and bring the bull into my sights. A bull such as he, with murder on his mind, can cover a great deal of ground in just two or three seconds. I was under no delusion whatsoever: if the bull were to charge, only powder and lead would stop him in his tracks.

The matter of obtaining the coveted photo went unsettled for several days until one afternoon when I observed the bull chewing his cud at the edge of a small meadow only a half-mile from the house. Then I decided to settle the matter for good and get it off my mind, and by hook or by crook get the photo I wanted. And I believed I could with a little assistance from Lillian.

I brought the matter up in a casual sort of a way, saying, "I believe we could get a photo of Old Cantankerous this afternoon." Lillian knew exactly what I meant by "getting a photo." It just meant stalking to within ten or fifteen feet of the bull.

She wrinkled her nose. "We?"

"If you'd like to handle the camera while I cover with the gun," I explained, fumbling a little over the words.

Maybe I was hoping she'd say, "You won't get me within forty yards of the brute!" and then perhaps I'd have scuttled the whole idea. But instead she began pulling on her overshoes in a very matter-of-fact way, as if obtaining the photo was as easy as apple pie.

While she was piling on layers of sweaters and pulling into a pair of stout mackinaw britches—it was twenty below outside—I got her snowshoes from the shed and pummelled their leather harness until it was well softened up. Then I checked the box camera. It held four unused negatives.

One would be enough. I then took the rifle down from its peg on the wall and fondled it briefly, passing my hand along its scarred stock. The old gun had been a close companion since 1923. It had provided us our meat. I had shot more coyotes and timber wolves with it than I could possibly keep track of. It had had its fair share of bears, both black and brown. It had faced pouring rain in summer, snow and bitter cold in winter. That old .303 had shared every bit of the wilderness with us and was perhaps a part of the family.

"Ready?" I asked. And as an aside, I told her, "You look fat as a little Eskimo wench bundled in all those sweaters." A compliment to which she was deaf.

But she was all set to go, all one hundred and fifteen pounds of her, and obviously anxious to get the business over with. I stared thoughtfully at the shells in my hand and hoped I wouldn't have to use one. Then dropped the cartridges into the magazine and stepped onto my snowshoes.

A packed trapping trail took us within a hundred yards of the meadow. The bull hadn't moved; he was still out in the open, fifteen yards from the brush. He half turned in his tracks as we came in view, watching us with lazy indifference. The approach across the meadow was difficult and slow, for here the snow was virgin and thirty-six inches deep. It clutched at our snowshoes, and each time we lifted a foot, three pounds of snow came up on the webbing.

"Think you can manage it?" There was a faint hint of anxiety in my words.

"I'm doing fine," she came back steadily.

With me breaking trail, we moved cautiously to within thirty yards of the bull. He looked as big as a mountain, and was now eyeing us with bold intentness. I stopped and slid a shell into the breech of the gun, and pulled the moosehide mitten from my right hand. Now there was just the thin woollen glove between my finger and the trigger. I glanced speculatively at the bull. As long as he stood with his ears up and mane down, we hadn't too much to fear from him. Now he was twenty yards from us, and still displaying no outward sign of animosity. I thought, "Maybe this isn't going to be so bad after all."

At this point Lillian must step around in front of me and assume the lead, for the camera had to have a clear field of vision between it and the bull. I stepped aside and allowed her to pass.

We shuffled forward again, and now there were only fifteen yards between us and the bull. I stopped and asked softly, "How does he look through the finder?"

"I can try one picture now," responded Lillian, still without a tremor in her voice. "But another five yards would be better still."

Another five yards! That would put her within thirty feet of a bull moose packing as much danger as a case of dynamite. Almost subconsciously, I slipped the safety on my gun. There was no sense in taking any chances.

"Unbuckle the heel straps of your overshoes," I suddenly ordered. Free of those straps, she could still move forward but in an emergency could step quickly out of the shoes and dodge. She unbuckled the straps and looked at me as if to say, "What now?"

My eyes held steadily on the bull. He was watching us with what now seemed to be amicable curiosity. Maybe this wasn't going to be so hard after all.

"Okay." I inclined my head. "Another five yards, but not an inch closer."

But those five short yards were a distance not to be travelled. The words had barely left my mouth when I heard the old bull grunt. Both his ears whipped back against his neck, his mane bristled, and his eyes rolled to show a bloodshot white.

My heart started to pound furiously. My lungs grabbed for breath.

"Quick, shoot now!" I said, meaning the camera.

Then the old bull charged. A scream forced itself from Lillian's lips, one that she could not stifle. "Shoot! For God's sake, shoot yourself," she cried, meaning the rifle.

Even in the wink of time it took for the gun to jump into my shoulder, for my eye to look down its sights, he was almost on top of her. Thank God my heart was again beating normally, my breath coming evenly. Here was no time for panic, but for cold calculated action. It had to be a brain shot —that's what my own brain said. No other could possibly drop him before his front feet began pounding Lillian to a pulp. It had to be a brain shot—nothing else counted now.

A good many thoughts could have been hammering at my mind in that swift second or two of ordeal. I might have been cursing myself, as of course I later did, for exposing her to this danger in the first place. I might have been thinking of a one-hundred-mile trek with team and sleigh for a doctor, or of how very much alone and shut away from other people we were here. Actually, but a single thought pounded at my head: it has to be a brain shot.

I deliberately held my fire, knowing full well that there would never be time for me to reload. Somehow I managed to keep pressure off the trigger until he was ten feet from her snowshoes. Then I held the sights steady between his eyes and fired. A brain shot, I said, it has to be a brain shot. And, thank God, a brain shot it was. He was dead when he hit the snow.

Slowly, and reluctantly, my eyes lifted to meet Lillian's.

"I'm sorry," I began, fumbling for words. Then for the moment I could say no more. The fear that had been in her still clung on in the tenseness of her face, pallor of her cheeks, dilated pupils of her eyes. And it was a fear of which she need never feel shame. To see Old Cantankerous at a distance, chewing his cud, was enough to tingle the roots of one's hair; to see him ten or fifteen feet away, charging, was a vision of hell itself.

I looked down at his body, still quivering in death. My thoughts flashed back to the gulch and the yearling, to those others of his kind that he was forever bullying. Then my thoughts looked ahead, to days to come when Lillian or Veasy might be out tending their traps and now without fear of Old Cantankerous. Then I nodded my head. This was all for the best.

Weeks passed before we ever mentioned the bull again. The roll of

A photo-op gone bad: the moose flattens his ears in anger (left), then, mane bristling, turns and charges Lillian, who snapped these photographs despite the terrifying circumstances.

film was sent off for processing, and it was almost two months before we received the prints back. Of course it never dawned on me that Lillian might have actually taken a photo of the bull as he was charging, but when I glanced at the prints I saw that she had. There he was, ears back, mane on end, hoofs churning the snow. And though I hated the sight of that photo, I knew it was one I'd never part with.

I passed it over to Lillian. "Look," I breathed quietly.

She took it from my hand, then dropped it. For a quick moment the old fear was in her eyes again. "I don't want to look," she said, dropping the picture on the floor. Yet somehow, right then the fear was gone.

Chapter 17

If your home is in the wilderness, you seem to realize the omnipresence of danger to a far greater extent than do those who move forward through life bumped by the elbows of their fellow men. Death is there in the swaying treetop, for who can rightly tell when that tree is likely to crash to earth, snuffing out the life of all on whom it falls? Death is there on the snow-covered lakes and creeks and rivers, for beneath the snow lurks many a treacherous air hole ready to devour instantly all who might stumble into it. Death rides watchful and expectant with the breath of an arctic wind, for intense cold numbs both the willpower and strength of all who have to face it, breeding within them an almost irresistible temptation to sit down and snatch a moment or two of rest. And if they succumb to that temptation? Instead of a few moments of rest, they are likely to sleep the sleep of no awakening.

Death momentarily revealed its presence to Lillian when the bull moose bore down upon her. And there was one other occasion at least when for a fleeting moment death hovered but a few feet away from her before turning his back and gazing the other way.

Lillian was out in the woods at the time, picking blueberries. Veasy, seven years old now, marched along at her heels. August was almost gone and the pea vines and vetches of the timber already smutty with rust. The woods themselves had a quietness and innocent serenity about them that exists in no other place but the deep woods. In berry season Lillian often went into them alone, or with Veasy, into the deep shade of the jack pines where the berries grew plump and lush. Sometimes I went too, although my fingers were slow and clumsy when they tried to pick blueberries. On this particular afternoon I had hitched the team to the mower and was cutting an acre of hay. Veasy and Lillian were alone, the endless forest about them.

The blueberries were a fruit of the forest that Lillian could not altogether claim as her own. There were others living in the woods who also demanded a share. It was to the heart of the blueberry patches that the ruffed grouse led her chicks. As Lillian's fingers flew from vine to vine, stripping them of their berries, a dozen mischievous red squirrels were within inches of her hand, helping themselves to the fruit. In blueberry time even the coyote forgot his appetite for meat and became a temporary vegetarian. There were others too who claimed some right to the berries, those who crushed the delicate vines with their own ponderous weight and growled a throaty challenge to any who questioned their right.

Even in the shade of the pines, the afternoon was hot and sultry. Yesterday it had rained and now steam oozed up from the moss. On hands and knees Lillian moved from vine to vine. A thin cotton blouse covered the upper part of her body, the despised slacks, her legs.

"You can't pick berries in a dress," she told me when, after lunch, I saw her pulling on the slacks and winced a little as she did so. A dozen or so yards from her, Veasy was making a half-hearted effort to fill the tin cup that he had toted along. Like me, Veasy considered that picking blueberries was no job for a man. His lips and cheeks were a smear of purple, for again like me, with every one berry that went into the cup another went into his mouth. But after a while neither cup nor belly would hold more, so with a big sigh of contentment he lay down in the moss and within seconds was fast asleep.

The sun slipped slowly into the west, and equally slowly the ten-pound lard pail beside Lillian filled to the rim with berries. In her urge to get it chockablock and start back for the cabin in time to get the supper, she moved sixty yards from where Veasy was sleeping. About her all was very still, save for the rattle of berries against the pail and the small talk of the squirrels.

Her left hand was about to pull a berry-laden vine toward her when her body quickly tensed and she was seized by the realization that now she wasn't entirely alone, that another was standing close by. Slowly she brought her head around. She stifled the cry that jumped to her throat. There between her and the boy was a monstrous, full-grown bear.

She doubted that the bear had yet seen her or Veasy. But it too sensed the presence of another, and clumsily came erect on its hind feet, head swaying from side to side, nostrils plucking questioningly at the air. Again a scream was born in Lillian's throat; again she forced it back. For now she could see that the underbelly of the bear was almost naked of fur, and that its teats were red and raw from the sucking. It too was a mother, and somewhere close by were the cubs.

With the cubs lay the danger. Usually, any bear will beat a hasty retreat at sight or scent of a human being. But not so in the case of a she-bear with cubs.

A blur of movement in the bushes a few feet from the boy drew Lillian's attention. A body took pattern, black, furry and round. Immediately behind it another similar form took shape. Lillian swayed a little on her knees, and her heart pounded as she watched the two cubs.

The cubs moved within a few feet of Veasy without noticing him, then, rolling over on their backs as bear cubs do when a-berrying, their little fists shot out and began pulling vines to their mouths.

Their mother dropped back to all fours at sight of the little ones, and she came slowly around in her tracks, staring fixedly at them. A growl suddenly rumbled deep in her throat, and the black mane at her shoulders bristled with brute rage. She had winded Veasy, or Lillian, or perhaps both.

Lillian wanted to cry aloud, to waken Veasy, as if such an act could conceivably shield him from the deadly danger that had now arrived. But again she held back all impulse to cry aloud and instead her lips began moving in silent prayer. For if Veasy should suddenly wake up, rubbing his eyes, and begin glancing about him, his very movement would attract the bear. Intent upon protecting her cubs, the she-bear would charge.

Realization of that told Lillian what must be done. Somehow she must try to draw the bear's every attention without waking Veasy. Slowly, steadily, then, she came up from her crouched position in the moss, compelling both mind and muscles to the task. At her sudden movement the bear swung around and faced her. Holding her own eyes on the bear, trying desperately hard to keep her every movement slow and steady, Lillian began backing away. Now the bear was upright again, jaws hanging open, yellow spittle frothing its lips. Backward Lillian went, cautiously, an inch or two at a time. But her eyes never lost their fix on the bear. Then the cubs saw her, and they raised their little snouts from the blueberries and rolled over from their backs, whining a little as their nostrils sought the scent of their mother. Then they saw her, and with short whoofs of delight they moved into her flanks. Again the she-bear came down to all fours. Her mane dropped, and the flare of anger left her eyes. She greeted the two cubs with a soft cough of affection and licked their woolly coats. Then, without another glance at Lillian or Veasy, the three bears turned away and loped off through the forest.

Despite the mental agony that Lillian must surely have undergone during those few fearful moments of her encounter with the bear, she took Veasy back into the selfsame berry patch the next day and the next, and continued to visit it until she had close to a hundred quarts of berries sealed down for the winter. Not until the last jar was sealed did she casually tell me of the incident.

"Why didn't you tell me at the time?" I exploded, on hearing her out

"What good would that have done?" she countered.

"Well, I might have gone along with you the next time, and maybe got a shot at the bear."

"A she-bear with cubs?" She arched her eyebrows. "And what would become of the cubs without the mother? You would have had to shoot them too." That was the fantastic quality of Lillian—even amid such great danger, she still cared whether a she-bear with cubs was killed.

"You should have told me anyway," I argued grumpily.

Veasy was working at his arithmetic, but now he laid down his pencil, shoved back in his chair and began listening to the argument.

"Carry on with your work, Veasy," Lillian bade him sharply. Then, carefully folding a dish towel that really didn't need folding, she placed it back on its hanger, patted her hair and said primly, "You didn't tell me about Veasy and the wolves, did you?"

Again Veasy dropped his pencil, and this time Lillian didn't get after him about it. "Why didn't you tell me about the wolves?" she persisted.

"Wolves?" Looking suspiciously at Veasy, I asked, "Did you tell your mother about that?"

Veasy stared me straight in the face. "You never told me not to."

My eyes went back to Lillian. A slight smile played at the corners of her mouth. "Let's just hear why you didn't tell me about the wolves." She said it mockingly this time.

I huffed my shoulders. "What was the use of telling you about that? Had I done so, every time Veasy went down the lake to look at his traps you'd be here fretting and worrying about timber wolves trailing behind in his tracks."

Lillian had me in a corner. She rejoined, "That's why I didn't tell you of the bear incident at the time. Had I done so, every time I went picking blueberries you'd be fretting about us getting mauled to death by bears."

~

Perhaps Veasy should never have been out on the ice, tending traps alone, in the first place. It happened the previous winter, in January. Veasy wasn't quite seven, wouldn't be for another six months. Still, he knew how to set the traps even if he couldn't pry their springs down with his hands. Instead he scuffed the snow from a windfall or rock, placed the trap on it and depressed the springs with his foot. And held a foot on them until he'd set the trigger on the pan, and they were now ready to catch things, even his own fingers, if they happened to bump the pan. No doubt this had happened, but if so, he kept the secret to himself.

He kept pestering me to let him set the traps out for himself until finally, a little against my will, I gave in. Lillian told me, "No, he's too young to be out on the ice alone, messing around with mink sets."

"Is he?" I wondered. And, glancing back to a hazy past, I began trying to remember how old I had been when I first shot a starling with a .22. Maybe seven or eight. And no one had been around to show me how to handle the .22 except maybe an older brother. Whereas Veasy had seen both me and Lillian setting out mink traps since he was old enough to slip along on skis.

"Is he?" I repeated. "Just a few traps set around the lake here at the house, well within hollering distance if anything went wrong? After all, it would give him something to do after school hours, and on Saturdays and Sundays. He's a bit young, yes, but maybe not too young to set out a trap or two and maybe catch a fine mink."

"He's too young," Lillian insisted.

"I've been over to the big lake on my skis," Veasy joined in. "Lots of times. By myself." By the big lake, he meant Meldrum, which was three-quarters of a mile from the cabin, well out of hollering distance. And sensing that I was wavering, even if his mother wasn't, he asked me directly, "Can't I put out just two or three traps at the lake by the house? I can ski awful fast now, quicker than you go on snowshoes." That part of it was fact. I said nothing, looking to Lillian for a decision. After at least five minutes of thinking it over, she said, "He does go quite a piece away on his skis. Too far sometimes. He was up the creek yesterday, gone for over an hour. And when I asked him where he'd been all that time he said halfway up the hill back of the house, to the old bear den where we smoked out our very first bear. That's a mile and a half from here." Then, with a small sigh of resignation: "Maybe it will be all right for him to be out on the lake, fixing a trap or two. At least I'll know where he's at."

So I gave him a half-dozen traps and went around the lake with him myself when he set them. I watched as he depressed their spring with his right foot. That part of it was all right. I watched as he made his trap cubbies out of pieces of stick. Nothing wrong about that either. And I watched as he took a piece of muskrat flesh from the small sack he was toting and placed it in the cubby. "Farther back," I told him. "The way you've got it, a mink or weasel could get away with the bait without touching the pan." And when he had pushed the bait farther in the cubby, using a long stick to do so, I said, "Now go to it. And whatever you catch is yours."

Despite the fact that timber wolves often left their track marks on the snow covering the frozen lakes, it wasn't often I saw a wolf in the flesh. In summer you often saw them, seldom in winter. In winter they got wild and cautious, hunting mostly at night, moving off into heavy timber at daybreak to sleep or cleanse their fur beneath the shelter of some overhanging trees. When Veasy went off down the lake on a late winter afternoon to look at his traps, Lillian told him, "Watch out for the wolves," just as a city mother would say, "Don't cross the street against the light." Timber wolves on the ice, like bears in the blueberry patches, were perhaps something that Lillian often thought of but never worried too much about. And I never lost much sleep thinking about timber wolves bothering Veasy either. Here in the wilderness one could, if he were that way inclined, spend countless hours worrying over all that might go amiss. But if you were so inclined you had no business living out in the wilderness in the first place.

I had been over to Meldrum Lake taking a peek at a lynx trap I'd set three days ago. The lynx was ranging a thicket of spruces, hunting snowshoe rabbits, and I'd arranged my bait pen alongside a well-packed trail, set the trap and tossed in a couple of handfuls of feathers for bait. On the chance that the lynx had got caught in the set, I took the .22 rifle along to finish him off. A lynx lived quite a while when held by the foot in a trap. Too long, in fact, for comfortable peace of mind. But I couldn't help that. The only traps that had ever proved suitable for the taking of such things as lynx were the leghold variety. Nothing else would do. But still, few professional trappers liked the thought of a lynx or anything else suffering in a trap, so the only thing one could do was visit the sets as often as possible before there had been too much time for suffering.

But the lynx hadn't been around; the set was undisturbed. And since it was late afternoon, and the January sun had set, I started back for the cabin to do up the evening chores.

I spotted Veasy at the far end of the lake by the house. He too was heading homeward after making the round of his traps. Even at that distance I saw that he'd caught a mink, for it was dangling from his right hand, nose almost dragging in the snow. And I knew that it was an extra-large mink that he'd taken out of his traps.

I squatted back on my snowshoes at the edge of the ice, thinking, "So you've made twenty dollars for yourself. Now what would a little fellow like you do with all that much money?"

Veasy was coming square up the centre of the lake and was now about a half-mile away, skidding easily and quickly along on the skis I'd made him from the pliable wood of a spruce tree. Head and face almost hidden by the parka lined with the soft fur of muskrats, feet and legs encased in knee-high buckskin moccasins, also lined with muskrat fur—that's how Veasy was dressed. The buck that supplied the skin came from the crest of a hogback a mile north of the cabin. The muskrats came from the beaver marshes. The thread was from the mail-order house. Lillian's needle had supplied most everything else.

Veasy angled away from the centre of the lake toward the west shoreline. He moved off the ice, into the timber to look at another trap set out in the spruces. In a couple of minutes he was in sight once more, again travelling the ice. But now there were others there too.

The five wolves trooped out onto the ice from the timber. They came noiselessly and suddenly. A second ago there might not have been a wolf within miles of the cabin as far as my hearing them or seeing their sign was concerned, but now, out of nowhere at all, there were five of them out there on the ice, within a half-mile of where I was squatting.

They paused a moment at timber's edge, heads high, ears forward, noses measuring the air. Then, in single file and not more than a couple of hundred yards behind him, they began trailing Veasy. There were two blacks, two grays and one wolf almost as white as the snow it trod. Any one of them weighed a hundred pounds or more; any one could badly maul a fourteen-hundred-pound moose if the animal panicked at the sight of them.

I started to come upright, then, shaking my head, squatted back down on the webbing. Instinctively I picked up the .22, then slowly laid it down again. Veasy was still five hundred yards away, the wolves slightly farther. The .22 was as useless as a pea shooter.

The gap between child and wolves was lessening; they were only a hundred yards behind him now. They travelled softly, like phantoms, without noise, the soft snow they were treading muffling their footsteps.

I wanted to gulp air into my lungs and let it go in one desperate, explosive cry. "Veasy, look behind you, timber wolves!" That's what I wanted to cry out. But didn't. That would never do. It would fluster Veasy, and throw him off mental balance. And maybe he'd panic and start running as fast as his legs could carry him for me. And the wolves would know he was scared of them, and if they acted true to their species they'd probably take after him as they would after a panicky moose or deer. I could do nothing but sit and watch.

Then Veasy stopped. He turned around, saw the wolves and stood rooted to his tracks. And to me, watching impotently, time and most everything else was at a standstill. My lips began to move, forming soundless words—"Don't panic. Don't run. Just keep on coming steadily up the ice. Remember what I told you about timber wolves and moose? No wolf or combination of wolves in British Columbia will tackle a moose if it turns and faces them, bluffs them out. But if it panics and runs, they'll tear it down before it's gone a mile. Don't panic, son. Just keep moving naturally up the ice as if you had the whole lake to yourself."

Stout little legs moving again now, pushing the skis over the snow. Limp body of the mink swinging to and fro from a small mittened hand. Fur-lined ear flaps flopping up and down against healthy red cheeks, like ears flapping on a foxhound when it's hunting up scent. Thus, up the ice he came, steadily, with never a telltale back glance to see what was going on there.

And behind him, still in single file, perhaps only seventy-five yards behind now, five lusty timber wolves, any one of which could break a man's leg at a single crunch of its jaws.

I untied the flaps of my own fur-lined parka and tossed them away from my face. Beads of perspiration were now tickling my cheekbones. "Keep coming, son, steady, just like that. Don't let them bluff you, don't drive those skis any faster. You're not scared of a no-account timber wolf, are you? Steady—steady—steady—"

And at last Veasy reached me, puffing a little, eyes blinking. A couple of hundred yards off the wolves stopped and bunched. My eyes went to the .22, quickly left it again. It was too far, but if they'd just come a little closer … Then one of the blacks trotted a few feet to one side, hunkered back on the snow and, forelegs braced, lifted its nose to the sky and howled, dismal, sad and spine-chilling. Then, sorting themselves out, and again in single file, the five wolves trotted off the ice and moved silently away through the timber.

"Were you scared, son?" It seemed a foolish question to ask, but I asked it just the same.

He nodded. "Just a little."

I said, "Shucks, never get scared of a timber wolf. Wolves'll never bother you. Curious, that's all they were." I made out that I was examining the mink. "Say, that's a lulu of a mink you've caught yourself. Should get twenty-five dollars for a mink like that."

But I have never told Lillian about the wolves. Somehow I thought she might not appreciate the picture of her young son being trailed by five wolves. Women are fussy about things like that. There were some things we told one another, some things we hardly ever mentioned. Such as she-bears in blueberry patches, timber wolves on ice, and little things like that.

Chapter 18

There wasn't a mare's-tail of cloud in the sky, and the soft westerly breeze sent nightcaps tagging each other across the lake and mosquitoes scurrying back into the grass whenever they dared to leave it. The alfalfa patch was beginning to purple with blossom, the timothy was knee-high. Radish and spinach were almost ready to eat, and almost every other seed recently sown in the garden was now a husky plant. It was the tenth anniversary of our first coming to the creek, to the very day.

"Let's celebrate," suggested Lillian as soon as the breakfast dishes were put away, the cabin broomed out and dusted spic and span.

"You name it," I grinned.

She wrinkled her forehead, and then said, "Let's go visiting."

"To Riske Creek?" I didn't like the idea of that. "We were there a couple of weeks ago."

"No, not to Riske Creek." And laughing, she went on, "We just came from Riske Creek—ten years ago."

"Then just who are we going to visit?" I was curious to know.

"No one." Lillian took a loaf of bread from the bread tin and began slicing it. "We'll take our lunches with us and just ride down the creek, and sit around the beaver ponds, and loaf in the sun, and things like that."

So Lillian made the lunches, and Veasy wrangled the horses, and I ran a rag through the barrel of the .303 rifle and pocketed a half-dozen shells, just in case we ran into a buck deer that would nicely fill the crocks.

The trail winding in and out of jack pine and spruce timber along the banks of the creek was a very different trail from the one that was there ten years ago. Then it was only a thin game path, good enough for moose and deer but difficult to follow by anyone on horseback. So first we had widened the trail out so that we could get over it with pack horses in tow and without their bumping their packs against the trees. Later we widened it still more, so that we could get over it with team and wagon or, in winter, the sleigh. The beaver marshes downcreek were far larger than those at the head of the watershed, and consequently there was far more fur around them. At a strategic spot alongside the creek, five miles from Meldrum Lake, we had built a cabin, small but neat, floorless but warm. In winter and early spring, when trapping muskrats or other fur in that part of the country, we moved a light camping outfit down to the cabin and stayed there until trapping operations were over. That's where we headed for now, for the cabin downcreek.

We visited every dam within easy reach of the trail, loafing there a while, looking for mink tracks in the mud or just lying on our backs in the sun, staring up at the sky, I thinking my thoughts, Lillian hers, Veasy his. And whatever our thoughts were, we kept them to ourselves, for it was easier to lie on our backs thinking them than to put them into words.

It was noon when we pulled up in front of the cabin, and Veasy proclaimed the fact by stating, "I'm hungry."

I said, "Climb down from your horse then, and build a fire for the coffee."

Lillian darted into the cabin and came out scowling. "Pack rats," she scolded. "They sure litter the cabin up. I'll have to broom it out before I do another single thing."

If Lillian ever hated anything, then that thing was pack rats. No matter how many got caught in the traps we left set for them, there were always more to take their place. And if Lillian left a bit of curtain over the window to give the cabin a sort of homey appearance, the rats soon chewed it to shreds when they had the cabin to themselves. And they chewed harness, and nipped the strings off the saddles, and generally fouled up anything they could reach that was chewable. When Veasy was two years old and asleep in his cot, a pack rat jumped up on the cot and bit him in the ear. You just couldn't get along with pack rats no matter how hard you tried to humour them.

While Lillian broomed every last vestige of pack-rat manure from the cabin and Veasy tended the coffee pot, I lay on my back, eyes partly closed, busy with my thoughts. There was much that was comforting about them, too.

Now, every beaver dam on the creek that could be patched up and repaired *was* repaired. Every saucer was full and overflowing. In recent years fur prices had been good, and now my mind was no longer plagued by financial worry. There were muskrats galore on the watershed now, as well as in the landlocked lakes about it. So many, in fact, that the matter of trapping them when their fur was fully prime was becoming quite a problem. We only had so much time to do it in, and sometimes ran out of time before all the marshes were trapped. The muskrat pelts were at their best through March and early April, but once the ice began rotting in the lakes the quality of the pelt deteriorated and fetched but half the price it would have brought in March.

Others, too, on the creek had benefited from all we had done to it in the ten years we had been here. Now, even in the driest summer, there was never a shortage of irrigating water for the crops in the valley below. Every landowner down there had water in his ditches wherever and whenever he needed it. There was no longer any blotting paper above to soak up every bit of moisture that fell. It spilled out of the saucers and fled on down the creek.

When first we came to the creek, not too many domestic cattle grazed the summer range about it, and those that did were in constant danger of perishing in the bog holes whenever the summer was a dry one. But now some three thousand head of Hereford range cattle were trailed back to

173

The same stretch of Meldrum Creek as pictured on page 56, this one taken after the Colliers had repaired the beaver dams.

the timber range along the head of the creek in early July by the ranchers, and left there until mid-September. And wherever the cattle ranged, they were seldom more than a half-mile from a clear and firm water hole and never did one become bogged down in the mud.

Yet despite all that had been accomplished, there was still something lacking. Though the old breeding grounds of the beavers were again all under water, and their old dams repaired, they still lacked one thing— beavers. A vacuum was there, and we knew not how to go about filling it.

"Coffee's ready!" Veasy's call took my mind from beavers to the more tangible fact that I was hungry. Lillian came from the cabin, brushing the door sill on the way. "Pack rats," she grumbled, squatting cross-legged by the fire and unwrapping the lunch. "God save me from them!"

Riding back home late that afternoon my thoughts again wandered to beavers. Ten years was a long time to want something and still be without it, yet right this very moment we were as far away from having any beavers in the creek as we were ten years ago. At least, so I thought.

And so we rode home, me brooding about beavers, Lillian sizing up the blueberry vines alongside the trail and once in a while stating aloud, "There'll be a good crop there this year," and Veasy perhaps thinking about things that had nothing to do with beavers, or blueberries either for that matter, the three of us blissfully unaware that shortly, within a few days' time, we were to be visited by one who was to play a vital role in not only giving Meldrum Creek back its beavers, but most every other watershed in the Chilcotin too.

∾

R.M. Robertson, a native of Glasgow, Scotland, migrated to Canada in 1910. He homesteaded on the flat plains of Saskatchewan in 1914, owner of one hundred and sixty acres of untilled prairie, his home a small hut with a sod roof. If it had not been for World War I, Mr. Robertson might today have been a prosperous prairie farmer, the hut with its sod roof a memory of a day when he hitched his team of horses to the doubletrees of a walking plow and turned the very first furrow in his rich Saskatchewan loam.

But by May 1919, when he stepped out of khaki, all he had in his pocket was a month or two of back pay, plus a hundred or so dollars of gratuity money. He took a two-bit piece from his pocket, flipped it into the air and closed his eyes. Heads he went back to the plow, tails he sought other employment. Tails it was, so with a shrug of the shoulders the ex-machine gunner turned his back on Saskatchewan's sod and pushed westward into British Columbia.

Outdoor life had ever had a magnetic attraction for Robertson's keen mind, and in 1920 he joined the staff of the British Columbia Game Department with the rank of game warden.

Game Warden R.M. Robertson never limited his activities to enforcement of regulations alone, or to apprehension and prosecution of offenders under the Game Act. He was more interested in what led a pair of Canada geese back to the few acres of water in which the hen bird had nursed her brood to maturity since first she laid an egg. Or the horns and skull of a bighorn sheep, now crumbling to dust before the indifferent

175

stare of the weather, yet still visible on the slope of a hillside that had not been trodden by the species within the memory of living man—what catastrophe, natural or man-made, had wiped these big game animals from the face of the land? These and a host of similar questions were ever demanding explanation from the game warden, who, whenever other duties allowed, was out on moraine-littered slope or in sombre conifer forest, eyes searching for some clue that might lead him to the answers.

When I first met Robertson in 1941 he was a divisional inspector and had already devoted twenty-one years of his life to the promotion of sensible wildlife management in his division. Those twenty-one years of duty had been spent mostly in the "dry" belt of British Columbia, where beneath the broiling summer sun the eroded soil of the hillsides became thermogenic dust, and the plant life it supported shrivelled upon its stalks for want of water to slake its thirst. Yet here, as elsewhere, there was no lack of evidence that the land had not always been so parched. Once upon a time moisture seeped out of the dry cleft here, and over there that gravel-bottomed depression scarring the slope of the hill had once been a vigorous stream. And there were so many scars, so many depressions, now all dry save for a moment or two in spring when the melting snows trickled into them from above.

The divisional inspector followed many a stream bed from source to mouth, examining the foliage that still clung tenaciously to the banks, seeking answers as to why they were now dry. And he too sensed that in the prostitution of the beavers lay at least part of the answer.

Remote though we were in our lonely isolation, not too much touching upon wildlife matters in his division went unheeded by Inspector Robertson. Though no game warden had ever set foot upon it—at least, not since we had come to it—not only its existence but also something of our activities to do with its beaver dams had reached the inspector's ears. And believing that secondhand knowledge is a sorry substitute for that gained from personal observation, Robertson wrote me that he had decided to visit us and learn of our goings-on for himself.

One day in late June of 1941 I saddled up my own horse and, trailing a spare behind me, rode out to Riske Creek to meet the divisional inspector and guide him back to our cabin at Meldrum Lake. For at that time it never occurred to me that any mechanical vehicle could possibly navigate the rock-littered track.

He was cooling his heels at the trading post when I arrived with the horses. About five feet nine, graying slightly at the temples, his one hundred seventy-odd pounds of well-knit flesh told of a body well tuned to vigorous outdoor exercise. "He knows what the drag of snowshoes is like on a soft day in March," I deduced as we shook hands and I proceeded to tie his war bag behind the saddle. I was watching from the corner of one eye as he took the bridle lines and put a foot in the stirrup. All government departments have the occasional square peg trying to insert itself into a very round hole. An inspector of the British Columbia Game Department should surely know how to handle horses.

Robertson fitted perfectly. His left hand holding the reins was at the cheek strap of the bridle as it should be, his right on the saddle horn, and not fumbling with the cantle. When he hoisted up he came lightly to rest in the seat, right foot instantly finding the stirrup. The inspector was as used to the unpredictable manners of horseflesh as any cowpuncher working for the ranchers hereabouts.

Not too much talk flowed between us as now at a trot, now a gallop, with the occasional walking gait between, our horses put the miles behind them. That was another thing I liked about the man: instead of bothering me with small talk, he held his breath and gave all his attention to the countryside, marking a deer track when one crossed the road, or the dusting place of a grouse whenever we passed one.

Before getting back to Meldrum Lake, one minor incident took place that told me much of the mettle of the man who rode thoughtfully at my side. We were skirting a small lake whose shoreline was fringed with a waving growth of foxtail grass, now heading out. I was watching a brood of young ducks swimming parallel to the far shore. Suddenly the ducklings huddled together and in close formation moved in toward the shore and the foxtail grass. There they turned and swam parallel to the shore again for a few yards; then, breaking formation, two of them began moving toward dry land.

The divisional inspector too had his eyes on the ducks. Suddenly he braced back on his stirrups, brought his horse to a stop and sang out, "Whoa!"

After staring intently at the other side of the lake, he breathed softly, "Over there in the foxtail, fifty feet from those two ducks—can you see it?"

Then I did see it, something that might have been a clump of foxtail grass waving in the wind but wasn't. "Coyote," I announced.

"The tail of one, anyway," agreed the inspector. "The rest of him is hidden in the grass."

The bushy tail of the coyote was waving gently to and fro like a flag fluttering in the breeze, as coyote tails have been waving in the long grass at water's edge ever since there have been coyotes—and ducks in the nearby water foolish enough to fall for the trick.

"Curiosity," observed the inspector, "killed a darned sight more than the cat. The owner of that tail is trying to bring one of those ducks within pouncing distance of its jaws by the simple trick of lying flush on his belly and using his brush as a decoy. Inquisitive things, ducks, especially young ones."

One of the ducklings was now out of the water, perched on one leg, watching the movement of the tail. Then at a clumsy waddle it started toward the grass and the predator that lurked there.

"This," the inspector murmured, "we cannot allow." And taking a deep breath, he got rid of it in one noisy shout.

The coyote heaved upright and for a split second stood broadside to us, ears in our direction. Then his keen eyes spotted us, and wheeling, he streaked off through the grass.

Quacking noisily, the inquisitive duckling scrambled for the water and splashed out to the others. And breasts low to the water the brood moved into a clump of bulrushes, out of our sight.

"Ever see that type of hunting before?" Robertson asked.

"Only once," I replied. "That time it was a young goose, and the coyote nailed it."

"I wonder," he mused, "how many ducks and geese have fallen for that shabby trick since coyotes first got on to using it?"

The divisional inspector spent close to a week riding our trapline with me. He fitted into the life as a shoe fits the foot of a well-shod horse. Come time to wash the supper dishes, he was out of his chair with the dish towel, drying as Lillian washed them. He fired questions at Veasy, not only those relating to muskrats or mink, or deer and moose, but also many others to do with mathematics and geography and history and other subjects usually talked of in a schoolroom. And to Lillian he said with a wink, "The adage 'spare the rod and spoil the child' doesn't apply here."

On the final day of his stay with us, while staring thoughtfully out across one of the marshes, he said musingly, "It seems to me you could well use a bit of help in looking after all these dams. Did it ever occur to you that if one happened to go out, the sudden rush of water would likely take a few others out below?"

The thought of that had been bothering us for quite some time now. At the time of spring freshet, or indeed when swollen by summer thundershowers, Meldrum Creek now more resembled a young river than any minor creek. A river, moreover, that was barricaded here and there by some twenty-five dams lacking any proper spillway. So far, none of the dams had been badly breached, thanks mainly to the mass of spruce boughs re-enforcing them. But eventually the boughs must rot, and the dams settle, as some were doing already. And if one of the major dams were to give, it was a highly debatable question whether those below it could withstand the sweep of water that would come pressing in on them.

As if arriving at some major decision within his own mind, but saying nothing of it to me, he repeated, "Yes, you obviously need some help." But of what such help might consist of or where it was to come from he offered no clue at all. Nor were we to be enlightened for a little while yet.

Later in the year, writing in the *Report of the Provincial Game Commission*, Inspector Robertson had this to say: "While on a recent patrol of inspection covering the trapline of Eric Collier, of Meldrum Lake, the potentialities of wildlife propagation were amply demonstrated on this trapline. With use of only a pick, shovel, and wheelbarrow, Mr. Collier dammed up some twenty-five of the old disused swamp lands which were once the habitat of beavers, muskrats, and other fur-bearers. These areas ranged in size from eighty to five hundred acres each. The runoff of the winter snows were held and the swamps reflooded. This was followed by the rapid appearance of muskrats and other fur-bearers, waterfowl and big game, as numerous tracks testified. In fact, the whole situation and appearance of the country changed from one of apparent stillness and dearth of life to animation and restoration of its pristine condition. The irrigation problems of an area contiguous to the Collier trapline have been largely solved as a result of the above project. The Collier project on the headwaters of Meldrum Creek is a brilliant example of what can be done in this very fertile field of endeavour."

These then were the thoughts of Inspector Robertson of the British Columbia Game Department concerning the events that had befallen Meldrum Creek since we came to its headwaters. But not until early the following September was I again reminded of his suggestion that "you could well do with a bit of help in maintaining all these dams."

It was 10:30 A.M. Lillian was busy with her sewing, stitching her winter mittens. Veasy was hunched over the table, exploring the mysteries of algebra. And I was checking traps to make sure their triggering was all right before we set them out in the woods.

Suddenly Veasy's back straightened and he sat bolt upright, listening. "What's that?" he exclaimed.

I too listened a moment, then shrugged my shoulders indifferently as the faint hum of a motor came to my ears. "Only a plane following the Fraser River north," I said. For Canadian Pacific Airlines was now operating a plane service between Vancouver, B.C., and Whitehorse in the Yukon, and their aircraft often passed high over our cabin.

"That's no airplane," Veasy insisted.

"Then what the heck is it?"

"A car."

"A car? Back here in this neck of the woods!" I shook my head. It was inconceivable.

"It is a car," persisted Veasy, now from the open door. "It's back there in the jack pines yet, but it's a car and it's coming in here."

Lillian was at my heels as I heaved out through the door, and together we stood there, gawking in amazement.

"Veasy's right," I said slowly. "It couldn't be, but it is a car."

The uneven throb of an automobile motor, hauling its chassis over a track that was far more suited to steel-tired wheels than one moving on rubber, was now certainly no trick of imagination. A car was out there on our road, still perhaps a half-mile or more from the cabin but getting closer by the minute. Soon we caught a flash of its blue body among the jack pines, moving very slowly and cautiously but moving just the same. And we stood there, blinking and wondering.

The automobile eased to a stop alongside us, and its driver lurched out of the seat, staggering a little as one is likely to stagger who suddenly finds his legs after being seated far too long. He was lean and tall, between forty-five and fifty, his eyes glazed for want of sleep, and yesterday's stubble still on his chin. But who was he, and what was he doing back here?

The stranger himself quickly answered that question. "Game Warden Mottishaw, Quesnel Detachment, B.C. Game Department," he introduced himself crisply. "You're Eric Collier—right?"

I inclined my head. "Himself. And this is my wife and son—Lillian and Veasy."

The game warden touched his cap, smiled a little and said, "I've already heard about Lillian and Veasy." Then his eyes went to his car. He frowned. "What a road! Two blowouts, a broken spring, a buckled fender and a leak in the radiator. I stopped that with chewing gum. Why in heck don't you move some of those rocks and roots out of the right-of-way?" he barked.

"We've only been back here ten years," I grinned. "Never got around to fixing up the road yet. Hope to someday, though."

The game warden dropped down on a block of wood and pushed back his cap with a slow, tired movement. He wasn't wearing any uniform, just an old pair of tweed pants and a coat of similar material. "Never mind," he said. "I got here even if I did have to drive all night to do it. But they're still breathing, and that's all that counts."

Veasy's every attention was being devoted to the automobile. He was fascinated by it. He walked slowly around it, examining its tires, fenders and springs. Then he went down on his hands and knees, looking at its underbelly. He peeked into the cab, at the instrument panel and the gearshift. Then he stepped away, nodding his head, as if all that he'd seen was good.

Making wild guesses as to who "was still breathing," I said to our visitor, "Step inside; it'll only take Lillian a jiffy to brew a pot of coffee and get you a bite to eat." He certainly seemed in need of food and drink.

But apparently he didn't hear me. He was at the rear of the car, fiddling with the handle of the trunk. "Well, where are you going to put them?" he asked sharply.

I looked at him in bewilderment. "Put what?"

"Haven't got the faintest idea, eh?" he said. "Here, maybe that'll explain." And he tossed a somewhat soiled envelope over to me.

I tore open the flap and unfolded the single sheet of paper inside. The words danced at me as I slowly read them, and their full meaning sank in.

"Guard them and care for them as if they were children. They're worth their weight in gold and if anything happens to these you'll not be getting any more from us."

That's what the paper said, and the brief note was signed R.M. Robertson, I/C C Game Division.

I dropped down on a fender of the car, trying to steady my voice and my thoughts. "You mean they are—" I began falteringly. Then I broke off, trying to collect my wits, eyes glued on the open trunk of the car. "Beavers?" I gulped, scarce daring to utter the word.

"Two pairs," the game warden affirmed crisply. "Live trapped at the Bowron Lake Game Reserve for liberation on Meldrum Creek. And I'd have you know that game reserve is two hundred and fifty miles north of here, and those beavers have been cooped up in the trunk of the car too long now. We've got to get them into the water, and the sooner the better. Where are you going to liberate them?"

The irrigation dam was the closest and most logical spot in which to set the beavers free. Each beaver had an oblong tin box all to itself, and one at a time we carried the boxes onto the dam.

"One pair are two-year-olds, the others three," the game warden informed us as he opened the drop doors of the cages. Each box had to be tilted on end before its prisoner would come out.

One at a time the beavers were coaxed away from their containers, and one by one they crouched low to the ground, eyes blinking stupidly at the sudden light, nostrils working. Then the largest one of the lot, a male, I judged, went erect on the webbing of its hind feet, forepaws doubled against its chest, as if in prayer.

"Smells mighty good, doesn't it, big boy?" chuckled the game warden. "And it'll feel a darned sight better than it smells. So get going."

Now that he winded the nearby water, the buck beaver waddled clumsily along the dam a few feet and then slid into the pond. And with scarce a telltale ripple vanished into its depths. One at a time the others took to the water at the selfsame spot, and in a few seconds not a trace of them was to be seen.

The day was very still, not a breath of wind in the air. Nothing disturbed the glassy surface of the pond. Lillian and I stepped farther along the dam and stood there, watching the water.

Game Warden Mottishaw seemed to have suddenly taken on new life. Some of the tiredness went out of his eyes, he straightened his cap to the correct angle and braced his shoulders. "Did you say something about coffee and bacon and eggs a while back?" he grinned.

"Will it be three eggs or four?" I asked the game warden, sensing a real outdoors appetite.

Then Lillian suddenly whispered, "Look!" She was pointing to a ripple cleaving the water some sixty yards out from the dam. I followed the point of her finger and was just in time to catch a glimpse of a large dark head thrusting out of the water. Then the head was gone and there was a resounding plunk, as if some very flat object had flailed down on the surface of the pond. Then all was quiet again, and Lillian's eyes were on mine, mine on hers. And right that very moment, we both knew that not one single day of the last ten years had been in vain. The beavers had come back to Meldrum Creek.

Chapter 19

For three suspense-packed days we were kept in a mood of gnawing uncertainty: would the newcomers stay? It was a haunting question too, for there were no fences or other barriers to prevent any or all of the beavers from going wherever they pleased. They were ours only so long as they remained within the boundaries of our trapline; if they crossed those boundaries there was no way we could possibly bring them back again, for once off our trapline they became the property of some other trapper with trapline adjacent to ours.

Early on the fourth day following their liberation, I stepped out of the door to fill the two water pails at the irrigation ditch. The water in the irrigation dam had remained at a fairly constant level that summer. The ditch itself was deep and broad enough to hold most of the flow coming into the dam, and we usually left the water in it from early spring until well along in the fall, since the ditch was only a few yards from the cabin door, and this saved us packing the water buckets to the creek whenever they needed filling.

The pails slipped from my hands when I reached the ditch. I stood motionless, staring at it, mouth stupidly gaping. Last night the ditch had been full of water, but now there wasn't even a muddy puddle there. It took all of ten seconds for realization to dawn on me as to why the ditch was now dry. When it did, I hurried back into the cabin and announced excitedly, "They've plugged the irrigation ditch. Let's go up to the dam just to make sure."

As fast as we could, Lillian, Veasy and I followed the ditch to the dam. Its intake was tightly plugged with sticks, weeds and mud.

"Look over there." Veasy suddenly broke the silence. "It's a beaver." And a beaver it was, fifty feet out from the dam, swimming high in the water, a six-foot length of willow gripped in its mouth and trailing along behind it.

Wetting a finger, I held it above my head. "Wind's coming toward us," I said. "Drop out of sight in the ditch and maybe he won't see us." So we scrambled into the irrigation ditch and dropped to our knees.

In broad daylight a beaver's vision is as poor as his nose is good. If downwind from a coyote, he can scent the predator at a distance of two hundred yards or more, and he can scent the presence of a person at perhaps a greater distance. But if one is downwind from a beaver and remains perfectly still, the beaver will sit combing his fur, or peeling the bark from a cottonwood stick, a dozen feet from the watcher without knowing he is there.

We were only fifteen feet from the plugged intake of the ditch when the beaver arrived with his stick and waddled out of the water. Now he gripped the willow in his forepaws, his flat scaly tail toward us. He slid the willow over the top of the dam, butt downstream, and to the noise of a series of soft grunts, rammed the butt firmly against the wall of the ditch. In a few moments I was to try and free the willow from its anchorage, but so securely had it been placed there, it was only with great effort that I was able to do so. And with that stick laid so firmly in place perhaps rests the answer as to how a beaver dam remains intact despite the pressure of water that sometimes comes against it.

Two more sticks were floated in from the pond and pushed into position. Then the beaver shot out into the pond and upended in a floating bed of pondweed. Suddenly the wind switched and the beaver smelled us. The pondweed was abandoned. There was a resounding splash as his tail thumped down on the water. His dark body went down into the depths to surface again a dozen feet out from the ditch. He swam furiously to and fro, whiskers twitching. Then his tail drubbed the water once more and gracefully he dived, and we were able to follow his course upstream by the broad V on the water.

"At least we know that one is still here," I said with relief. And a couple of days later we were quite sure there were two. By that time a round structure of sticks had begun taking shape above the water. A beaver lodge was in the process of construction. Early in the morning and at sundown, one of us, either Lillian, Veasy or I, cached ourselves among the brush at water's edge and sat patiently, watching the lodge. Finally Veasy was rewarded by seeing two beavers hauling in material for the house at the same time. So one pair had reconciled themselves to their new quarters; not for another two weeks were we to know what had happened to the others.

We followed the dams downstream for evidence of their presence but found nothing of them there. Then we searched upstream to the head of the watershed with similar result. We next covered the entire shoreline of Meldrum Lake and there found a clue. We found three cottonwood trees that had recently been felled by beavers. But little of their bark was eaten, none of the wood skidded into the water. Beavers too had apparently inspected that shoreline, but, as if not liking what they found, had moved on elsewhere.

A small spring-fed brook dribbled into the lake from the west, such an unpromising trickle of water that it hardly seemed worth investigating. Yet explore it we had to, riding our saddle horses through the timber on the west side of the lake and following a game trail that crossed the brook a half-mile above the lake. When we arrived at the crossing we found that now there was no water in the stream, its bed bone dry. And that was funny, for only once before had we seen the stream altogether dry, and that was nine years ago.

We tied our horses and walked up the stream bed. A little farther up, the brook wound its way through a small meadow hemmed by aspens.

As the meadow came in sight, the riddle of the dry watercourse below was instantly solved. Now the meadow was under water, and where the stream flowed away from it there was now a dam, four feet high and some twenty-five feet long.

It looked as if someone had surely gone berserk with an axe in the surrounding aspens, chopping them down senselessly. Many of the trees were lodged, unable to fall to earth; others had toppled over into the water and been trimmed of their every branch. But many had fallen on land, and lay as they had fallen, as if those who had been responsible for their felling wanted no part of them now that they were down.

There was no doubt about the identity of the woodcutter. His house told us of his presence, even if the evidence of his teeth were not sufficient. And the lodge was too large to have been thrown up in such short order by any one beaver. A pair must have followed the stream up from Meldrum Lake and decided that the meadow was the place for them. So, not only had the beavers returned to Meldrum Creek, but apparently they were here to stay.

This seemingly reckless destruction of their food supply—the cutting down of trees for no apparent reason whatsoever—was a puzzle we were quite some time in solving. When we went around the shoreline of the irrigation dam, we saw that in places the aspens had been felled by the score, yet not one in ten had been made use of.

"Why all the waste?" I pondered aloud.

"There's a reason for it, no doubt," Lillian said.

"There's a reason for almost everything that goes on in these woods," I grunted. "But some of them are darned obscure."

"You mean we're too stupid to understand," she laughed.

Veasy was examining one of a pile of chips scattered around the stumps. Tossing the chips away he contributed his bit to the discussion by saying, "Maybe they don't like the taste of the bark. Maybe it's sour or something."

"Then why cut it down?" I was quick to come back.

He said, "We'll know why someday." And one day of course we did.

By freeze-up, both beaver lodges were cemented over with twelve inches of mud. Enough food was cached down in the water in front of the lodges to last their occupants all winter and until the ice went out the following spring. But for quite some time after most of the ponds were iced over, the beavers somehow kept the water open around the entrance to their houses. Then early in December, when the mercury fell to fifteen below zero, the leads of open water to the lodges froze over. Not until the following April were we to see our beavers again.

~

It was mid-May. One more winter behind us, another summer ahead. Mid-May, and the garden plot plowed and harrowed and fertilized with squawfish. The stench of the decomposing fish still came out of the soil as we worked it, but we didn't mind that. There are worse smells than rotting fish. And in a few days' time the smell would all be gone, the seeds sprouting and thin lines of green showing where now there was only dark, smelly soil.

It didn't take long to plant the seed once the ground was ready for it. I went along with the hoe, making the drills. Veasy came next, spilling the seed into them. Then came Lillian in a wide-brimmed straw hat, yellow-ish with age, shielding her head and face from the bold stare of the sun, raking the dirt back into the drills and padding it down with her feet. By "It's time to go cook supper" the last row of seeds was planted, and I relaxed on the handle of the hoe and said, "Okay. You go cook supper and Veasy and I'll make the ditches for the water." And as she started off for the cabin, I watched her retreating figure and murmured to Veasy, "What a wonderful woman! I don't know what the heck we'd do here without your mother."

"Think you'd stay here without Mother?" Veasy asked. I made no answer because I doubted very much that I would. Without Lillian, none of it all would make sense.

I glanced at Veasy, studying him thoughtfully. How the boy was shooting up! Be thirteen come July, I thought. I ought to buy him a real rifle for his birthday. I could get a real good one for ninety dollars, new too. Ninety dollars for a rifle. More cash than we had to our name when we first rode our wagon into the wilderness. We had come a long way. Not that Veasy didn't make good use of the .22. He killed a buck with it last fall, about as big as bucks come. I saw the track in a skiff of snow, half a mile from the cabin. For a little while I thought of getting the .303 and hunting the critter myself. But when I came to the cabin I'd changed my mind. I told Veasy to take the .22 and a dozen long rifle shells and track the buck until he jumped it, and then circle the tracks, watching real close. "You'll have to get him in a vital spot with a light gun like that," I told him. "Don't shoot at all unless you can line the sights on its heart or lungs." In a couple of hours he was back, blood all over his clothes. He'd jumped the buck, and circled it, and got within sixty feet of it before touching off the trigger and plugging it right through the heart. Yes, it was time I got the boy a real gun, and it would fit nicely into his approaching birthday. I'd get him a 30-30; there was a gun he could kill almost anything with if he held the sights right.

How the boy was growing, mentally as well as physically. Does he ever find it lonely back here? If so he never says anything about it. But once in a while he stares off into space as if far beyond the horizon there's something he's thinking mighty hard about. Wonder what it is? Maybe someday he'll get up and start out for that horizon, and he'll not come back until he finds what lies on the other side. And maybe he won't come back to the woods then at all. I shoved such thoughts from my mind. They weren't too pleasant anyway.

∻

By the time Lillian sang out, "Supper!" the irrigation marks were scuffed out neat and straight alongside the rows of seeds. There had been no rains since the snows melted, so we'd have to irrigate right away and soak the dry soil.

First thing in the morning, while Lillian was getting breakfast, I went to the head of the ditch and turned a stream of water into it. Breakfast over, and the dishes washed, the three of us went to the garden and began distributing the water down the irrigation marks. We had the water on about half of the garden when suddenly it seemed that we didn't have enough water for what was left. I scratched my head and said, "That's strange. Where's it all going to?"

Lillian walked over to the main ditch, looked at it and sang out, "There's hardly any water in the ditch."

"Then where's it gone to?" There'd been lots there twenty minutes ago.

"The beavers must have shut it off." And with that Lillian burst out laughing.

"That's a fine kettle of fish," I grumbled. "By golly, they can't do that to us. We've got to have irrigating water or we'll have no garden or hay."

But the beavers were as determined to stop water from escaping down the irrigation ditch as were we to get it to the garden and hayfield.

A beaver knows nothing about irrigation. His every concept of water conservation is based on the principle that nowhere along his entire dam must the water be allowed to escape in one concentrated channel. Providing the escape of water is spread evenly over the whole of the dam, the beavers don't seem too perturbed. But should the water start to cut a channel in any one place, whether over the top of the dam or around it, instantly the cut must be dammed.

As soon as the two beavers in the dam realized that spring that they were losing the water, and in the one spot, they soon remedied the situation by neatly and quickly plugging the mouth of the ditch.

Eventually the problem was solved by an arrangement satisfactory to us both. Taking sly advantage of the fact that a beaver is mostly nocturnal, working at his dam by night or in the first hours of daylight and sleeping through the day, we were able to turn water into the ditch and irrigate from shortly after sunup until sundown. But as quickly as the sun set, the beavers floated down from the lodge and plugged the ditch tight. Or if we turned it down too early in the morning, when they were still active, they shut it instantly.

The plugging of the irrigation ditch at night resulted in a greater flow of water running away over the top of the dam, and it soon became obvious that the beavers weren't going to stand for that. And no healthy beaver will for long tolerate a situation that can be quickly remedied by application of a little labour on his part. In this case, perhaps working without break the whole night long, the pair in the irrigation dam went to the chore of raising the height of the entire dam. And therein lay a hazard.

The irrigation dam differed from all others we had repaired in this respect: in the creek channel proper, no boughs were used as re-enforcement. There, for a span of thirty-odd feet, the dam consisted of a straight dirt fill, and its top had been held at least twelve inches higher than the remainder of the dam. The line of reasoning that prompted us to dispense with boughs in the fill was that if it were held to a certain height well above the remainder, no water could possibly spill over it and hew out a channel. Elsewhere, of course, the dam was strongly re-enforced with boughs, and there the water could run over the top without doing any harm.

But as inch by inch the beavers raised the level of the remainder of the dam, the water correspondingly inched its way higher up the dirt fill until only some three inches of dirt was showing above the level of the water.

Then calamity struck, swiftly and decisively. A three-hour downpour in early September resulted in near-flood conditions on the creek. Far more water was feeding the irrigation dam than could possibly get out unless somewhere it was able to find a weak spot where it could hew itself out a channel. It found that point of weakness at the dirt fill.

Overnight the water in the dam rose until it was spilling over the top of the fill, nibbling away at the dirt. In a matter of minutes a channel was cut, and into this channel raced the freshets swelling the creek. The breach widened, became deeper, and the strength of the water surging through it was so great that when I stepped into my hip boots and waded out into the torrent to see what might be done to save what was left of the fill, I had to fight not to be swept off my feet and carried downstream.

With the help of Lillian and Veasy, large boulders were rolled out onto the dam and skidded into the cut, in hopes that they might provide some sort of cribbing against which dirt could be dumped. But the wild strength of the water swept the rocks over the brink of the dam as if they were made of paper and we stood there, watching the fill disintegrate before our eyes, not knowing what to do, reconciling ourselves to the fact that the entire fill would go out and the pond go dry. But we were reckoning without the beavers.

A violent splash from the vicinity of the beaver lodge reminded us of their presence. The water rippled, and a form took shape, lining straight for the dam. The beaver approached to a half-dozen feet of the fill. He turned, swimming parallel to the dam, then coming swiftly around, floated almost into the current sluicing through the fill.

The presence of the beaver gave me a sudden idea. "Run back to the cabin and get an axe," I bade Veasy. And when he returned with the axe, I said, "I'm going to chop a few spruce trees down and lop off their limbs. And we'll dump the limbs in the water a little way from the cut and maybe—"

"You're crazy," cut in Lillian, reading my mind. "No two beavers can possibly shut that force of water off."

"They can maybe try, can't they?" I retorted. "One thing is certain: it's no use us trying to do anything until the dam drains out."

So I had my way, and we packed bundles of limbs along the dam and piled them about twenty yards from the breach. Then went back to the cabin to await what might happen.

At nightfall the water was still rushing through the cut. Now the channel was four feet deep by fifteen wide. Nothing but a bulldozer with a heavy blade could possibly shut that flow off—at least, so we thought.

Early the next morning I stepped outside the door, listening. Last night the roar of water rushing through the breach was so loud that we almost had to shout to make one another heard, but now all was quiet and still, even the customary murmur of the creek below the dam muted. Carefully I followed the irrigation ditch up to its source and stepped out onto the dam. I looked at the spot where we'd dumped the spruce boughs. Not a limb was to be seen. And where yesterday there had been a miniature canal scarring the fill, now there was a dark, tamped surface of shiny mud. And beneath the mud were the spruce boughs, weighted down with rocks, which ranged in size from small pebbles to some as large as a football. Thus had a single pair of beavers, in a single night, shut off a head of water that man could have shut off only with heavy earth-moving equipment.

~

The evening patrol showed up about a half-hour after sunset, and was as regular as the sunset itself. But never was there more than one beaver in the patrol. Sometimes the buck, sometimes his mate—for now we well knew male from female, but never saw the two together. From our hiding place in the irrigation ditch, and if the wind was in our favour, we could see the beaver surface shortly after leaving the house via an underwater exit and watch as he or she swam leisurely down to the dam, head lifted slightly above the water. But the patrol never moved right into the dam, at least not when we were spectators, but instead stayed off from it some ten feet, swimming ever so slowly parallel to it until one end was reached. Then the sole member of the maintenance crew pivoted around and floated gently back until the other side was reached. Following this ritual, and if all was well with the dam, the patrol moved away and moments later we heard the chatter of teeth as an aspen stick was peeled of its bark among the flooded willows out from the shore of the pond.

The sensitive guard hairs of a beaver's dense fur are the instrument that detects the presence of any major leak in the dam. No need for him to waddle along its top, relying upon eyesight or ear to inform him of a weakness somewhere. The slightest pull of water escaping in one place registers against the tips of his fur as the beaver makes the patrol, and should any such leak exist, within seconds he goes about the business of sealing it tight.

The feed bed lay in a clump of willows in two feet of water, a half-dozen feet out from the edge of the pond. I built a natural blind on the shore consisting of bundles of willows propped against an aspen that had lodged when the beavers felled it. And then I drove two stakes in the muck and wired a rail to them, thus making the observation bench.

And if the wind was coming toward us, we squatted down on the bench in the even light, stifling the desire for a cigarette as we sat waiting patiently and expectantly in the blind. Of course no beaver would come to the table if cigarette smoke hung on the air, nor would one come if the wind carried our scent to them. Once in a great while they came when there was still light in the sky, but usually all was in shadow when the incoming wavelet on the otherwise smooth surface of the water warned us we'd better sit very still, and be cautious even in our breathing.

The wavelets widened and in a moment or so a beaver came gliding silently through the water, to crouch down on the feed bed with decidedly humped back. First he must rid his guard hairs of the water that clung to them, a ritual speedily accomplished by a vigorous shake of the body. Then the fur was combed fastidiously down in place, the long nails of his webbed hind foot sufficing for a comb.

Now he was ready for whatever might be on the feed bed, and always there was food there. If a litter of aspen or willow already peeled of their bark floated in the water around the feed bed, there was always one stick there, sometimes willow but usually aspen, with sufficient bark left on it to furnish any beaver an appetizer for the more trenchant meal to come. The stick was gripped firmly in his front paws, and like a squirrel shucking a pine cone the beaver's teeth soon cleaned it of all bark. The peeled wood was them sometimes dropped on the feed bed, but more often tossed away into the water, at some later date to be floated downstream and perhaps become a part of the dam.

That stick attended to, the beaver slipped quietly into the water and with a few swift strokes swam out of sight. But not for long. Soon the telltale wavelets again warned us to sit tight and still, and behind the wavelets came the beaver. Now there was a two-foot length of aspen fast in his teeth, though where the stick had been cut we hadn't the least idea. We had heard no crash of a falling tree and could only surmise that the stick was part of one already felled.

Now the feed bed was again stocked with a food supply, and for the next ten or fifteen minutes the rhythmic castanet sound of teeth informed us that the beaver was really hungry. Finally, his belly was filled, and dropping what was left of the food on the feed bed—there was always some left—he moved off through the water.

So dark was it now that wavelets were almost lapping at our feet before another beaver moved in on the feed bed. This time the ripples were not quite so strong as before; a smaller beaver was coming, the female for sure. She too hoisted out of the water onto the feed bed, shook the water from her fur and then proceeded to comb it. She too completed the job of peeling the stick left behind by the male, eating its last shred of bark. And she too slipped away from the table to return a minute or so later with a fresh stick of food. And though now it was so dark that we could scarcely see the outlines of her body, we could still hear her teeth clicking as she gnawed the bark from the wood. Then she was gone, with only the far-off squawk of some roosting mallard to denote that life was still there in the pond.

I got up from the bench, kicking the cramp from my legs. But Lillian sat there a little while longer, looking toward the feed bed she could no longer see. Veasy wasn't with us tonight. He'd stayed home with a book that evening and kept a fire in the stove, and water boiling in the kettle for us. We never knew how long we might have to sit in the hide before the beavers came, and some nights they never came at all. Even in summer it got a bit chilly sitting there on the bench, the sun gone for the day, stars winking down at us, and hoot owls muttering in the spruces. A hot cup of coffee went down very well when we got back to the cabin.

I waited a moment for Lillian, then said a bit impatiently, "No sense in you sitting there any longer."

She got up, stretched her legs and said musingly, "I was just thinking about something."

It was so dark I could scarcely see her face. "About what?"

"The feed bed. They always leave food on it for the next beaver, don't they?"

"Always," I said.

Together we started for the cabin. We were about at the door when Lillian suddenly asked, "Why aren't people like that?"

I stood with wrinkled forehead and eyes to the ground for several seconds before replying, "I guess that beavers do instinctively what mankind must learn to do eventually. It seems a contradiction that a humble animal like the beaver can follow the golden rule while man can't. People, Lillian, are just different from beavers—and that's the pity."

Chapter 20

It seemed as fantastic as it did ridiculous: destroy a beaver dam with dynamite after waiting ten long years for the beavers that had built it? It was crazy! Coyotes, timber wolves, cougars and other natural enemies of the beavers, yes, it was a foregone conclusion that we would have to wage continual warfare against them, but never for a fleeting moment had it occurred to me that we'd be compelled to dynamite a dam. Yet there was the dynamite, tied behind our saddles, fuse and caps too. And a loon out there on the water, flexing a wing and chuckling as loons sometimes do chuckle, at the seeming absurdity of it all.

At two years of age a female beaver seldom gives birth to more than two kits, usually only one. At three she might have from two to three in the litter, but not until reaching full maturity at four or five does she become really prolific in her breeding. Quintuplets born to beavers of six years of age and up are the rule rather than the exception.

But with only two pairs to begin with, beavers multiply slowly. Not until four years following the liberation of our original two pairs on Meldrum Creek was the creek able to boast a half-dozen active colonies along it, or some thirty-six beavers. From that point on the increase was far swifter.

Conservation of any wildlife resource is not without its problems, and where beavers were concerned we certainly were not lacking in ours. There was the problem of the beavers who would not vacate their pond even though they had hacked down every deciduous shrub within a sixty-yard radius of the water. Then they began cutting conifers, a wood as foreign to the diet of a beaver as aspen bark to man. It was as plain as the water in the pond that if this state of affairs continued in the colony, its occupants might become diseased, and the disease would spread to other colonies. Downstream a few hundred yards was Meldrum Lake, verdant stands of aspen and willow crowding its shoreline, yet not boasting a single colony of beavers in its entire four-mile length. Yet for reasons that were known only to themselves, the obstinate tenants of the pond a short distance away from this land of milk and honey refused to move downstream. Finally we decided that we ourselves would assume full responsibility for providing the colony with a proper food supply.

There were plenty of aspens among the conifers a quarter of a mile back from the water, but this food supply was beyond safe reach of the beavers. If they ventured that far from water they would most likely fall prey to a marauding wolf, coyote or bear. But this food could be snaked through the conifers and to the edge of the pond at the horn of a saddle, and once that idea took root in our minds we made twice-weekly trips to the colony, cutting down some fifteen or twenty aspens and snaking them in to the pond.

This experiment in beaver culture lasted all of two months, and it seemed that the more food we were willing to drag into them, the greater became the appetite of the beavers. Once I revisited the pond twenty-four hours after the usual supply of food had been hauled down to it. Every tree was peeled of its last square inch of bark, every limb cut off and taken into the water.

Enough is enough. This comedy of errors had gone on too long. Trying to keep those beavers in food was like pouring water into a sieve. My eyes wandered thoughtfully to the dam, which was about ninety feet long, six feet high and broad enough on top for one to drive a four-horse freight team over it if the sticks and other debris would support the weight of the horses—which very probably it would.

A dark and deadly idea began shaping in my mind. Without that dam, there would be no pond, and without the pond, the beavers would have to move! Maybe here was a solution to the matter, one that would do the beavers no harm, but instead would actually benefit them.

The next day, saying nothing to Lillian of our intent for fear she'd voice womanly objections, Veasy and I rode back to the pond, sticks of blasting powder, caps and fuses tied behind our saddles. Eight round holes were punched in the top of the dam and eight sticks of powder, complete with fuse and caps, inserted into them. To allow us plenty of time to gain the protection of some stout tree when the fuses were ignited, each fuse was cut an inch longer than the last, all eight being timed to explode simultaneously, but giving us about two minutes to get the heck and gone away from the dam when the explosion took place.

Kicking a sliver of pitch wood from a rotten log, I lighted it and moved along the dam, touching its flame to the fuses. When all eight were spitting out sparks I raced for the tree where Veasy was already crouching. For a couple of pent-up minutes we hugged the tree trunk, squelching the urge to peer around it and see what was happening at the dam. Then, like the sudden firing of a twelve-inch cannon, the detonation came. Water plumed high into the air to spank down again on the pond a hundred yards from the dam. A shower of sticks, mud and rocks shot high above the treetops, some of the rocks returning to earth perilously close to our hiding place. Then all sound was blotted out by the roar of water spewing out of the pond.

After the powder smoke had lifted a little we came out from behind the tree to inspect the result of our work. A gap twelve feet wide and at least six feet deep had been blown out of the dam, and through this gap the pond was making its getaway.

"Guess that'll take care of the situation," I confidently told Veasy. "Now they'll follow the water downstream and maybe resettle in Meldrum Lake."

"Think so?" said Veasy noncommittally.

I glanced sharply at him. "Don't you?"

He considered a moment before replying, "Beavers built the dam in the first place, didn't they?" And when I made no retort he went on, "Maybe instead of moving out they'll stay and plug up the dam again." Veasy took nothing for granted.

Three days later we returned to the scene, and I for one went back with the firm conviction that every beaver in the colony would now be elsewhere. But as we neared the dam site, all seemed far too still. Why no sound of running water? All could not have drained out of the pond in such short time. Then the dam was in sight and when fifty yards away from it I sat on a rock, shaking my head. The impossible had happened. The gap in the dam was a gap no longer. The beavers had completely filled it up again.

That taught us a lesson. It taught us that it is a waste of powder and time to try and eject beavers from their own selected homesite by blowing up their dam. If the colony looking after it is an "active" one—if it has from four to six beavers in it—the dam will be repaired almost as fast as it can be blown out.

"What now?" asked Veasy, trying to smother a laugh.

"Just a minute, boy," I said sheepishly. "Let me have a bit of time to figure things out."

For twenty minutes I never moved, sitting there with my cheek in my hand, thinking it all over. Then, slapping my thigh, I heaved up and announced, "We'll bell trap them, that's what we'll do. If they won't go peacefully we'll eject them by force."

The following afternoon saw us back at the pond, each leading a pack horse, each horse toting three ten-gallon kerosene drums into which small latch doors had been built. One of the horses also toted a small tent and blankets and provisions, and tied behind the saddles of the two horses we were riding were a half-dozen traps and three small horse bells. The jaws of each trap had been heavily bandaged with canvas wrappings.

We pitched the tent well back in the timber, a hundred and fifty yards from water, where our scent wouldn't carry to the sensitive noses of the beavers. The horses were staked on picket ropes at a pothole meadow a half-mile away. We ate supper, ruminated over the campfire for a few minutes, then moved down to the water and set the traps.

The ends of the trap chains were fastened to stakes driven solidly into the ground, and the slack in the chain tied to a slender willow with a horse bell fastened to its top. As soon as a beaver got into a trap his first jump back into the water would result in the instant ringing of the bell. And there is no noise quite so jarring as the sudden jangle of a horse bell on the hush of a wilderness night.

There was still a little light left when the pounding of clapper against bell galvanized us into action. Veasy hefted the pitchfork, which recently had boasted three tines but now had only the two outer ones. I hoisted a kerosene drum on my shoulder, and we cut through the trees to the pond, the furious din of the horse bell guiding us straight to the trapped beaver. It was a huge beaver, too, that threshed water at the end of the trap chain, an old male weighing close to seventy pounds. Heaving gently on the trap chain, I skidded him up onto dry land. Veasy made quick use of the fork, holding the thick neck of the beaver down with the tines and pressing its head firmly against the ground in such a position that its teeth could do us no harm. Bearing down on the trap springs, I eased the beaver's foot free of the jaws. We had made a good job of bandaging the traps; they had left no mark on the beaver's foot at all.

The kerosene drum stood on end at my side, makeshift door open. I took a deep breath, then signalled Veasy, "Okay." And as the pitchfork tines relinquished their hold on the beaver's neck, I took a firm two-handed grip on his flat scaly tail and with one sudden heave deposited him in the drum and quickly closed the door.

By midnight each of the six drums had a prisoner. I kicked the campfire coals ablaze and brewed a cup of coffee. I sat over the fire, sipping the coffee, ears perked for a quick splash of water, which would denote that there were still beavers left in the pond. Thrice I heard the far-off lament of a timber wolf. A half-dozen horned owls held noisy convention

202

in the treetops across the pond. A moose suddenly belched from within a stunted acre of second-growth pine. But noises such as these can be heard almost any night in the wilderness if one cares to sit sleepily over a camp-fire listening for them. But there was no splash of a beaver's tail against water, and as the first light of dawn brought grayness to the woods, I crawled into the blankets for a couple of hours of sleep.

Though slightly cramped of limb, the six beavers were little the worse off for their confinement when some dozen miles to the south, and six hours later, they were tipped out of the kerosene drums on the shingle of a fair-sized landlocked lake that not only had a plentiful supply of beaver fare along its banks, but also bore slight but certain evidence that nearly a century ago there had actually been beavers there.

One by one the "catch" was released from the cages, and one by one the beavers sniffed suspiciously at the air before waddling into the water. And there we left them, free once more to shift for themselves, and re-loading the drums on the pack horses we returned to our camp and reset our traps.

That night the bells rang but twice, and within a few moments of their ringing two more woefully puzzled beavers were shut in the drums, to be liberated several hours later with the remainder of the colony. It was impossible to determine how many stayed in the lake, but when we revisited it a week later a good-sized lodge had been built, and some fifty or sixty aspens lay across the shoreline, all trimmed of their branches. Some had stayed.

∼

According to British law, a man is innocent until proved guilty of the crime with which he is charged. No man can rightfully point the finger of accusation at his fellow man and proclaim, "That man is a murderer" before all evidence has been examined and a jury has rendered its verdict.

Thus it was with the coyotes. If we had suspicion that they were indeed killing some of our beavers, suspicion was no excuse for our adjudging them guilty and passing sentence upon them. First we must have evidence beyond shadow of doubt. And it took me most of one summer to collect that evidence. For three months, wherever I travelled the game trails, my eyes were alert for any coyote scat (manure) deposited on them. The scats were carefully examined for the evidence I must have before rendering verdict. And there was no lack of evidence. An analysis of some ninety-six coyote scats revealed that twenty-seven of those coyotes had recently gorged themselves on a fare of domestic veal. It is an acknowledged fact among cattle ranchers that coyotes do kill the occasional calf. Fifteen scats told of mule deer that had been slaughtered. Five were composed of moose hair, though in this case it is likely that the coyotes had been helping themselves to the leftovers of a moose killed by timber wolves. Coyotes are too cowardly to tackle a moose themselves. The feathered content of some eleven scats confirmed that the head of many a mallard and other duck was being chopped off by the coyotes. Seventeen scats were composed mostly of legitimate fare such as squirrels, mice and snowshoe rabbits. It was the content of the remaining twenty-one that gave us the evidence we sought. Each of these contained the well-digested remnants of beaver flesh, mixed with scraps of the furry hide. That clinched the case. A suspect had been found guilty beyond all measure of reasonable doubt; but executing a sentence was a different matter indeed.

In 1941 almost any well-furred coyote pelt could be sold for ten or fifteen dollars, cash or trade, so consequently every trapper and home-steader in the country was out hunting his skin. But in 1943 coyote fur went out of fashion and the fur trade no longer wanted their pelts. The fact that now the coyote's pelt had little cash value automatically brought to a halt the hunting and trapping to which he had been subjected for so many years gone. This resulted in a spontaneous increase of coyotes. And the more coyotes, the more beavers they killed.

Reluctantly, perhaps, for he had meant so much to us in the early days of our exploits on the creek, and by use of every trick that we could devise, we now waged merciless war against the coyotes. Once again the matter of survival hung in the balance, not our survival, but that of the beavers. After a short period of preliminary skirmishing, testing different ammunition, so to speak, we came to the conclusion that poison bait was the most efficient, if not the fairest, means with which to decimate the ranks of our adversaries. But no matter how heavy might be the casualties we inflicted upon them, we never lacked coyotes. Now, with the many beaver dams and different species of wildlife around them, Meldrum Creek had indeed become a land of milk and honey for all carnivorous predators. Hundreds of young ducks were now hatching on the marshes, and practically every beaver pond had its goose nest. Every acre of water with a food supply for them now teemed with muskrats. And then of course there were the beavers. In 1943 the pelt of an average beaver was worth from forty to fifty dollars, so whenever a coyote killed one he was helping himself to a somewhat expensive meal at cost to no one at all but us. With such a seemingly inexhaustible larder for them to draw upon, it was hard to keep the coyotes in reasonable check. The tracks of one were soon filled by those of another. But through spring, summer and fall there was never a moment of truce, and slowly but surely the beaver colonies increased, though at but half the rate they would have had there been no coyotes to reckon with at all.

And there were timber wolves, too. Perhaps it was the moose herds wintering in the second-growth beaver cuttings along the creek and ponds that attracted so many wolves to the scene. Moose or beaver, it mattered not to a timber wolf; the flesh of the one would fill their gut as quickly as that of the other.

We quite often chanced upon the rotting carcass of a timber wolf that had gulped down one of the poison baits and trotted off through the forest to drop dead in his tracks perhaps three miles from where he swallowed the bait. There might have been a shade of regret but certainly not of pity in us as we gazed at the fly-blown carcass. By this time we'd often sat on top of a beaver lodge in late spring, listening to the pitiful whimper of some three or four kits within, huddled in the lodge together, starving, waiting in vain for a suck at the dugs of a mother who would never come back to the lodge. Timber wolf or coyote, it was all a pattern to us. Now we were learning how harsh at times the wilderness can really be. And a lot of its iron was in our souls too when it came down to the matter of protecting the beavers from predators. Timber wolf or coyote, it mattered not a bit. It was a job and one that had to be done.

I don't know how many timber wolves were accounted for by the use of poison bait and rifle in the years that the war raged on, but recollection of one certain wolf is still vivid in my mind, as it rightly should be. I never had a more skillful opponent. It took all of four years and every bit of woods knowledge that I possessed to settle accounts with him.

Chapter 21

There was black rage born in my heart, an oath on my lips, the day I stalked broodily around one of our finest beaver colonies and marked the telltale evidence of the havoc that Wolf's penchant for murder had wreaked upon the beavers. There was the offal of one's guts here, a few bedraggled scraps of fur there. There was the half-eaten carcass of an old buck beaver alongside a recently felled cottonwood tree, and that was ample indication to me that Wolf was almost full of belly before ever he sank teeth into that one.

But it was the killing of the old mother beaver that fanned my rage into wild and terrible flame. There she lay, belly to the sun, not more than a dozen steps from the lodge, bloated and stinking, dark underfur speckled white with blowfly eggs. She was an old beaver, true, but right in her very prime where motherhood is concerned. She was an old sow beaver who could be reckoned upon to give birth to four or five sturdy kits each June for many a year to come. But now she was dead, killed by a single crunch of Wolf's rapacious jaws. Yet not an ounce of her flesh had Wolf eaten. Here before me was the wilderness in its sourest mood: a mother beaver killed for no useful purpose whatsoever—at least, none that I could think of.

It was mid-June, and the aspens and willows were properly leafed out.

Water lilies and similar aquatic plants pushed their stems to the surface of the water, and a raft of newly hatched geese had been perched on the beaver house when first it came into my view. Young wilderness life was everywhere, and rotten though the underbelly of the old sow was, I knew that her udder had been full of milk when Wolf snuffed out her life. I stepped on to the lodge, reluctantly, and stood there a few moments, listening for what I knew I must hear. Then suddenly I heard it, the faint whimper from deep within the lodge that told me of the kits, dying the lingering, bitter death of starvation.

That's when I lifted my face to the sky and vowed, "I'll get you if it takes until the crack of doom to do it!" But it was a threat easily spoken, not quite so easily fulfilled.

Despite all the damage he did us in the four years of our feuding, never at any time was I able to consider him entirely an enemy. There was a bond linking us together that the whole bloody score of his crimes could not altogether sever: we were both a part of the wilderness, both reliant upon the wilderness for our daily bread. Whenever I took a mink, muskrat or otter from a trap, I was killing. The wilderness insisted that I kill or else pack up and leave it and never come back. No man can hope to survive long in a wilderness without killing.

That's how it was with Wolf. He could no more deny himself the pleasure (or the need) of killing than a bull moose can deny the fever of the mating season. His sanguinary lust for destruction was his by right of heritage, born in him and nurtured in him at the dugs of the shaggy furred bitch that whelped him.

His huge footprint in mud or snow where he ranged will-'o-the-wisp over our trapline often stared me in the face during those four years that I hunted him, yet only once did I catch sight of him in the living flesh. That was in mid-December when I was trapping for mink and otter in a warm spring of water that boiled up unfrozen among the spruce trees girding a muskrat marsh. Such springs are not uncommon on any northern trapline, and their water stays open even at a chill forty below. I had ridden a horse down to the edge of the marsh but then tied it to a tree and crossed the ice on foot. My heavy gun was in its scabbard on the saddle, a single-shot .22 slung over my shoulder in case there should be a live mink or otter in the traps.

A gray form suddenly took shape among the bulrushes, so large that at first I thought it was a deer. But as it turned to run I knew that at long last Wolf and I had met, with only one hundred twenty yards of ice between us. For a half-dozen seconds the killer wolf stood broadside to me, a capital shot for any rifle powerful enough to drop him. But the .22 on my shoulder might as well have been a slingshot for all the good it was. Then his head turned and he broke into swift flight, an elusive flash of gray in the blinding winter sunlight, and melted from sight beneath the vague shadows of the spruces.

I angled over to the bulrushes to see what he had been up to now. The answer glared at me from the ice. The roofs of four muskrat houses were levelled to the ice, which to my reckoning meant that four muskrats had died limp and bleeding in Wolf's jaws.

The total sum of the losses he occasioned us in the four years that I hunted him is beyond reasonable tally. Some of his crimes were minor affairs—for a wolf—but they hurt just the same.

Such as the time he happened onto my sets in the spruce timber and without so much as a by-your-leave devoured two prime mink that were dead in the traps. Mink pelts at the time were in very active demand, worth fifty dollars apiece. He stole one hundred dollars from us then with a couple of licks of his jaws, and, to show there was no ill feeling on his part about it, cocked his leg and urinated on the empty traps to boot.

Oh, he was sharp, as sharp as the keenest razor ever honed. If I carefully concealed three No. 4½ wolf traps under the dry spruce needles and tied the head of a deer above them for bait, what did he do? He circled the whole package, cocked his leg against a bush and moved on to kill a deer of his own. Yet if a lynx or a mink were caught in the traps, he'd walk in, scornful of the scent of steel, and stow the fur-bearers away in his own cavernous gut. According to Indian folklore, all cultus (bad) Indians returned to Earth after they'd died in the form of a timber wolf. If that is really so, the reincarnated Indian who had taken on the form of our wolf must have been a very cultus one indeed. Clever, too.

Wherever the phantom killer journeyed, you could be sure that at least a half-dozen coyotes would be padding along at a safe but respectful distance in his backtracks. Opportunists that they were, coyotes are ever willing to let a wolf do the actual killing while they bring up the rear to feed at the leftovers when the wolf moves on. There was no lack of leftovers while Wolf ranged our trapline.

I was running a line of traps up the shoreline of Meldrum Lake. The lake ice, eight inches thick, was clear as a sheet of glass. I could look down out of the saddle and see shoals of fat squawfish beneath the horse's hoofs as if there were no ice at all. But the caulks in my horse's shoes were new, so there was little danger of the horse skidding and spilling me on the ice.

A sliver of land jutted out into the lake, and there an inch or two of snow covered the frozen ground. I left the ice to shortcut over the peninsula, and as soon as my horse was on snow, I knew there had been murder committed somewhere close by. The coyote tracks on the peninsula told me that. Just before hitting ice again, I cut a track that dwarfed those of the coyote's as a cougar's would a house cat's. I knew who had made those tracks as soon as I saw them. "He's at it again," I bleakly informed the horse. "Wonder where?"

It was a question answered as soon as I rode onto ice again.

I'd seen the two deer, a doe and a fawn, sunning themselves on the spine of a ridge above the lake a couple of days earlier. All that was left of them now was a crimson smudge on the ice and a tuft or two of hair. Force of habit impelled me to drop seven or eight strychnine baits on the frozen blood and scrape deer hair over them with a stick so that magpies or blue jays wouldn't find them and haul them away to the top of some nearby tree. Since Wolf had begun raiding our trapline, I always carried a few poison baits in my travels, spurred by the hope that someday he'd blunder and gobble one or two down.

Then I neck reined away from the ice and circled up into the timber.

I located the fir tree beneath which the doe and fawn had bedded. Their tracks in the snow led in wild leaps to the lake, Wolf's loping prints moving in behind. The deer had no hope of survival when they began skidding crazily on the ice.

Two days later I was again tending the Meldrum Lake traps with but slender hope that Wolf might have returned to the scene of the kill and picked up one of the baits. As I hove in sight of X marks the spot, I saw two coyotes forty yards from the kill, stiff in death. Just where timber and ice met was a third coyote that had also fallen victim to one of the baits. But Wolf hadn't been back. He was perhaps forty or fifty miles away by now, for distance mattered little to him in a few inches of snow. He travelled here and travelled there, moving all the time, as if the guilt of his many crimes would not allow him to rest.

As time went on I lost all count of the coyotes that perished in traps, snares or from poison bait set expressly for Wolf. But not for a moment did I swerve from my vow to bring him to justice.

The fourth winter of my hunt was a "heller," as we call such winters back here. I've lived through a half-dozen such winters, and each has left its claw mark on me somewhere. As usual, Wolf had been ranging our trapline all fall. I was only a hundred or so yards behind him the day he chased a two-year-old cow moose out of a litter of windfalls and pulled her down on the edge of a two-hundred-acre beaver pond. I arrived on the scene in time to find her guts beginning to ooze through the gash he'd ripped in her flanks. But of course he heard me coming and was a half-mile away, maybe, when I got there.

Between Christmas and New Year's Day a muddy overcast shoved in from the north. About midnight I was awakened by the banshee howling of wind. I got up and right then and there knew we were in for a "heller." I could feel the bitterness of the wind seeping in through the house logs. I loaded the heater stove with wood and crawled back into bed, thinking about all the traps that were set and wondering when I'd get to visit them again.

In the morning, as I headed for the barn, I faced a north wind that almost cut me in two. Slanting in with the wind was a pitiless lash of snow. When snow falls in wet, feathery flakes, I know that the storm will soon blow over. It's the harsh granulated fall carried by screeching arctic winds that gives me cause for concern. You never know when it will quit or what its depth will be when it does.

For three days there was scarce a let-up to the blizzard. Perhaps there was a lull of sorts around lamp-lighting time, but after supper we could again hear the snow spitting against the kitchen window.

Lillian's flower garden was fenced by mesh wire, five feet high, and I sat broodily watching the snow inch steadily up the wire. When only a little of the fence showed above snow level, I decided I'd better jar myself loose, saddle up the horse and go pull some traps set in the overflow of the beaver dams to the west.

Despite the sheepkin coat, fur chaps and moosehide mittens with woollen ones inside, I came near to freezing solid as I went from dam to dam. It was only twenty-three below when I pulled away from the house, but the drive of the wind and snow chilled the marrow in my bones. I bucked the storm for eight cruel hours, pulled my traps and was rewarded with a couple of mink and an otter. In all that bitter travel I never cut the track of a single animal, never set eyes upon a bird. It was like riding through a kingdom of the dead.

Only a few inches of the wire fence were in sight when the snow ceased falling. The overcast broke and by night a swollen bitter moon bathed the forest in frigid light. The air became deathly still, not a single branch moving beneath its weight of snow, and a silent, searing cold stalked remorselessly across the wilderness. Water buckets in the kitchen froze overnight, and cans of milk and jars of fruit were frozen up too. The sting of the cold made me retch and cough as I went about the outside chores. Frost covered the horses when I opened the barn door in the morning, and at any moment of the night we could hear the monotonous crunch of snow outside as moose moved to and fro, trying to keep warm by the simple process of forever keeping moving. Our thermometer ceases registering at fifty below. For six mornings in a row the mercury was cuddled despondently at the bottom of the glass, unable to go any lower. Was it sixty below or sixty-five? That's a question I'll never be able to answer, but there were moments when I'd have sworn it was eighty.

January was almost spent when the chinook finally came. A warm wind spewed in from the Pacific, driving back the mass of polar air that had crucified the wilderness for so long. For thirty hours the mild air pushed in from the ocean, licking at the snow, moistening it, yet barely lessening its depth. Then, as suddenly as it had arisen, the wind died, stars pricked the heavens, and the snow started to freeze.

"The snow will hold a twenty-five-pound coyote by morning," I uneasily remarked to Lillian. "And by the following morning, a full-grown wolf." I might have added that it would give beneath the hoofs of a moose or deer, but that would have been superfluous; Lillian knew all about that.

That evening, when filling the water buckets at the water hole in the ice, I suddenly tensed, listening. What I heard welled up faintly from out of the east, mournful and eerie. It wasn't exactly an oath and it wasn't exactly a prayer; it was just the dismal, spine-chilling anthem of a timber wolf hunkered back on its haunches, howling at the moon. And I shook my head; death was again unleashed upon the land.

Was it *our* wolf? That I couldn't say, but I had every intention of soon finding out. The cry came from downcreek, in the neighbourhood of our trapping cabin, I judged. By the time the water buckets were filled, I knew just what we had to do and returned to the cabin and conveyed my thoughts to Lillian and Veasy.

"Timber wolf on the loose somewhere around the cabin downcreek," I said. "Reckon we'll pack up and move down there for a few days of look-see."

At the slight lift of Lillian's eyebrows, I went on, "There'll be blood on the crust come morning, maybe deer, maybe moose, but one or the other for sure. Maybe—" I shrugged and shifted course. "Might just as well be down there as up here."

"Just when are we going to move down?" Lillian asked with a frown.

"Day after tomorrow. I'll bust a track through in the morning." I knew the sheer impossibility of ever getting through to the cabin with a loaded sleigh unless I first broke out a track with the loose horses.

"That's not giving me much time to get things ready," she complained.

No, it wasn't. "If we don't get down there right away," I explained, "the son-of-a-gun might be clear out of the country when we do." For time, tide and timber wolves wait for no man.

"I'll have to bake bread, make up some pies and do a lot of other cooking," groused Lillian. "Drat the timber wolves anyway. Why don't they behave themselves?"

"They *are* behaving themselves," Veasy slipped in. "They're doing what comes naturally."

Veasy was a realist. At fourteen years of age he could run a line of traps as competently as men with a lifetime of experience at the job. Seldom did a buck deer get away from him once he latched onto its tracks. Of course, Veasy had a little Indian blood in his veins and sometimes that blood asserted itself. He could find his way out of the deep woods in the middle of the night if need be, and without trail or star to steer him. To Veasy, trapping was a means of making money, hunting a means of getting meat. Both were just a part of the daily chores, like packing water or splitting wood. Another job to be done, and the sooner done the better.

His mind was miles ahead of his years. At an age when other children were still reading comics, Veasy was reading Karl Marx (though not agreeing with all that he read). And instead of giving his mind to whodunits, he gave it to Lewis' s *Theory of Economic Growth*.

By the time he was fifteen Veasy had killed three timber wolves and collected a forty-dollar government bounty on their scalps. A coyote that came within the sights of his gun was dead when he touched off the trigger. But he got no enjoyment out of killing either. At a very early age, the granite realism of his wilderness upbringing taught him that every muskrat killed by an owl, or beaver by a coyote, was a financial loss to us. Yet he knew that all predators were born to fulfill a purpose, and that when taking the life of another creature they were merely "doing what comes naturally."

The trapline cabin was only four or five miles away. The road we had cut to it followed the downward course of the creek, and when the ice of the beaver ponds was safe we travelled it where possible.

Five miles! I could snowshoe there in an hour and a half given the right kind of snow, yet it was to take me all of three days to get there with a loaded sleigh. I struck out at sunup in the morning, riding my saddle horse and driving the harnessed team ahead of me. They weren't hitched to anything, just breaking out the track. The front legs of the horses were bandaged in canvas wraps, much as the traps were bandaged when we live-trapped the beavers. If they hadn't been, the crust would have slashed their skin and drawn blood within a half-mile of leaving the house.

Travel was woefully slow, for the full depth of the snow hit the horses at the point of their shoulders. Coyote tracks criss-crossed the road every few yards, and about a mile out from home I cut the track of a single deer. On the windward side of the deep furrow he'd left behind in the snow were the claw marks of three or four loping coyotes. I thought, "They'll haul up to the critter before it's gone a mile." By now there'd be a crimson splash or two on the snow here, a few scraps of hide there, and maybe a thin scattering of offal. But no more. The deer had no chance at all.

It took four hours to get through to the cabin, and the horses were gray with frosted sweat when I hitched them to a cottonwood tree close to the building. The wrappings on their legs were slashed to ribbons, but that didn't matter now that the track was broken out.

I took a half-dozen pack rats out of the traps that had been left set for them, and cursed those that hadn't been caught but had left their droppings all over the table. I started a fire in the sheet-iron cookstove and fried a half-dozen rashers of bacon. The bacon was hanging on a wire from the ridge logs where pack rats couldn't get at it. The cold had given me an appetite, and after mopping up the grease with soda biscuits, the world seemed a whole lot brighter, and I was ready for the trip back.

Before I could haul a load down, though—hay and oats for the horses, bedding and provisions for ourselves—I first had to plow out the track with the front runners of the sleigh. This took most all of a second day, so it was close to light-the-lamp time on the third day when we reined a tired team alongside the cabin door and began tossing out gear.

Late the previous October I'd killed a bull moose about a mile and a half from the cabin. After quartering the bull out and loading the meat on pack horses, I'd liberally sprinkled poison bait around the innards and other offal in certain expectation that either a wolf or a coyote would happen along for a meal. And that is what had lured me to the cabin now: the slender chance that perhaps acute hunger had brought Wolf to the leftovers, and that when pawing in the snow he'd make a mistake and swallow one of the baits.

The weather sided with me that night. Half an inch of powdery snow fell that would allow me to follow clear-cut sign on the crust. I knew I could make far better tracking time on snowshoes than on horseback, so I softened up the snowshoe harness with coyote grease, pocketed the venison sandwiches Lillian had packaged for me and struck off through the woods, rifle cradled in my arm, hope warming my heart. The crust under my webs was as solid as set cement, and I clipped along at a good three miles an hour.

I braked up a little as I neared the site of the kill, for now I was cutting coyote tracks, lots of them. There was little left of the guts. Coyotes had dug down in the snow and got most of them. I didn't take time out to circle for dead coyotes. About a hundred yards from the old kill was a bare knoll with a single massive fir tree growing square on the top. I knew that wolves have a penchant for lying in such spots, where they can see all that is going on around them. So I moved over to the knoll.

I was almost on top of it when I stopped the soft swish of my snowshoes. I was looking down on a track that had not been made by any coyote.

"Wolf!" I said slowly. For by now I knew his track when I saw it as well as I knew that of my own saddle horse. I was looking at the pad marks of the wolf that had been cheating me out of my beavers, the wolf that had killed countless scores of moose and deer, that had robbed our traps of their catch whenever he came across them. He'd bellied at the foot of the tree long enough for the heat of his body to melt the crusted snow. He knew exactly where the moose guts were, but he hadn't come closer than a hundred yards of them. Oh, he was crafty, ever suspicious of any meat he hadn't just killed himself.

I circled the knoll and picked up his tracks leading away to the north. He travelled the length of a pothole meadow, wove through a stand of spruce as thick as the fur on a lynx. He climbed a drear, timberless hogback, dropped down the other side and suddenly swung sharp east into scattered pine timber. Here he stopped abruptly and crouched down in the snow.

Fifty yards ahead of me a single deer had furrowed through the snow. Thin lines of blood on either side of its trail were visible from where I stood. "The crust," I told myself. "It's slicing the deer's legs."

Wolf had trotted up to the deer's trail and nosed the blood. Then he broke into a lope, keeping on the windward side of the sign. The one-sided contest had commenced.

Beneath a huge pine I was able to read the deer's tracks clearly. They had been made by either a very large buck or an equally large doe. Wolf's tracks lengthened, and a half-mile farther on I came to where the deer was jumped. Wolf's stride let out a little. The deer bounded off through the crust in lunges twenty feet apart. Wolf's stride let out still more. The deer tracks began to weave crazily; here and there the doomed animal had staggered. Now Wolf was loping with every ounce of speed he could summon.

He caught up to the deer as it broke out of the timber and started across a clearing. There it piled up in a ten-foot snowdrift. It may have died from fright and exertion even before Wolf's teeth ripped through its liver. Anyway, I hoped so.

Wolf had eaten the heart and the liver, strewn guts over the snow and chewed off most of one hindquarter. That was all he ate, so by that I knew that this wasn't his only kill since the snow crusted. A really hungry timber wolf will eat a deer at a meal.

I judged that the deer had been killed around daybreak, so Wolf had at least a four-hour start on me and might now be a dozen or more miles away. But the whole afternoon was ahead of me, so I ate my sandwiches, sucked at a mouthful of snow and inspected my snowshoe webbing. Then I slipped forward on the tracks.

Wolf had bedded down under a tree for maybe an hour, then struck east again at a steady trot.

"He'll come out at the Big Lakes if he holds in that direction," I calculated aloud. The Big Lakes, six miles long, marked the eastern boundary of our trapline.

As I neared the lakes I saw considerable moose sign. The lakeshore was heavily fringed with willow, and here the moose were yarded up. Though some of the tracks were quite fresh, Wolf paid them no attention as he moved steadily eastward.

Almost within sight of the ice I came out on a narrow avenue that I had cut through the thick spruce as a trail for saddle horses and pack animals when scattering traps out along the lakeshore. Coyotes, foxes and an occasional wolf travelled this easy path through the spruce, so I had a few snares set out on it now that had been there since late fall. They were beneath the heavy overhang of leaning trees, where a deep fall of snow wouldn't put them out of action.

Wolf's tracks shortened as he came in sight of the snow-covered ice. I noted where he had bellied down in the snow a moment before getting up and moving on. At the edge of the ice he stopped again and I wondered, "What's on his mind now?" Then, as my eyes swept the ice, I exploded, "You damned murderer!"

Tufts of dark hair were scattered over the ice ahead, and the snow was spangled with blood, as if a half-dozen moose and as many wolves had battled there at the same time. But at closer range I saw that a single calf moose and the one wolf had made all the sign.

Wolf had played with and tortured the calf as a cat plays with a mouse. On a full stomach, too. I wouldn't have begrudged Wolf even that calf if his belly was truly empty. But he had already gorged himself at the carcass of the deer.

The tufts of hair and blood in the snow told their own sordid tale of what had happened next. The calf moose was about to cross the ice when Wolf darted out between it and the shore. The killer drove the calf still farther out on the ice, then headed it off as a cow pony heads a steer. And every now and then, whenever the fancy struck him, Wolf closed in on the calf's flanks, leaping up at it with slashing fangs that drew blood with every leap. Wolf could have finished the job quickly there on the ice, but he preferred to prolong the calf's agony and his own sport.

Following the tracks on the lake I saw where Wolf had bellied down in the snow and allowed the calf to lurch ashore. I studied the belly mark in the snow a moment. I could picture Wolf lying there, an unholy grin on his face. And I thought, "You know the calf can't get far. You'll let him get into the timber, then you'll haul up on him and enjoy another round of blood-letting."

I followed the calf's tracks into the timber. There Wolf's sign cut in again, in long lopes. Up through dense willow and thinning poplar the tracks took me, and spruce loomed ahead. I could see the blazed trees that denoted my trapping trail, along which snares were set.

I moved onto the trail, glanced along it and suddenly rooted down in my tracks. My eyes bulged, and my heart beat slightly faster. "The snare!" The cry that leaped from my lips was one of surprise, and pent-up excitement. "Ye gods, he hit the snare." Then the huge gray body dangling at the end of the snare seemed to move. "He's alive!" I muttered aloud. And quickly I bolted a cartridge into my rifle and snapped the gun into my shoulder. Then slowly and foolishly lowered it. "He's dead as salt salmon," I told myself. It was the gentle movement of the tree to which the spring pole was fastened that swung his body to and fro as if indeed there were life in him yet.

Then I saw the calf, down in the snow thirty feet beyond the snare. I forgot for the moment about Wolf and slid past his dangling body to look at the mangled calf. It would never come to its feet again, even though a beat or two of life was yet left in it. So I put the muzzle of the gun behind its ears and gently squeezed the trigger. It was better thus.

Again I turned to Wolf. I judged his weight at one hundred and ten pounds. Certainly he was the largest dead wolf I'd ever seen. I squatted slowly back on my snowshoes, grappling with the question of how and why he had blundered. In cold blood Wolf would never have thrust his

Eric poses with the hide of a wolf that had ranged their trapline for four years; when it killed an old mother beaver for what appeared to be sport, Eric became determined to hunt him down.

head into that snare, camouflaged though it might be. Wolf had smelled the steel of too many snares for that. Perhaps it was the old, old story of a pitcher going to the well just once too often. Momentarily blinded to all else but his desire to haul up to the calf, Wolf had thrust his head into the snare without having time to scent its whereabouts. His first frantic lunge had released the trigger that held the tip of the twenty-five-foot pole to which the snare was fastened. As the pole raised, Wolf was lifted into the air, and though he struggled to escape the clutch of the thing that was choking away his life, the snare, like Wolf himself, knew nothing at all of pity. All that it caught it killed.

Thus Wolf died. A murderer all his life, he died a murderer's death. With wind sobbing mournfully through the treetops, and moon's first crescent staring sardonically down, seeing much, saying nothing.

Chapter 22

Half a roasted mallard resting easily inside me, a quarter of blueberry pie there to keep it company. Old sun about ready to quit for the day, old moon, fat as a fall turnip, awaiting his cue to hoist up above the treetops in another part of the world altogether. This was the hour I liked best.

A flock of noisy bluebills scolding one another in the cattails, doe and fawn deer standing belly deep in the water just across the pond from me, quenching an evening thirst.

The evening patrol coming away from the lodge, floating down the pond to make professional scrutiny of the dam. I thought, "There must be a dozen beavers in that colony this year if there's one."

Another day's toil behind me, and something accomplished, something done. Maybe another cord of wood sawed, split and piled in readiness for the winter ahead. Or the head of an old beaver run located at the other end of Meldrum Lake, now occupied by a pair of otters. Likely as not they'd be visiting that run when the lake was again shut by ice, and most any man of the woods knows how to chop a hole through the ice at the underwater entrance to an otter hideaway, drive a couple of poles down into the mud and set a trap. A well-primed otter pelt was worth twenty-five dollars.

Or maybe a half-dozen horned owls thrown out of the traps, for the owls had to be kept in check too; they preyed upon the muskrats. Or accounts finally settled with an old dog coyote who'd killed many a beaver in his time but would never kill another. Trivial chores these, but chores just the same. But they added to something accomplished, something done, and that's what counts in any man's life.

Eventide. Half the wilderness about ready to put on its nightcap, the other half just taking it off. The wilderness is never altogether asleep. It labours all day and it labours all night; the wilderness is never altogether still.

The young ones came out to play early this evening. Usually the mother tells them better stay in the house until night shuts down proper, and peering predacious eyes can't see, but tonight they slipped away from the lodge a few minutes after sunset, and all four of them trailed one another to the rock.

Maybe they think they're fooling their mother tonight, that they slipped away from the lodge without her being any the wiser. If so, they are only fooling themselves. She's there, lying still as a water-logged stick in the middle of the pond, and she knows right where the little ones are too. Can't fool an old mother beaver when it comes to watching out for the youngsters.

Let me see now: it'll be five years come next September since they first came back to the irrigation dam and Meldrum Creek. Maybe the old female beaver out there now is one of the original pairs, but it can't be proved by me. Some trappers say that an old sow beaver will live for twenty years or more if they keep clear of traps and predators, though how they figure that I don't rightly know. Our first two pairs of beavers took to the waters of Meldrum Creek in 1941. Nine years in all were to pass before we set our first trap and caught our first beaver. By that time not only was the creek itself stocked to carrying capacity with beavers, but many of the landlocked lakes about it too. Other creeks, other lakes, miles from our trapline had their beavers back too. As the throwing of a pebble on water spreads ever widening ripples, so, by 1950, did the beavers spread over much of the Chilcotin.

There's hardly room on the rock for more than one of the kits at a time, and each seems to think that he's the chosen one. They're ten weeks old now, thrice the weight of a muskrat, and when their tails pound the water you'd swear it was only the splash of some mighty trout rising to a fly. They learned that trick from watching and hearing the older beavers splash their tails on the water, and it's one they'll never forget.

Now one has all of the rock to itself and for fifteen or twenty seconds manages to hold his own against the combined efforts of the other three to crawl up and push it head over heels into the water. But they know a thing or two about make-believe warfare, do the young ones. While two of them wage a frontal attack, the third steals in from behind, sneaks stealthily up the rock and, with one sudden rush, tosses the tough guy off the rock and back into the water.

It all reminds me of a game I used to play as a boy long years ago in England, when all I knew of the Canadian wilderness came to me by way of James Oliver Curwood or Fenimore Cooper. To a boy crowding nine or ten, make-believe is often far more real than life. A field of ripening wheat is an endless and mysterious forest, a brook some mighty river that somehow has to be forded. And if you close your eyes long enough and squeeze them real shut, those little mounds of earth aren't mole hills at all: they're beaver lodges heaving up from the water of some lonely mountain lake.

One of the boys would hoist up on a stone wall that in his mind quickly became a castle's rampart and run along the top of it, thumbing his nose at his playmates trying to catch up to him and wrestle him back to earth. Man child or beaver child, make-believe is for both.

∶∿

Five years have brought changes around our wilderness home. They have brought changes to the bit of a hill that slopes away from the water behind where I sit. Five years ago cottonwood trees grew so high and thick on the slope of the hill, one couldn't see the sun when it was nooning, at least not when the trees were in leaf. And almost all of them were mature trees, ten inches through at the butt.

The good earth on which they stood produced little vegetation but a cover of sour timber grass that nothing seemed to eat. The thirst of the cottonwoods themselves took all nourishment and water from the soil, leaving none for anything else that might have a mind to use it. And how can the richest soil produce edible crops if the sun is denied a peek at it when young life wants to grow? The sun and the wind and the rain, and the heavy winter snows—it takes a combination of all for earth to produce its finest.

Now not a mature cottonwood is still standing within thirty yards of water's edge. The beavers mowed them down as the binder mows a wheat field. At first it didn't make much sense to us, since the trees were mostly left windrowed one on top of the other with little or none of their bark or limbs being eaten. Waste, that's how it looked to us when the beavers first massacred those cottonwoods.

But five years brings understanding too. It wasn't waste at all, it was part of a grand design. With the cottonwoods down, the sun was now able to take a long look at the soil, putting some sweetness into it. Juicy pea vines pushed up through the sod where before there was only the sour timber grass. Blackberry bushes sprang to sudden life too, and black bear and ruffed grouse came to eat their fruit. Deer moved down from the conifer forests to browse the purple-flowered vetches, and when the pea vines podded out, Canada geese and ducks waddled out of the water to feast on the laden pods.

None of this could take root so long as the cottonwoods stood there, draining all that the soil could offer. But the beavers felled them, and since the soil was rich to begin with, soon a half-dozen species of tender deciduous shrubs were sprouting where before there had been but a single cottonwood.

Now these many shrubs were shoulder high to a saddle horse, providing capital winter feed for the moose when they trailed down from the higher country. In summer their leaves provided both breeding place and food for insects, which in turn fed many a half-fledged bluebird and other feathered youngsters. Thus had the activities of one form of wildlife—the beaver—provided both habitat and food for a great many others. Perhaps before Columbus was born the watersheds of the North American continent were once so richly endowed with wildlife that the lands adjacent to them had to be continually farmed if all were to be assured an adequate food supply. And perhaps the beaver was the agent Nature employed to go about such farming. His dams held and conserved the water upon thousands of major and minor watersheds, subirrigating the soils around them and keeping them cool and moist during the hottest days of summer. Nothing was wasted that might contribute to the welfare of life moving through the forest or swimming in the water. No rich topsoil was borne away to an ocean, but was instead deposited upon the floor of lake or stream to nourish and fertilize the beds of aquatic plants that were food for the fish and the waterfowl. No deciduous tree at water's edge was allowed to thrust its upper limbs up so high that members of a deer family beneath were unable to stretch their necks and reach them. All water that could possibly be conserved behind dams was conserved, for wet cycles are followed by dry cycles, and enough water had to be conserved in the kind years to last through the lean. Ever were the watersheds and forests able to support the wildlife they harboured, and such calamities as erosion of soil and dry, stinking creek channel were never felt at all. Then onto this tranquil scene walked Man.

∻

I can no longer see the old mother floating in the middle of the pond, for over there all is shadow. She's there somewhere, though, nose diagnosing the air for the possible presence of a predator. So long as the little kits are at play, mother is close by watching.

Somehow or other, three of the youngsters have managed to hoist up on the rock at one time, and fists are flying, arms tugging, and there's many a hostile grunt as the free-for-all gets underway. Then all three gladiators tumble head over heels into the water and the fourth, who has been patiently biding his time, climbs up on the rock and sits there proudly—the victor.

Five years have brought changes to the pond too. Much of the water is hidden by the broad leaf of the water lily beds, now in yellow blossom. Five years ago there was an isolated stalk here and there, but no really profuse beds as there are now. The floor of the pond is kept in a state of continual cultivation by the activities of the beavers. Tons of mud have been dredged up from the bottom to seal the long dam tight, and in fall the lodges too are plastered by a thick coating of mud to seal them off from the nip of the sub-zero temperature shortly to come. This continual scuffing of the subsoil of the pond results in a well-farmed bed for any aquatic seed deposited there.

Not only do the beavers plow, disc and harrow, but they also plant too. The pod of a single water lily plant holds within its rind a goodly number of seeds, but how can they be broadcast in other waters if there is no one there to carry them? In late summer, when the seeds are fully ripe, the beavers float slowly from plant to plant, eating a pod here, another one there, until their bellies want no more. Several hours later the seeds are again given back to the water, but at a spot perhaps a mile or more from where they were consumed. If the soft rind of the pod has been digested, the seeds remain to be cast away with the droppings of the beavers. Embedded in the manure, they sink to the bottom and lie there dormant through the winter, to thrust out tiny networks of roots in the spring. Thus is a bed of water lilies established where not long ago there wasn't a single plant.

~

Spank! Mother floats idly on the pond, scouting for lurking danger. Spank! Now her tail has sounded the tocsin, and so mighty is the splash it can be heard far off in the conifer forest. The little kits slip silently off the rock and scurry off through the water. They'll not be back tonight. But still I sit there, wondering what was bothering the mother that she had to break up the game and call the kits back to the lodge. I haven't long to wonder. There's a quick cleavage of water up-pond slightly from where I sit. No beaver or muskrat is responsible for those wide, swift ripples, of that I am sure. Someone is coming who can glide silently along through the water at twice the speed of any kit beaver. Beneath it too, for that matter.

A dark, velvety, snakelike head comes in sight, and I see the thin line of rich brown fur where an inch or two of the back protrudes above water level. Then I see the thick, tapered bullwhip of a tail, and it tells me who the intruder is. He's an otter, an old dog otter, one who could break the back of any kit beaver with a single snap of his jaws.

But he'll not dine on beaver meat tonight. The long arm of experience has taught him that if he tackles any mature beaver, all he'll get for his troubles is a slashed and bleeding hide. And now the little ones are safe in the lodge, mother guarding its entrance, for even as the otter was nearing the rock, her sensitive nose detected his presence. The splash of her tail on the water warned the kits of the danger, and they were quick to heed its warning and get back to the safety of the lodge.

On my way back to the cabin, carefully picking my way through the litter of fallen cottonwoods, I stopped at one such tree with a stump girth of almost two feet. Though the beavers had gnawed off a little of its bark and pruned a few of its limbs, most of the tree was intact. I squatted down on its trunk, wondering, "How many years will it lie here before time and the elements completely destroy it?" Then, answering my own question, "Forty or fifty, maybe." But eventually every shred of bark, every grain of wood, would be gone from the eyes of man, the cotton-wood again an organic compost of the soil whence it had first sprung to life. And that's how it was all around the pond, and in the conifer forests too—a blowdown here, a beaver-felled tree there, slowly rotting away, until eventually nothing would be seen of them. Yet maybe the trees still lived. They lived on in the form of the humus that their own rotting flesh had created. And soon, and from out of that selfsame humus, a tiny shoot would peep upward, and another tree be born. Unless man himself signs the death warrant, the wilderness never altogether dies.

Chapter 23

In winter, weather was the master, we its slave. If weather said, "No, you're not running any traplines today, you're staying put in the cabin," we didn't run any traps, and stayed put in the cabin. And read a book, or combed and brushed the mink pelts, or made another dozen muskrat stretchers, or, for plain want of exercise, went outside to take a reading on the thermometer that had said fifty-two below at sunup but now said forty-five below. That was just five degrees too cold. At forty below we could tell one another, "Yes, weather says we can run the traps today providing we don't squat down on a windfall and rest for more than a minute at a time," but from forty downstairs we knew that weather intended that we stay put in the cabin and see what the book said, or shine up the mink pelts, or whittle away at a bit of board and make another muskrat stretcher.

From the fall of 1937 on, we could, when weather said stay home, move a couple of knobs and at the twitch of a squawfish's fins be in San Francisco, or Seattle, or some place in New Mexico that we'd never before heard of. Or if we wanted to get away from Meldrum Lake but still be in Canada, we could move a knob an inch to right or left and land on our feet on the prairies, maybe at Regina, Saskatchewan, or Calgary, Alberta, or some other place boasting those mysterious somethings called transmitters.

The radio, an RCA Victor, cost us four mink and a coyote pelt. By the fall of 1947 we'd been a part of the wilderness for so long, trapping for almost all that we possessed, that instead of saying, "That's going to cost us forty-one dollars and fifty cents," we said, "That'll be four coyotes and a weasel." And the coyotes and weasel were ever there in the woods, sometimes within a hoot and a shout of the cabin.

But when weather got really mad, and slapped us back whenever we ventured outdoors, we rubbed the magic lamp, turned on the radio, and music from a thousand miles away soothed our troubles away. And of course just before Christmas, it came right into our cabin and sang for us "O Holy Night." A radio may seem an awfully common and ordinary thing to a city family, but to us it was often our only tie for months on end with the outside world.

We seldom tried to buck weather, to quarrel with it, for we knew that we'd always come out on the losing end of the stick if we did. Instead, we tried to get along with it, to understand it, and if possible figure out its shifting moods in advance.

Though November's moon had been a kind moon, with little snow on the game trails, we knew that December's would probably usher in a condition that all trappers dread but that so far none have been able to do much about: day after day of intermittent snow driving in against the windows of the cabin, and when once again the stars and the moon came on in the heavens, a bitter cold snap to hold the wilderness in its grip.

Now, few fur-bearers move above ground, all having sense enough to stay down in the bowels of the earth, where even if empty of belly they are at least shut off from the foul sting of the weather above. And at a temperature of forty or more below, we stayed in the bowels of our den, but if the mercury hovered around thirty-five below we were out tending our traps, Lillian taking care of her line, Veasy his, and I mine.

For the surge of arctic air now worrying at the land could not last forever. Eventually the polar air must retreat, and some measure of warmth return again to the wilderness. When this came to pass the fur-bearers would again move freely above ground, seeking food for their ravenous bellies. But to take full advantage of opportunity while it was there, our traps must be in proper working order and baited with fresh scent before the movement got underway.

Weather was the deciding factor. We have long since reconciled ourselves to the near certainty that December's moon will bring ever deepening snows, January's the prolonged cold snaps that usually follow them. We might forecast with some degree of accuracy that February's lengthening days are likely to be punctuated with slightly more warmth than cold, a warmth that sometimes puts such an iron crust on the snow that the hoofs of cow or bull moose will not puncture it as the big deer wander in search of browse.

But of March we are not so sure. March is the erratic month of the winter, cunning and deceptive, kind and cruel. Sunshine today, storm tomorrow. Warm south wind at the dawning, snow-laden northwester come nightfall. Twenty above zero when we go to bed, twenty below when we awake the following morning. You can never tell about March.

Of all the months of the year, March is the one I dread most. For March is the time of the muskrat harvest, when the leather in the pelts is heavier than at any other time of the year, the fur at its finest sheen.

Now, no matter what be the moods of the weather, Veasy and I must be out on the windswept ice, placing our traps in the houses, fumbling with fingers that have lost almost all feel of everything among the floating mass of aquatic weed forming the floor of the feed bed. Through the years I had my moments of adversity running the traps in December, January and February, but to March belongs the day whose events will be fixed crystal clear in my mind perhaps to the end of my time. Though spring and the cry of a wild goose were just around the corner, it's the day I'll never forget.

It was tolerably warm when Veasy and I set out the traps. We left the house at daybreak on horseback, snowshoes resting across the pommel of the saddle, pack horse trailing behind with its load of a hundred-odd traps. The lake we intended to trap lay six miles to the east, with never a shank of trail between it and home. When crossing open meadow the snow was chest deep on the horses, and travel was frustratingly slow.

I knew that the lake would still be covered by close to two feet of snow, with possible flood water beneath it and the old ice. That's where the snowshoes proved their worth. Ice is treacherous stuff when hidden by a mass of snow, and if in places it might support the keel of a battleship, in others, where hidden air holes force water into the snow, it might give under the weight of a man unless he moves delicately from rat house to rat house on skis or snowshoes.

It was crowding 9:30 when we broke away from the jack pine timber and came in view of the lake. I tied my horse to a tree and began kneading some softness into the leather of my snowshoe harness. I then took the traps from the pack saddle and began laying them out in piles of a dozen each. Then, stepping onto my shoes, I stared out across the lake.

Though the fringe of bulrushes around its edge was now pretty much hidden by snow, it didn't matter. The black tips of our markers were still visible to lead us to where each muskrat house was. Without those markers we wouldn't be able to locate one house in four. They had been stuck into the roofs of the houses in early November last, when sufficient ice had formed to support our weight on foot. They were slim wands of willow, axed along the shoreline, and now only their tips protruded above snow level. But anyway enough there to tell us where our shovels would lay bare the muskrat house beneath.

I took three dozen traps and slung them in a gunny sack over my right shoulder. Veasy hoisted another three dozen across his back, pushed back his parka and commented, "Think we can get seventy-two set by noon?"

"Can try," I replied. "You start setting at the south end of the lake and I'll begin at the north." And as he shuffled off I sang out after him, "Bank the houses good with snow after you set because—" But then he was out of earshot, and probably hadn't heard me anyway. So I shrugged my shoulders indifferently. He'd been setting muskrat traps since he was thirteen, so why should I bother to tell him about the banking? Veasy hated your telling him anything that he already knew anyway. "Waste of good breath," he'd grumble.

231

Banking the houses with snow was a prime essential of the trapping, for of March we knew so little. Though maybe fifteen above zero at the moment—it might possibly have been twenty—a very slight shift in the wind at nightfall might plummet the mercury to twenty-five below by morning. But if each muskrat house was heavily insulated with snow after being opened up for the trap, even should the mercury skid to thirty below, the water on the feed bed would remain free of ice and the trap in proper working order.

By four in the afternoon one hundred and ten muskrat houses had been opened up, a trap set on their feed beds, then closed and banked with snow. Beating the snow from the webbing of my snowshoes, I hoisted them into a tree. I retightened the cinch of my saddle, tossed an unuttered query to Veasy, and at a nod of his head we swung up into the saddles and began the homeward journey.

Night was shutting down when we got back to the house. After stabling the horses I took a peek at the thermometer. It had dropped eleven degrees since morning. The wind too had veered from east to north. "Below zero for sure by morning," I muttered to myself, kicking the snow from my overshoes so that Lillian wouldn't scold me for leaving puddles of water on her linoleum.

Eric sets a trap in a muskrat push-up. (Push-ups are "mini-lodges" that the muskrats build beyond their main lodge. They serve as resting places or feeding stations.)

But that thought didn't worry me too much. If the morrow dawned clear and bright with promise of sunshine through the day, we could open up the houses, take the overnight catch from the traps and reset, at a temperature of anything down to ten below, providing, that is, that there was no north wind. From ten below down, we'd squat tight in the house and let the traps sit too, secure in the knowledge that all would remain in proper working order.

The mercury was at eighteen below when I looked in the morning. I met the question in Veasy's eyes with a shake of the head, telling him, "Better let them sit today. If it isn't any warmer tomorrow we'll go down and pull the traps, and not reset until it does warm up."

After breakfast Veasy suddenly suggested, "How about me going out for the mail today and meeting you at the lake tomorrow morning?"

"That," I conceded, "is a mighty bright thought." For we had neither received nor posted any mail these three weeks gone.

Since January Veasy had been covering the twenty-five miles between us and the post office on skis. That thin line of ski tracks was our only path to the outer world, and the only path we were likely to have until perhaps along in mid-April when the spring runoff commenced. For January's snows had been prolonged and deep snows, and by the end of the month we abandoned all hope of being able to keep a sleigh road open.

Those narrow twin indentations in the snow passed within a mile of where our muskrat trapping operations were now underway. Veasy could ski out to the post office today, stay there overnight and meet me at the lake in the morning.

"You'll be there for sure with the horses in the morning then?" he asked.

"Come hell or high water," I assured him. Which at this season of the year meant no matter how cold it might be.

I both sensed and heard the polar wind that was born in the black of the night. I came over on one elbow in bed, listening to its growl through the treetops. I could feel its chill seeping in through the logs,

233

and I crawled out of bed, put more wood in the heater and then walked to the window and peered outside. Snow beat in against the glass with a dry rustling sound. I moved over to the door and inched it open a little. As if waiting for just such an opportunity, the wind flowed in through the crack, dusting the kitchen floor with a fine film of snow. I coughed as the cold hit my lungs, then banged the door shut.

Lillian too was half awake now. "He'll not start back in weather like that," she said sleepily.

"Remember what I told him when he struck out? Come hell or high water I'll be there. And come hell or high water he'll be there too." And in an endeavour to perhaps comfort her in a situation where little comfort was in sight, I added, "Maybe blow itself out by morning."

With break of day the wind cleaved sheer from the jaws of the north. Its nip shrivelled my flesh as I headed for the barn. The smooth, well-packed trail of yesterday was now blanked out by the swirling, drifting snow. I wallowed through the drifts, losing all feel of the trail a dozen times before reaching the barn. I watered and fed the horses, stared sourly at the saddles hanging on their pegs and then slung them onto the horses.

Nothing but sheer force of habit made me check with the thermometer after breakfast; no matter what the thermometer said, I had to go.

"How cold now?" Lillian wanted to know when I stepped back into the kitchen.

"Only twenty below," I managed to grin back at her. And twenty below zero with a wind from the north is colder than forty below with no wind at all.

"You can't handle muskrat traps in weather like that," she said. "No, not if each pelt was worth twenty-five dollars." Actually, the skins would bring us about a dollar and a half apiece. Recently the price of muskrat pelts had been improving.

Again I reminded her: "Come hell or high water I'll be there." And come hell or high water Veasy would be there too. A rendezvous made in the wilderness is a rendezvous that has to be kept.

I wrapped the lunches Lillian had made up for us in three layers of canvas and tied them behind my saddle. But despite the wrapping, I knew the bread and the meat would be frozen solid before I got a mile away from the house. Then, hitching the pack horse to the tail of the animal I was leading down for Veasy, I climbed reluctantly up into the saddle and struck out into the snow.

The cold hauled up to and clawed me before I was a half-mile down the trail. It seeped through my moosehide mittens, pawed at the woollen ones inside them. The wind licked at my overshoes, somehow found entrance and pried at the felts within. Even my heavy sheepskin coat failed to weaken, still less halt, the probe of that wind. My eyelashes became icicles, and a sudden stab at my left cheek warned me I'd best pull my mitts for a quick moment and tie the hood of my parka tighter around my chin.

I came to a long sliver of open meadow, its stunted Arctic willow just showing above snow line. The dark outlines of a cow and calf moose took on shape a few feet from the brush. I was almost on top of them before they lifted from their beds in the snow. The cow trotted some thirty yards, then stood broadside, eyes flaring ill temper. I could have hit the calf with a stone as I rode by it, so close was the little fellow to the horses.

I hunched over in the saddle, turning my face from the wind. "Right this very moment," I gloomily addressed the two moose, "we three are the coldest warm-blooded creatures in all of Canada." And the moose hadn't budged an inch when I rode out of their sight at the other end of the meadow.

Then I came out at the lake. I could see little of it for the clouds of drifting snow that careened across the ice. "It will be hell out there on that ice," I mumbled, hitching the horses to trees. "And if we have to pull our mitts and go down after any rats—" The possibility of that only added to my gloom. For the rubber gloves we usually wear when rat trapping would be as useless as silk gauntlets today. Somehow or other there's a little warmth to woollen mitts, even if they are soaking wet. At least they break the wind. But there's none whatsoever to a thick skin of rubber.

I peered hopefully at the south end of the lake, to where Veasy should come in. If he was now down there, moving from rat house to rat house, I'd see him despite the drifting snow between us. For all of a minute I stood very still, straining my eyes to the south. But Veasy wasn't there. I had all of that ice to myself, and it was the loneliest place on earth.

My snowshoes sank almost to the bottom of the twelve or so inches of new snowfall. Each time I lifted them up the end of my shovel handle played a tattoo on their frame, ridding them of their load of snow. Tap-tap-tap, like a blind man walking the pavement. And so I began the cruel task of pulling up the traps.

∿

In the large-scale cropping of muskrats, there's slightly more to the matter than just setting traps. Every house must be staked in fall before heavy snows blot them from sight. Each trap set must somehow be marked when trapping operations begin. If they are not, and if between seventy-five and a hundred traps are set out on a single piece of marsh, in the event of an overnight fall of snow several of the traps are not likely to be found again.

When muskrat trapping, Veasy and I use a system of cards, numbered from 1 to 100 depending upon the number of traps set out. A foot or fifteen inches is broken from the top of the marker stakes, the remainder used as a toggle to slip through the trap ring. A card is then affixed to the broken piece of stake and placed upright in the snow alongside the house in which the trap is set. So if the last trap looked at was number 4, and we then move on to number 6, we instantly know that the fifth trap has been missed and retrace our steps to find it. Without using such a system, one would of course never know that he had missed a trap until all had been gathered and counted.

We've trapped several thousand muskrats on the beaver marshes of Meldrum Creek since first we came to the watershed, but never in such appalling conditions as confronted us on that unforgettable day in March. The snow had duned the outer fringes of the shoreline in drifts five and six feet high, and with each heave of the wind the drifts became deeper. The wind had carried some of the cards from their sticks, and carried them no one knows where. With these markers missing it was impossible to locate the traps. I thought, "Out of the hundred and ten we've got set, we'll be lucky to retrieve eighty."

Above the clamour of the wind I suddenly thought I heard someone whistling. I glanced southward down the ice and discerned the dim outline of someone moving out of the timber and onto the ice. Come hell or high water, Veasy had kept the rendezvous. And now, for some reason or another, that desolate, frigid lake was not nearly as lonely as it had been a moment or so ago.

The cards 14 and 15 were gone, as had been 7 and 10. Though I prodded here and there in the snow with the shovel handle for feel of the soft mass of house beneath, I was rewarded with only the jar of wood against ice. At number 17, I had to peel off my right mitt, roll up my sleeve and go down in the water with naked arm and hand for the muskrat. For twenty inches of chain was fastened to the spring of each trap so that immediately upon getting caught the muskrat would go down into deep water with the trap and there quickly drown. No true man of the woods can abide the thought of any fur-bearer suffering long in the traps if means can be found to end its life quickly after it has become trapped.

But once in a while both rat and trap became firmly entangled in the bulrush stems below the ice, and then we had to roll up our sleeves and go down into the water with bare arm and hand to work the trap loose.

It took me a couple of minutes to disentangle the trap, and a deadly numbness paralyzed my hand and arm the second they became exposed to the outer air.

The gunny sack over my shoulder was heavy with soggy rats. I'd lost all track of how many I'd taken from the traps thus far pulled, but figured it at around thirty. And a healthy northern muskrat weighs from two or three pounds. Under my breath I cursed the clumsy snowshoes that weighted me down. A huge temptation was in me to disengage from the harness and flounder on afoot. But the dark saucer of many a treacherous air hole was visible when we set the traps out, holes that the long frame of the snowshoes could safely span. It would be foolish and dangerous to discard the shoes now, for now the air holes were hidden by drifted snow.

I watched Veasy cut across the lake a quarter of a mile away, awkwardly lifting his skis straight up from the snow with each step. He weaved and staggered and almost went down a dozen times before reaching the timber where the horses were hitched, weighted down as he was by the load of muskrats and mail on his back.

Sight of Veasy heading for timber reminded me that I was hungry. I thought, "I'll give him ten of fifteen minutes to get a fire going and then pull off the ice myself."

Numbers 33 and 35 were missing, but I made no effort to find the houses in which the traps were set. It was sheer waste of time. My legs were now beginning to buckle each time I brought a shoe up from the snow, and an aching fatigue wracked my every muscle. My body was almost shrieking aloud for respite, so sticking my shovel upright in the snow, I shouldered my load of muskrats and struck out to join Veasy.

He was down on his knees in front of a tree, still trying to get a fire going. I saw one of his matches flare and then go out. "How are we coming?" I asked meaninglessly, dumping the rats out in the snow.

He glanced with little interest at the muskrats, struck another match, grumbled a little when it went out before igniting his shavings, then said simply, "I'm getting by. But I can't get the fire going."

Then I glanced at his hands. Red and swollen they were from too much exposure to the water beneath the ice, and intense cold without.

"Have much trouble in finding the traps?" I asked, knowing full well he'd had plenty.

"Nothing but." Another match flared and went out. "I'll be out ten or a dozen by the time they're all pulled." He tossed me the matchbox. "Here, see what you can do. I guess my hands are too clumsy."

"They're too darned cold, you mean," I said, striking one of the matches against the side of the box and cupping it in my hands.

But the match only went out before it could do anything with the shavings, as a dozen more did before finally they caught and the fire blazed feebly, and I gently fed it sticks, fearful it would go out on me before it was able to throw any warmth.

"Helluva way of making a living, isn't it," I said, breaking open the lunches and placing the sandwiches on spits in front of the fire to thaw out.

That fetched a faint smile to Veasy's face. "It'll all be forgotten in a day or so."

I shook my head. "I'll never forget today."

The three horses stood with hindquarters to the wind, rumps covered with snow, heads hanging dejectedly. Man or beast, the blizzard had mercy on none.

We bolted down the lunch, piled more wood on the fire and crouched by its heat. It took both mental and physical strength to wrench away from that fire. But there were yet many more traps to retrieve, and the longer we stayed by the fire, the bleaker became the thought of going back to the ice. So, banking the fire with wood so that there would be some flame left when we returned, we resumed the ordeal on the ice.

By late afternoon, after retrieving all the traps and their catch that could be retrieved, my legs had turned to rubber. For the last six hours my snowshoes had been lifting several pounds of snow at my every stride, and suddenly I thought, "I'm not going to lug them around another foot." I hauled up in my tracks, unbuckled the heel straps and stepped off the webbing. And I was plowing forward through the snow, shoes, muskrats and traps over my shoulder, when the snow suddenly settled away from my feet, and I was chest deep in water.

A large occupied beaver house thrust its white bulge up above the bank of the lake twenty-five yards away, and I had gone through the thin ice above the beavers' winter food cache. That cache is perhaps all that saved me from going out of sight, for the mass of peeled cottonwood and willow around the underwater entrances to the lodge offered tricky support for my feet. But at least it was support. Hurling rats, traps, snow-shoes and other gear off onto solid ice, I pawed frantically at the water, half swimming, half wading, like a deer fighting flies at a pond on a hot summer's day. For a half-dozen yards the ice continued to break as I clawed at it in an effort to drag myself from the water. Finally, at the edge of the cache it strengthened, and I was able to drag my body out. And now there was no doubt about it: I was the wettest, coldest, most miserable piece of humanity in the whole wide world!

Veasy had seen me go through the ice, and had reached the beaver house by the time I was back on my feet. He steadied me as my toes found the snowshoe harness, and I buckled the heel strap tight.

"D'you mind toting the gear?" I asked, knowing perfectly well that I couldn't. And together we moved into the jack pines and kicked the fire ablaze.

I stood over the flames, swaying a little, hands feverishly searching my pockets for cigarette papers and tobacco. I found both, as wet as the skin of a fish. And Veasy didn't smoke. "Heck of a life," I complained through chattering teeth.

Steam billowed up from the front of my mackinaw britches; their rear was a sheet of ice. I kept turning slowly around before the flames, like a side of barbecuing beef.

Veasy was separating rats from traps, mentally tallying each. Then, loading both into sacks, he turned and said, "Sixty-eight rats, seventy-five traps." So thirty-five traps with whatever fur they held were still somewhere out on the lake, buried under the snow. And there they would remain until the ice began to rot and they sank to the bottom of the lake.

For the next half-hour I pivoted slowly around in front of the fire, trying to get my clothes dry. And when Veasy had loaded all the gear on the pack horse and tied his diamond hitch in the lash rope, I wrenched away from the fire and moved stiffly over to my saddle horse.

"Think you can make it home?" asked Veasy, more from sheer formality than for any other reason.

"Think I'm going to stick out here in these cursed jack pines all night?" I retorted sarcastically. Then with a feeble grin: "Sure I can make it home. Let's get going."

Plod-plod-plod. You cannot trot or gallop a horse when his chest is breasting snow. And on the poorly broken trail leading back to home, their hoofs could only go down into the print of their previous steps. If they missed that print and their knees struck the snow bridge between it and the next, they stumbled and went down on their noses. Plod-plod. Out of the lengthening shadows ahead I could hear Veasy mildly cursing his own horse, which was stumbling now and then. From between teeth that were chattering with the cold I was also cursing my own. But the horses weren't to blame; there was but the one gait at which they could travel, and a very rough one it was.

The cow and calf moose were still there on the meadow, and both lurched away toward thicker timber when our three horses loomed in sight. The calf bogged down in a snowdrift at the edge of the meadow, staggered to its feet, made a few faltering steps and then went down again. The calf was very weak and emaciated; the winter had not been too kind to wildlife, especially the young ones. It was still lying in the drift when I last looked back on it. I thought, "Wonder whether the little beggar will live to see cottonwood leafing time in the spring?" Then: "Wonder whether I'll live to see that house again?"

To me those last couple of miles were a nightmare of physical and mental torture. Mechanically I kept kicking my horse's flanks with feet that lacked any feeling. My bridle lines were looped over the saddle horn, the horse plodding slowly but faithfully along without any guidance from me. With folded arms braced against the pommel, I slumped forward over the horse's withers, my face touching its mane.

I'd lost all sense of direction, and couldn't even see the pack horse a few yards ahead of me. But now and then Veasy's query of "You all right?" told me that I was in the land of the living.

A faint pane of light loomed up from out of the night. I half straightened in the saddle and tried to fix my eyes on it. Soon I could smell the smoke from our stovepipes, but the light seemed miles away. Finally the house was reached, and Lillian stood at the door, fervently greeting us, "Thank God you're back!" Then, as I slumped down off the horse, she asked anxiously, "Eric, what's the matter with you?" Trying to gather my wits I solemnly assured her, "Apart from the fact that I'm both frozen and drowned, nothing at all." I stumbled down from the saddle, picked myself up from the snow and clutched at Lillian for support. "Let's dance," I suggested.

Veasy dumped the fur at the door and moved on to the barn with the horses. A small shack where we do most of our skinning in winter was only thirty yards away, a fire laid in its stove only awaiting a match. But now those few yards were so many leagues.

So I dragged the sack of muskrats across the kitchen floor, spilling them out on Lillian's shiny waxed floor. In balmier moments this might have evoked a storm of protest from Lillian, who didn't like having her floor mussed up like that. But not tonight. I thought, "She's a good kid. She knows when to scold and when not to."

I dropped into a chair by the stove and began pulling off my overshoes. They were frozen to the felts within. So yanking overshoe and felt off together, I next began peeling my woollen socks. Frozen to my—well, almost so.

As the heat of the stove began seeping into my body, all coherent thought began fleeing my mind. I shed my sodden underwear and began pulling on the dry underclothes Lillian had laid out for me. I gazed stupidly down at the muskrats.

"Worth their weight in gold?" I blurted out.

"What's that you're mumbling about?" spoke up Lillian from among her pots and pans. But it didn't really matter, and I was too tired to answer if it did.

242

Chapter 24

The wind was from the north when we first became aware of the fire. Lillian was the first to detect the presence of smoke on the air. She'd been trowelling a flower bed, fixing the earth ready for the seed, sifting it through her fingers to make it friable. The sun was just at the setting, and Veasy and I were indoors, patching up a fishnet that had got snagged when last we dipped for squawfish. We both glanced sharply up when Lillian came running through the door, face streaked with samples of mother earth.

"Smoke!" she said tensely. "I can smell smoke."

At mention of that dread word, smoke—for we were all rightly scared to death of forest fires—I heaved out through the door and stood there smelling the air. Lillian was right; there was a forest fire burning. But where? A glance into the north told me. There, a dense pall of smoke was riding above the forest. To the north of us, but how many miles to the north? And why this early in spring? Too early yet for thundershowers, so we couldn't blame it on lightning. In June or perhaps July, when we could expect electrical storms, but not this early, on the fourteenth day of May.

I tried to soothe Lillian's fears, and some of my own too, by telling her, "I doubt whether it will run very far now. Woods aren't quite dry enough yet for a fire to hit full stride. It will likely go out before getting a chance to do much damage."

To the west of us, far to the west, there was seldom a year went by but that somewhere the woods were on fire. In that country, the Indians of the Aniham reservation cut hay for their cattle and horses on a scatter of wild hay meadows that dotted the jack pine forests like raisins in a pudding. Some say that the Indians have been setting the forests on fire ever since there have been Indians and forests. Others say no, it was the white man who taught them the habit. Still, it is an acknowledged fact by all who hunt meat in the forests that it is far simpler to see and kill a moose or a deer in timber that is lifeless and without underbrush than in timber that is green. Then too, deciduous growth will quickly take root when the conifers have been temporarily destroyed. And aspen, willow and alder are prime moose and deer browse.

But nowhere yet has any forest fire resulted in establishing permanent pasture for big game animals that rely upon deciduous plants for their food. Eventually the conifers will return, and when they do, so dense will be their young growth that one could not see either moose or deer among them should any be there, and of course they won't be there. For when the conifers do return, there will be no room among them for any shrub or plant that would please the taste of moose or deer.

And so the torch is set to the forest again! Lay low the thickets of second-growth fir and pine, destroy the windfalls that clutter them! Then any hunter, Indian or white, can rein his horse through the clearings and shoot his moose or deer without coming out of the saddle.

Seldom a year has passed since first we came to the watershed that some large tract of forest far to the west has not been ablaze. For the only answer to fire, if used as a means of creating moose or deer browse, is more fire. There is no other agency that can keep the conifers in check.

Conifers will always come back, providing there is sufficient soil for a tiny seed to take root in. Without topsoil, little of anything will grow. And then the land is barren, unable to provide food for any cloven-footed animal. That's how it is with countless thousands of acres of forest far to the west of us. So often has the country been fired there that now almost all of its topsoil has been scorched and burned until only gravel and rock are left.

Now no tree, deciduous or conifer, grows there with the exception of the odd, almost leafless, stunted aspen. One could ride a saddle horse among the charred windfalls that litter the underfoot and see a bull moose or buck deer at a distance of almost a mile. But there are no moose or deer out in those burned-over acres. There is neither shelter and food nor moisture for any game animal. Fire has taken all.

~

The floor of the forest was still fairly moist when we first saw the smoke. But three weeks had gone since the last of the snow melted, and the days had been cloudy. No flame could lick far into the forests so long as their underfoot was moist. So we dismissed all thought of fire from our minds, believing it could do us no harm.

But sometimes a flame once kindled is stubborn about becoming altogether extinguished. Especially one that has been born in the virgin forests. It might lie dormant and unseen, smouldering slowly away within the punky wood of some rotting windfall, or entirely under ground level, feeding on the roots of a tree that has died upright yet stubbornly refuses to go down. It will sometimes smoulder with scarce a wisp of smoke to show that there is any fire there at all.

May was about gone, and the smoke that had been in the north forgotten, when the clouds went away from the sky, allowing the sun to glare down on the forest as it lifted and stooped from horizon to horizon. And the wind came down from the west, a keen wind that, if cool and pleasant against the skin, drove little puffs of dust ahead of it when it touched a naked game trail.

And with the wind came the smoke once more. Though barely noticeable at first, soon it was pluming up into the sky to the north. Uneasiness began needling my mind. Ever since coming to the woods to live, I have dreaded the advent of forest fire. Even when the fires were ablaze far to the west, many miles away, I would climb the high timbered hill whose spine is but a mile from the house, and from its top focus my binoculars on that country to the west, trying to track the path of the fire and wondering if a sudden shift in wind would drive the flames toward the headwaters of Meldrum Creek and so onto our trapline. All trappers dread the possibility of fires burning their traplines, for after the flames have gone there is little left in the burned-over area for carnivorous fur-bearers to track down and kill. A forest fire brings death.

Now, with the northern skyline darkened by smoke, I suggested to Veasy, "How about you saddling up a horse and riding to the top of the hill for a look?"

Two hours later he was back, his face set in serious mould. "The whole country around Devil's Lake is on fire," he said sombrely. Then with a shake of the head that suggested much: "The wind is carrying it this way, toward Meldrum Lake."

Devil's Lake bordered the northern reaches of our trapline. There the country was littered by boulders and scarred by almost impassable ravines. Long fingers of forbidding muskeg thrust out from the lake and into the forest, like fingers from a hand. The lake itself stank like a cesspool of decomposing vegetation and slimy alkali mud. It was these evil characteristics of the land about it that gave the lake its name.

As the crow flies, about seven miles of fir and jack pine forest lay between the south end of Devil's Lake and the north end of Meldrum. The woods between were criss-crossed with moose and deer paths, yet none were wide enough to balk the fire when a brisk west wind was egging it along. Falling trees acted as a bridge that enabled fire to cross a trail.

Supper was eaten when Veasy saddled up his horse and rode to the top of the hill again. It was dusking when he got back. At sundown the wind had calmed down a little, and without wind or encouragement from the sun the fire would mark time through the night and not resume its march until bright of day in the morning.

"We'd better wrangle the horses first thing in the morning," I told Veasy, "and follow the east shoreline of Meldrum Lake to where those traps are hanging at the north end. If fire hits either one of those spruce trees, the traps will be ruined."

When first we came to the creek, we only had some four dozen assorted traps, and some of these weren't much good, what with their springs having lost tension and one thing or another. Now we boasted all of six hundred. We had number 0's for weasel, number 1's for musk-rat, 2's for mink, fox and fisher, and 3's and 4's for lynx, timber wolf and otter. In recent years I had invested over a thousand hard-won dollars in such a large collection of traps, for now that Veasy was running his traplines too, we had so much more country to cover, many more traps needed to cover it.

Many of the traps hanging in the spruces at the end of the lake were number 4's, costing me forty dollars a dozen. There were several smaller sizes too. On any large trapline the traps are seldom toted back to the cabin when they are picked up from their cubbies. Instead they are col-lected in bunches and hung beneath spruce trees, there to remain until trapping season comes around again.

"How many traps are there up there anyway?" Veasy wanted to know.

I went to my desk and took out a well-thumbed ledger, and riffled through the pages until I came to the one that accounted for the present whereabouts of all our traps. When traps are scattered over a trapline thus, in bunches of a dozen here, another dozen there, it is easy to forget just where they are cached unless some written record is kept of them.

"We've got four and one-half dozen," I announced, "hanging under those two trees."

By morning the lake at the house was almost hidden by low-lying smoke. The smoke had settled overnight and now clung to every fold in the ground. Horses, too, are mortally scared of forest fire, and this morn-ing ours out in the pasture were as nervous as week-old moose calves, and almost as elusive too. Even Lillian's pot-bellied mare whom we could most always walk up to and catch showed us a clean pair of heels now. Around and around the pasture they galloped, keeping well away from the corral whenever they neared its wings. But finally Veasy was able to corner the old mare in a V of the fence and slip the halter over her head. And when she was led into the corral the rest trailed in behind her.

But it was closer to 11 A.M. than ten when we climbed into the saddles. And the sun had been astir for five or six hours now, and the wind was again briskly from the west. And the smoke had gone up from the folds in the ground and was now umbrellaing the hilltops.

Lillian was at the barn when we saddled up the horses, a bit of worry in her eyes. "Be careful," she murmured, as if she didn't want to say the words but somehow felt she had to. If there was one thing in the woods that Lillian was really frightened of, that thing was fire. She knew how fast a fire can run when it is burning in heavy spruce timber. She knew, for instance, that it can outpace a man afoot. And she'd seen snowshoe rabbits cremated in their tracks, and spruce hens and ruffed grouse limping along without a wing feather to fly with, and porcupines cowering down in treetops with fire spitting flame a few feet below. And she knew that many a wilderness cabin has gone up in smoke when flames jumped the clearing on which it sat.

"We'll be careful," I promised. "But there's nothing at all to worry about. Just the traps, that's all. We'll be back in a couple of hours." And to give added assurance, I said, "The fire will never get here. The beaver ponds will stop it cold in its tracks before it does that." That was our only hope. Still, I couldn't be sure.

Our horses had to swim at the crossing where the creek came out of Meldrum Lake. Below the lake a couple of hundred yards, the beavers had dammed the creek, backing the water up to the lake itself. I glanced downstream to the beaver dam, upstream to the lake. Then shot a glance over my shoulder toward home, and thought, "Thank God for the beavers!"

Clear of the water we put the horses to a swift lope. If the fire reached the other end of Meldrum Lake before us, our traps would be lost.

"Wonder who started this one?" Veasy said suddenly, half to himself.

"Some damn fool," I retorted. "Someone firing a ten- or fifteen-acre meadow maybe. Whites, I figure, not Indians." For there were no Indians in the near vicinity of the country where the fire had started.

"Why doesn't the Forestry Department do something about it?" Veasy was in a mood for arguing. "Why doesn't the Forestry Department catch a few of those maniacs that are forever dropping matches in the meadows and let them light their matches in a penitentiary cell instead of here in these woods?"

"What can they do?" Veasy's thoughts had often crossed my own mind, to be dismissed with a shrug of the shoulder. "How often have you or I actually seen anyone starting these fires? Never. And we're in the woods all the time. If folk living off the country haven't got brains enough to keep the forests green, there isn't much any government department can do about it."

The smoke was thickening now. We were halfway up the lake, drawing away from pine and fir timber into heavier growths of spruce. Our horses were lathered with sweat, and it was use of quirt on rump rather than kindness in the voice that urged the horses on. They were unwilling to face that smoke.

Now we could hear the crackle of burning spruces and occasional crash of a tree that had died in a matter of seconds. The timber grass was on fire to the right of the game trail our horses followed, and running along its edge, seeking a spot to cross, seeking a smouldering tree lying across the trail.

We were now almost within sight of the end of the lake, dodging stands of flaming spruce and neck reining our horses through aspen and willow thickets close to the shore. To our right a hundred yards was a litter of blowdowns, either felled by wind or fire of other years. On three sides the windfalls were surrounded by spruces that were losing their greenness and becoming gaunt spars even as we looked toward them.

Suddenly from among the litter of windfalls a form took shape out of the smoke, so still and lifeless that surely it was only my imagination that made me swear it was a moose. Yet a moose it was, an old cow with hair graying and rusting at the withers.

But why did the cow stand so still? Why was she there at all, what with the spruce trees on fire from toe to crown and spewing flaming brands all around her?

Then I knew why the old cow stood there. "Judas Priest!" I cried aloud. "She's got little ones in the windfalls!"

Veasy leaped out of the saddle. He quickly hitched his horse to a tree and muttered, "We've got to get them out of there."

The .303 Ross rifle was in its scabbard between my stirrup leathers, and I thoughtfully fondled its butt. "How? That's an old cow, and she's raised plenty of calves in her time. We'd have to put a bullet through her head before we could lay a hand on those calves. Better the loss of two lives than three. The cow will live to see another day, but the calves are goners already."

I knew just what Veasy was thinking. Go into the windfalls, hoist the newly born twin calves across the saddle and pack them down to water's edge beyond reach of the flames. That's what Veasy had in mind. But he was reckoning without the old cow. She'd never allow us to lay a hand on the calves; she'd charge if we tried to do that. And there was no sense in shooting her and trying to save the calves. Without the mother they'd die anyway.

"Judas Priest!" I sang out again. And keeping a watchful eye on the cow I urged my horse a little closer to the windfalls.

The calves—about a day old, I reckoned, all legs and awkwardness— were lying side by side by a blowdown, necks stretched flush with the ground. "Aiya!" I shouted at the top of my voice. "Get!" And the twins raised their heads, staggered to their feet, took a few hesitant steps toward their mother and then went down in a heap.

A flaming spruce began swaying on its roots. Its top leaned slowly toward the windfalls. The tree hesitated, as if unable to stand properly yet unwilling to go down. There were no needles left on it now, and the branches themselves were spitting livid fire. A shudder wracked the tree and then, unable to live any longer, it crashed to earth and died.

The top of the tree fell within a half-dozen feet of the twins. But neither moved. Head and necks on the ground, liquid eyes fixed on the smouldering tree, they lay there.

The tree continued to burn, throwing a molten heat. The stink of scorched hair and flesh came to my nostrils.

"Judas Priest!" My hand dragged to the butt of my rifle. I pulled the gun and bolted home a shell. "It's better this way, son," I murmured quietly to Veasy. I lifted in the stirrups and brought the gun to my shoulder. Its sights moved onto a calf. And I squeezed the trigger once, and I squeezed the trigger twice, and you could scarcely hear the shots for the awful roar of the fire. And the twins twitched a little and then became limp and still, crimson founts of blood gushing from their foreheads.

But the delay cost us our traps. The trees in which they were hanging were burning as we came in sight of them. Nothing could go near those trees. And the traps were a cherry red, and the temper would be gone from their steel, and they'd never be of use to us again.

Behind us was the intermittent thud of burning timber falling across the trail. The fire had by now, no doubt, jumped the trail at a dozen different spots and was seeking what it could find toward water's edge. I wheeled my horse sharply west and loped it down to the lake. The northern end of the lake was only two hundred yards away, but I could see nothing of its shoreline. All I could see was a sheet of brilliant flame.

I looped the bridle lines around the horn of the saddle and quietly told Veasy, "We're trapped!"

For while there was no fire over on the west side of the lake, the burning forest at the north barred our escape there. And we couldn't retreat the way we had come, for now the fire was on either side of the game trail and crowding down against the water. Forest fire to the north of us, to the south of us, to the east. And to the west there was only the water, in places forty feet deep.

I puckered my eyes and stared meditatively out across that water. A couple of loons danced their crazy devil dance out in the middle of the lake. They, anyway, were safe. So were the fishes. I glanced at my horse's ears, patted its neck. There was only the one way out: we must swim the lake.

"Tighten your cinch," I bade Veasy, slipping out of the saddle and tightening my own.

He looked at me for a second or two. "You going to swim the horses?"

I said, "I'd rather drown than roast."

In winter I'd often piloted my horse from east to west across the northern end of Meldrum Lake because that was quicker than going around the shoreline. It was around five or six hundred yards from east shore to west. But in winter there were two or three feet of solid ice beneath the horse. Now there was no ice. There was just a couple of loons making one hell of a racket, and the sound of wavelets lapping at the beach.

"All set?" I asked, swinging back into the saddle.

"Whenever you are." The reply was steady and measured.

I neck reined my horse into the water. The gelding snorted and fought to get the bit between its teeth and turn back to land. "Get going!" And I brought the quirt hard down on his rump. Unwillingly he breasted out into the lake, feeling with one front foot at a time for the bottom he could not see.

I slung my rifle over my shoulder and lifted my feet clear of the stirrups, bending my knees until my thighs were almost parallel with the seat of the saddle. I grabbed a handful of mane with my left hand and took a firm grip on the bridle lines with my right. Suddenly there was no jar at all to the gait of the horse. He moved easily along, head high, nostrils flared, tail floating. As far as movement was concerned, I might have been riding on a cloud. We were out in swimming water.

The gelding was a strong and willing swimmer once he knew that he was in deep water and unable to turn back. The water sheered away from his side, and his eyes were riveted on the opposite shoreline. My face was almost brushing his mane, my knees about touching my chin, calves of my legs pressed tight against the leather. Balance, I had to maintain balance. If I lost balance and leaned to either side, the gelding might be thrown off balance too and maybe roll over on its back.

"Veasy, all we can do now is trust in God and the horses!" There wasn't much else that we could put trust in.

"I'm trusting!" There was no fear in the words, and their closeness told me that Veasy was only three or four horse lengths behind me.

We were almost in the middle of the lake now, but far from the other shore. But the gelding was swimming easily, well up in the water, and his breath was coming evenly too. I wanted to turn in the seat of the saddle for one swift appraisal of how Veasy's horse was making it. But pushed the desire away. Movement of any kind might throw the gelding off balance.

"Look out, we've got company!" Veasy's voice sounded very close. I thought, "His horse must be outswimming mine."

From out of the corner of my eyes I saw a huge head take shape. The head was crowned with a set of antlers, which, though now a mass of velvety pulp, would in three months' time perhaps measure fifty inches or more across. "Gol' durned bull moose," I grunted.

The bull swam with the ease and swiftness of an animal as much at home in water as on land. It made two yards for every one my gelding was making, and was only a few feet from the horse as it passed. But it paid us no attention at all. Its eyes too were sighted on the nearing shore. Human being, domesticated horse and bull of the north woods, all out there in the lake fleeing a common foe.

The bull moose was perhaps a half-mile off in the timber when our horses touched land. "Swam like a moose yourself," I told the gelding, patting its quivering neck and loosening the cinch. "Got us out of one heck of a muddle-up that time, you did."

As we neared a windfall to sit down while the horses dried off and got their wind back again, a grouse fanned its feathers and came skidding on a wing toward us. The grouse, a hen, moved to within fifteen feet of us, then artfully trailing a wing to try and make us believe she couldn't fly at all, turned sharply away. "She's got chicks," I said.

Peep-peep. It came from almost under my feet, yet I searched for a few seconds before spying the chick. Peep-peep. Other chicks began piping for their mother. She was on a windfall, fanning her feathers. "Hatched yesterday," I judged, picking the chick up and examining it.

Then I set it down in the grass and repeated softly, "Only yesterday. And what a fire-torn country you've been born into."

And there across Meldrum Lake, and in the country to the north, thousands of acres of forest were on fire. There was jack pine and fir, spruce and aspen, willow and alder, all going up in smoke. And there were Franklin's and ruffed grouse chicks, wobbly moose calves, spotted fawns, little black bear cubs, soft furred fisher cats, baby rabbits, clumsily gaited porcupines, red squirrels and flying squirrels, bluebirds and robins, coyote pups and lynx kittens—all going up in smoke across Meldrum Lake and in the country to the north.

Next morning we could both see and hear the flames from the cabin door. They were only a half-mile away, and they had swept down the east shoreline of Meldrum Lake in seven-league boots. Then suddenly they marked time. Because at the creek, where it came away from the lake, they were halted in their tracks. Though they had destroyed a lot of our forest, they could not destroy our home.

When first we came to the creek, and at this time of the year, there was only a trickle of water moving downcreek from Meldrum Lake. Then, such a fire would have crossed the creek and leaped to our cabin without a pause. Now all was changed. Below Meldrum Lake, for mile after mile, lay the beaver dams. And their every gate was closed. Unable to press south, the fire turned, following the edge of the beaver ponds, thrusting here, reaching there, seeking a path to cross the water and march forward again on the other side. But there was no path, and there was only the water of the beaver ponds—and that no fire could cross.

Then came the rains. In mid-June the overhead clouded and rain beat down on the forests. Again the underfoot became sodden even as it had been when the last of the snows were melting. And so was the fire halted, and eventually extinguished altogether. And so our home was saved.

Chapter 25

Axe blades ringing, handsaws whining and, as if beating time to it all, the steady tattoo of the hammers driving the nails home. Stacks of lumber piled every which way close to the shingle of the lake, and kegs of spikes and nails, rolls of building paper, tiers of sweet-smelling fir shakes for the roofing scattered everywhere, all contributing to the smells and sounds of a new house a-building.

Shouts of "heave, hoist and roll" or "turn her over on her belly and notch her down another inch" mingling with the jargon of the tools, and another log leaves the ground, teeters on the skid poles, then rolls slowly up and is notched down into place. And the sun gets up and the sun goes down, and another four or five rounds of logs have been laid, or the floor joists spiked into place. Thus the mansion takes on form and meaning from a spot where but a week ago there was only a scrub patch of willow.

For sixteen years the little cabin with its sod roof and rough board floor had been the only home we'd known, the only one we could afford, and for that matter the only one we needed. But now the logs were settling, and the split timbers of the roofing buckling slightly. The ridge logs too were beginning to belly toward the floor beneath. Twice in the last twelvemonth I'd had to unhinge the door and shorten it an inch or two so that it would open and shut without scraping the floor. Ten whole days it took Lillian and me to build the cabin. So anxious were we to get the job over with and a roof above our heads, we weren't too fussy about its foundation. Now the bottom log was beginning to rot and crumble where it touched the earth, and for every inch it settled we had to lop another inch off the door or window; if we didn't we couldn't open them.

Lillian never nagged at me concerning the matter of building a better home, although she did grumble now and then when she caught a sliver scrubbing the rough floor of the old one. It was never worse than that. In the spring of 1945 (I'd just got through planing another half-inch off the door) I took a deep and serious breath and announced, "We've lived here long enough." Lillian looked at me sharply, and Veasy too, as if both wanted to say, "Then where will we live now?"

"We're going to get us another house," I went on to explain. "We'll build another one. And this time we'll put a proper foundation under it if I have to pack cement in from Riske Creek on my back to give it one."

The words emphasized the mood, and the mood set the pace for the action. "The logs," I rambled on, "will be thirty-six feet long and as straight as the track of a bullet. There'll be a sitting room big enough to dance in, a washroom, at least three bedrooms, a kitchen for Mrs. Collier and—come on, son, let's take axes and saw and go up on that hill over there to see what we can find."

We had to climb almost to the top of the hill to locate the sort of timber I wanted. They must be trees without hint of windshake or crook in them, free of major limbs, and as sound and as solid within as Gibraltar's Rock without.

We wandered from tree to tree, squinting up at their stems and testing them with our axes. "Your mother," I confided to Veasy, "is going to have the cutest darned house these funny old woods can give her."

Despite the fact that there were at least a million trees on the hill, it took us a whole day to locate and blaze the ones we wanted. We were choosy about our timber because, as I explained to Veasy, "We'll not be building another one, at least not in my time or your mother's either, for that matter."

It took almost all of a week to select just the right kind of timber, fell it and haul it onto a skidway and skin off its bark. But we worked old sun off its legs, and the ring of our axe blades on timber wakened the moon and the stars. When the sixtieth log was peeled and decked on top of the others, I squatted down on the skidway, built myself a cigarette and said to Veasy, "Know something? Now that the war is over, we're liable to see the craziest spree of spending the world ever heard about. Money will be flowing like water over a beaver dam. Every woman will be buying a mink coat. There'll be a pile of money in furs next winter." A prediction that came true.

And now, a year later, the seasoned logs were going up, round after round, though it had been a tricky matter hauling them down from the top of the hill with a team and sleigh when the snow deepened enough to cover the windfalls and rocks. For so sheer was the pitch of the hill, the sleigh runners had to be rough locked from top to bottom, and even when braked like this a strong arm and soothing voice were needed to curb the impatience of the team when breast strap and martingale put strain on hames and neck yoke.

But I had no part in that. Veasy decked the timbers on the sleigh, chained them to the bunks and steered the horses down the dizzy descent to the bottom. And when all were hauled, he took wedge, sledge hammer and axe, found a thicket of good straight pine and split out timbers for the roofing.

For those earlier years of pinch a penny here, clutch a nickel there, had left their mark on the three of us. Now, with a new home to be built, the moods and dictates of leaner years forbade us spending a single dollar upon any piece of building material that was ours for the taking in the woods.

Yet despite all that our woods had to offer, there was much that must be purchased outside and hauled in on the wagon. There were windows and doors, nails and flooring, cement and wall plaster, building paper and linoleum. And I was determined to pay cash on the counter for all, so that when the job was finished we'd not be owing any man a cent for what went into the building.

At first I thought that perhaps Lillian, Veasy and I could build the house ourselves; then I changed my mind. Lillian had been there at my side at the building of the old cabin, helping me fell the logs and giving the last ounce of her strength helping roll them into their notches. And I'd vowed then and there that if and when another was built, she'd share in none of the labour. Pots and pans, scrub brush and broom, darning needle and flatiron, such things as these and a great many more are tools that any woman should know how to use, no matter whether the home sits within hollering distance of a bear den or by crowded city pavement. But no woman should be called upon to share in labour fit only for man's coarse strength, though many there are sharing it, and without calling either.

"We'll contract that part of it out," I decided. "Yes, we'll put the logs on the ground and pay someone else to throw them up and round the job off."

Once that decision was agreed upon, I cautiously began sniffing around for the scent of someone who'd build the house in the right way and for the right wages.

I found my man at Riske Creek. His name was Wes Jasper. He could swing an axe or a hammer or coax the rhythm from a handsaw as well as any I knew. Jasper was a jack-of-all-trades. He'd tackle any job in sight that showed glimpse of a dollar's worth of profit. He could hoist aboard the meanest bucking horse in the Chilcotin and ride the outlaw to a standstill. Or rope and tie a maverick calf in seven seconds flat, or herd a band of wild horses out of the thickest acre of forest and chase them into the artfully concealed wings of a trap corral. He could plait a rawhide lasso rope, make a horsehair cinch and shoot the eye out of a blue grouse sixty yards away. Though a cow puncher by chosen profession, Jasper saw no disgrace in dropping his lasso rope and hefting an axe. So, after having run my man to earth and after a long evening of good-natured haggling over price, Jasper said yes, he reckoned he could build the house.

Lillian had little to say about the project at all until the logs were down off the hill. Then she had a great deal. She made almost daily visits to the spot where the home was to be built, measuring here, measuring there, shaking her head or nodding, smiling or frowning, or just sitting down on the logs, looking at nothing at all. Finally she said, "We must have proper plans for every square inch of space." I shifted uneasily in my chair and asked, "What do you mean by plans?"

She said, "How is everything going to fit in unless it is all planned out in advance?"

I sniffed. "This cabin was built without plans and it has been a mighty comfortable one too. Warm as a rack of buttered toast in winter, cool as iced lemonade in summer."

Lillian's eyebrows lifted. "One room?" She spoke mildly, but there was heavy emphasis on the "one."

"You think we should go down to Vancouver and hire ourselves an architect?" I asked sarcastically.

Lillian made no reply. Her eyes went to Veasy, and mine shifted there too. He strolled to the window and stood looking out, hands in pockets. And watching him I thought, "How he is shooting up." He lacked a half-inch of being six feet and weighed around a hundred and sixty pounds. He could hoist a two-hundred-and-seventy-five-pound buck across the saddle without puffing enough to blow a match out, or snowshoe or ski for eight hours straight without a single sit-down. Veasy lacked one vice that both Lillian and I had: he never touched tobacco. I was a heavy smoker, Lillian moderately so. Between us we managed to get away with a half-pound tin of tobacco a week, rolling our own cigarettes. I had been smoking since I was fourteen, but until going to the headwaters of Meldrum Creek with me Lillian had never touched tobacco. There she somehow acquired the habit, liked it and made no attempt to deny it.

We never did tell Veasy, "No, you mustn't smoke." Tobacco and cigarette papers were there on the table all the time, and had he taken a paper, filled it with tobacco, placed the cigarette between his lips and lighted it, neither Lillian or I would have said a word. Perhaps if Veasy had gone to school with other children the story might have been different. But Veasy didn't go to school, at least not to one where there were other children. And whether that is a curse or a blessing I wouldn't like to say.

He came away from the window, sat down again and said, his voice firm and steady, "Mother is right. A building of that size should be planned out on paper so everything will fit in."

I said, "You know I can't draw a line from A to B without it's got a crook in it."

"Veasy can," Lillian was quick to interject. "Can't you?" And her eyes went to Veasy for confirmation.

"I can try," said Veasy cautiously.

If the wilderness had treated Veasy kindly where physique and health were concerned, it had been tolerably kind to him in other matters too. He knew a little of the mechanics of geometry and not only had compass, protractor, set square and slide rule, but what is of far more importance, he knew how to use them. So between them, he and Lillian drew up the plans for the house, while I sat back in a chair, pretending to read but all the time straining an ear to catch whispered talk of "the clothes closet should fit in here," or "your bedroom goes there," or "the heater stove sits here." Once I peeked at them over the top of the pages and asked, "What, no deep freeze?"

But finally it was all there on paper, the lines neat and straight, and when Jasper and his crew arrived to start a-building, that's how it was built.

∾

In the early fall of 1945, almost any trapper with a nose at all could scent prosperous fur prices on every breath of wind that shivered the tops of the conifers. Our own traps were set out long before the snow came, unbaited and unscented, but there just the same, as we waited for the fur to become fully prime before adding bait and scent.

Four inches of snow fell in early November, and following the snow the temperature skidded sharply to zero minus five. Now all carnivorous fur-bearers were fully prime, so I scented and baited the traps, leaving

Veasy to the job of hauling the logs down off the hill. For somehow the house must be paid for, and I was determined to exact every cent of its cost from the wilderness about us. That wilderness was not to fail me.

In line with my earlier predictions, fur prices rocketed crazily. Mink hit an all-time high of sixty dollars a pelt for extra-large sizes, and since the muskrat cycle was at a peak there were plenty of mink around to prey upon the muskrats. Each muskrat itself was worth three dollars in cash, or still more in trade. Almost any small, dark and silky fisher cat that got tangled up in the traps was certain of fetching one hundred and fifty dollars, maybe slightly more if one haggled long enough with the trader.

On the outside, in the land of indoor plumbing and hardtop roads, money started flowing like water down a flume. And deep in the heart of the wilderness the trappers slid their snowshoes over the trapline trails, bowing their heads to the blizzard, silently cursing the frost that pricked their fingers as they adjusted the pan of the trap, but trapping just the same.

So it's trap, and trap, and trap, and it's skin, and skin, and skin! Step into the snowshoe harness when there's yet no light in the east to see things, bid the moose and the mule deer good morning as they lift from their beds at your coming. And drag back to the cabin by the light of the moon and the stars, cold, weary and all stiffened up from stooping down to the traps and lifting the catches from them.

Then, after a quick supper, all fur has to be stretched, by the light of the coal-oil lamps, or flickering candle if no other light is at hand. But cleanse and stretch the catch, for God and the wilderness willing, there'll be more to stretch with the morrow. The fur trade is hungry for pelts and, for this one fleeting moment anyway, cares little about what it pays for them.

I personally came nigh wearing the webbing of my snowshoes to a frazzle during that winter of high fur prices. It was one winter when the wilderness smiled benevolently. For day after endless day the mercury was at twenty above with the nooning, seldom dropping below zero at night. Not too much snow lay about the game trails, so once a trapline was broken out and packed, one could, if he wished, tote his snowshoes on his back and tend the traps afoot.

From mid-November until early in February, I had but one day's respite from the chore of running and tending the traps. It hardly seemed right to be out there in the snows handling traps on the birthday of Our Lord, so on Christmas Day I stayed in the cabin, resting, and doing full and proper justice to the feast that Lillian had been all of a week preparing.

As soon as the carnivorous fur-bearers showed a hint of' losing their winter sheen, I pulled the traps set for them. By that time Veasy had all the material for the home that could be obtained from the woods piled up at the site we had selected for its building. Now the two of us were able to give all our attention to the large crop of muskrats that had multiplied upon the marshes.

It was the hardest trapping of all. One hundred traps set out in the houses today might yield us some seventy or eighty rats on the morrow. All must be toted in off the ice on our backs, loaded on the pack horse, and the skins peeled from them and stretched by lamplight, when the mind and the flesh were begging aloud for rest.

Lillian's nimble fingers placed the skins on the stretcher boards and tacked each one in place while Veasy and I did the skinning. Seldom was there a night throughout the muskrat trapping season of 1946 that saw us in bed before midnight, seldom a morning that we weren't up and moving around by 5 A.M. at the latest.

By early April, when the ice began turning to slush, and the muskrat houses were collapsing, we three were so tired of it all that we could not have stood the pace of it any longer for all the gold of Ophir. It was with relief that we greeted the disintegration of the ice and muskrat houses. For the moment anyway we'd had our fill of trapping and didn't care if we ever saw the pelt of a muskrat again, or of any other fur-bearer, for that matter.

We sprawled on our backs for a few days of lazy relaxation under a swiftly warming sun outside the cabin door, watching squadron upon squadron of wild geese winging by overhead. The irrigation dam was a babble of quacking mallards and other ducks. Bluebirds and robins and multihued woodpeckers were busy with their nesting, and as the shore ice slipped its moorings, and open leads of water thrust dark and slender fingers from land, the beavers of Meldrum Creek came out of lodge and bank run, and threshed the water with their tails as if in salutation to the sheer joy of it all. Spring was back in the wilderness.

By mid-June Jasper and his work crew tacked down the final layer of roof shakes. The house was finished and ready for us to move into. Hitching the team to the wagon, we piled our mean stock of furniture and other effects in the box and quickly the move was made. And after sixteen years of eating and sleeping in that one-room, sod-roofed cabin, our new home seemed as big and important as Buckingham Palace.

∾

The lush returns from the winter's trapping not only paid cash on the counter for the new building, but were also responsible for bringing another revolutionary event to the changing tempo of our affairs. The

Eric, Lillian and Veasy in front of their new cabin, designed by Veasy and Lillian.

high prices received for our furs left us with a healthy bank balance after the house was paid for. The beavers were multiplying fantastically well. Temptation was strong in us to trap a few in the spring of 1946, for then a large beaver pelt was selling for seventy dollars. But somehow we dreaded the thought of trapping any of the beavers until we absolutely had to. A day was fast approaching when we'd have to trap beavers, to keep their numbers in check. But that day was not yet.

To me, and perhaps Lillian too, the infrequent pilgrimages to Riske Creek in spring, summer and early fall were just another chore, something that must be done every now and then. The return trip took two days no matter how early we got away in the morning. In winter, of course, sleigh runners replaced wagon wheels and then, if the snow lay deep in the track, we were fortunate if we got back in two days; more often it took three or four.

But still, we'd never known any swifter or easier way of travel, and what the eye doesn't see, the heart doesn't cry about. What if these times many of the ranchers, and many of their cowboys too, for that matter, had turned their backs on a mode of transportation that had served them so long and so faithfully and were now gripping steering wheel instead of reins, gearshift instead of whip? As far as Lillian and I were concerned, they could have their automobiles. We'd ever trusted in horseflesh, and were still content to do so.

But Veasy saw things differently. The horses were slow, the wagon rough. And anyway, why spend two days going out to Riske Creek for mail when the round trip could be made in four hours?

Reading his thoughts and becoming uneasily aware of the outlandish design shaping up in his mind, I decided to bring matters to a head. "What's ailing you these days?" I cautiously inquired one morning when I noted him standing by the wagon shaking his head.

He came slowly around in his tracks and said, "We need something out here that will run on gasoline and oil and not grass or hay."

I took a measured breath. "You mean an automobile?" Even the very words sounded bitter on my tongue.

He slowly nodded. "Why not?" Then, without flinching from the probe of my eyes: "There's a vehicle on the market called a Jeep. Willys Jeep. I saw one at Riske Creek a while back. Fellow who owned it told me all about it. Said you can go anywhere with one that you can with a team and wagon. Just the rig for us. It has a four-wheel drive and when you gear it down into bull low you can crawl along at two or three miles an hour. Fellow said it will go through eighteen inches of snow too."

Four-wheel drive? Bull low? Just what in hell was the boy talking about?

"We can pick one up secondhand for a thousand dollars." The way Veasy said it, a thousand dollars might only have been a five-cent piece.

"Oh, my God!" I squatted back on my heels, shaking my head at the absurdity of it all. Stink up this wilderness of ours with the exhaust fumes of an automobile? Over my dead body!

"Lillian," I suddenly cried. "Hey, Lillian, come here!" And when she came, I said weakly, "It's Veasy. He thinks we should buy some sort of an automobile. Jeep, he called it. Four-wheel drive—bull low—" And then words failed me.

"You want Mother to bounce over these rocks in a wagon for the remainder of her days?" Veasy asked jarringly.

"You want to stink these woods up with gas fumes?" I flared back. Then looking to Lillian for help: "Crazy, isn't it? Absolutely ridiculous."

Lillian neither agreed nor disagreed. She just shook her head and said, "I'm neutral."

My eyes drifted almost affectionately to the wagon. Fifteen dollars cash and one coyote pelt, that's what the wagon had cost me. Not too long ago either. Just how long, though? Only seventeen or eighteen years. It was a good wagon yet, a good stout wagon. In those days they made things to last. That wagon was assembled in times when a vehicle had to be good, true and strong, and last a fellow a lifetime, and maybe that of his grandchildren too. All that the wagon needed was a fresh coat of paint. Give it another coat of paint and it would be as good as new.

Veasy was reading my thoughts. "Needs new tires too," he informed me, as if he knew more about old wagons than I did myself.

"And the spokes are coming away from the felloes, and the hound gear is falling apart."

"Give it a good coat of paint and it's a fine wagon yet," I persisted doggedly.

Veasy wouldn't give an inch. "A Jeep would soon pay for itself back here. We'll have to start trapping beavers pretty soon, and as I see things a lot of that could be done with a Jeep. And a whole lot easier and quicker than we could do it with pack horses too."

Trap beavers with an automobile? At first it sounded preposterous. But after two weeks of mulling that over in my mind, the suggestion had lost some of its wildness.

When first we came to the creek, the only trails about it were game trails. In due time some of these trails were cut out a little so we could get over them with our pack horses. Maybe they could be cut still wider. And maybe with the use of a few boxes of stumping powder we could remove some of the rocks from the right-of-way. And by corduroying the track where it crossed the occasional strip of muskeg, and by bridging the creek here and there, maybe we really could get to several of the beaver dams with one of these "Jeeps," as Veasy called them.

The issue hung in doubt for almost three months. Veasy clung to his theme that much of the work now done with horses could be done better and quicker with a Jeep. "We could even stack the hay with one when it's cut." Or "Haul wood with it too." Then, sensing that I was wavering, he tossed in some more shots: "Could use it for hunting ducks and geese. Haul moose and deer in out of the woods with it maybe."

It still sounded outlandish to me, but now Lillian was neutral no longer. Veasy's steady, unyielding arguments had convinced her that a thousand dollars spent on a secondhand vehicle wouldn't be a bad investment at all.

Versus Veasy alone I might have held out, but with Lillian and Veasy teamed up against me I didn't stand a chance. We'd buy one of these confounded things with their four-wheel drive and bull low, and bring an end to all this discord that was disturbing the peace of our home. Inwardly I felt sure that such a contraption of gears, spark plugs, carburetor and other whatnots would come to a quick and sorry ending before it travelled many miles over our sort of roads. Or given an ounce of luck we might even manage to get it stuck in a muskeg, where it would soon settle from sight, to be neither seen nor heard of again. This latter prospect cheered me up no end.

In that fall of 1947—the year of mechanization, I call it—when finally we got the Jeep I was forty-seven years of age. Twenty-seven of those years had been spent in the wilderness or near-wilderness. Yet never once in all those years had I ever once laid a hand on the steering wheel or gearshift of an automobile. I was distrustful of any mode of transportation that did not rely upon something with heart, lungs and good stout legs for its motivating power. Now a team of horses hitched to wagon or sleigh, there was something solid, something a fellow could rely on. Through bogholes or snowdrift, upgrade or down, the horse always got you there eventually. They never left you afoot. And should some mild calamity befall wagon wheel or sleigh runner, it was usually one that could be easily repaired with use of pliers and haywire.

Now I was suddenly called upon to put my whole faith in a vehicle that had no heart or lungs, lacked anything resembling legs, and with so many innards beneath its bonnet that just staring down at them gave me a headache.

A friend of ours in Williams Lake drove the newcomer to Riske Creek. The three of us drove out from home with team and wagon to meet it. Veasy was humming a lively tune all the way out, Lillian had an air of expectancy about her, as if we just couldn't get to Riske Creek quickly enough, that maybe the thing would run away before we got there. I was crestfallen, hanging my head, thinking, "I should have never given in to all this foolishness."

And so we came to Riske Creek, and there the vehicle sat, spic and span. There it sat, but—how in heck were we going to get the thing home?

"Drive it, of course," said Veasy.

"Who?"

He shrugged his shoulders. "You, if you like. Or if you don't want to, I will."

"You don't know the difference between gearshift and toot the horn," I rudely informed him.

"But I can learn, can't I?"

"Okay," I said, "go ahead and learn."

Our friend gave a half-hour of his time to teaching Veasy how to use gas pedal and clutch, gearshift and instrument panel. Within an hour of first touching the steering wheel, Veasy was driving the vehicle up and down the road. It took me most of a year to learn how to drive a team of horses properly. It took Veasy an hour and a half to learn how to drive that Jeep.

Despite urgent advice from me that she'd better go back in the wagon, Lillian was perched on the seat beside him when Veasy headed the vehicle north, in the general direction of Meldrum Lake. I stood by the wagon, watching the cloud of dust the Jeep left in its backtracks. When I could no longer hear the purr of the motor, I turned to the friend and said, "Bet two bits he'll never get it home."

"Bet two bits he will."

It was a bet I lost. Two and a half hours after leaving Riske Creek, Lillian and Veasy were home. Trailing behind in the wagon I kept gazing ahead, expecting at any moment to see them sitting by the side of the track, the Jeep gone lame or something—and was perhaps a bit disappointed when it wasn't so.

The vehicle sat in front of the house for a week before I'd lay a hand on its wheel. Finally Veasy coaxed me into climbing on the seat beside him. "You've got to learn to drive it sometime," he argued, "so why not now?"

Eventually I tried. I said "giddup" as I moved the gearshift from neutral to first and stepped on the gas pedal, cried "whoa" when I wanted to stop. I ran the contraption headfirst into the irrigation ditch and had to shout for Veasy to come and get it out of there. I skinned the bark off so many jack pines when first I drove it out to Riske Creek that it seemed someone had newly blazed out the track. But finally I learned.

The wagon never did get its new coat of paint. In fact it has never had a team of horses hitched to it since mechanization came to the trapline. It sits

Once Eric purchased a Jeep, the wagon was retired. Here they are off to one of their beaver-trapping cabins; Eric and Veasy built all the roads and bridges on their property.

dejectedly under a pine tree, stoically enduring the taunts of the elements, tongue slowly rotting, tires loose on the felloes. And sometimes as the sun goes down and the softened murmurings of the wilderness are as an angelus in our ears, Lillian and I walk over to the wagon and squat there on its tongue, chins cupped in the palms of our hands, eyes on the ever present forest. Yet we scarce see the trees. Instead we see the wagon in front of the trading post, within its stout box all we can claim as ours. And when the night breeze touches our skin we barely feel its breath. Instead we feel the sharp jar of the wagon wheels as they roll from rock to rock. "Remember?" I suddenly ask of Lillian, sensing that her thoughts are mine.

She nods. "As if it were yesterday."

"Yesterday," I repeat. "Yes, but what a long way we've travelled since yesterday."

Chapter 26

It came on me suddenly, like raindrops from out of an almost cloudless sky, or a buck deer stepping out from behind a curtain of second-growth firs. It was the beginning of an ordeal and trial for Lillian that was to test her strength, her reasoning and, yes, her faith, as that of few other women has been tested either before or since. It was Lillian versus Wilderness, with the odds heavily against her.

It was Tuesday, in mid-December, and I was thinking about how in a couple of weeks another year would be gone, and we'd be at the jump-off of 1948. I was four miles out from home, snowshoeing over a trap trail that overnight had been covered by nine inches of new snow. It was a wet snow too, one that stuck to the snowshoes and made my every stride an unpleasant effort. Still, I was used to that. Snowshoeing ever has and ever will be a matter of cruel effort when one is plowing out after a recent snowfall which, had the air been but a few degrees warmer as it fell, might have been rain and not snow at all.

It was around noon when the thing hit me. A half-hour earlier I'd been fine, eager to get over the trail and see what the traps had caught. But suddenly I felt tired, and my legs ached, and I broke out in a cold sweat. I set fire to a pitchy stump, shovelled the snow aside with one of the snowshoes and quickly made myself a bed of boughs.

Despite the heat of the fire, I was shivering as I lay on my side on the boughs.

I took my lunch from the packsack, stared listlessly at the sandwiches and then pushed them aside. There was no appetite in me. The stump blazed cheerfully away but seemed to throw no heat. I lay as close to the flames as I could get without setting fire to my clothes, but still I shivered. And the longer I lay there, the weaker I seemed to get.

Snow began falling again. From off in the northwest I could hear the tumult of wind rushing through the treetops. A blizzard of sorts was moving in from the northwest, and while it might blow itself out in an hour or less, its passing would probably leave another three or four inches of snow on the trail.

A desire was in me to build myself a shelter of boughs and sit the blizzard out by the fire. Prudence, however, told me to do no such foolish thing, but instead to turn around at once and get back home while there was sufficient strength in my legs and willpower in my mind to get me there.

"Be all right if I can just get back home," I tried to comfort myself. "Guess I'm a bit sick right this very minute, but get back home and in bed and I'll be all right come morning."

Realization that I was sick turned my thoughts to Veasy. He was trapping out of the cabin downcreek. He was alone down there, trapping out to the east and north, while I stayed home with Lillian and covered the country lying south and west of Meldrum Lake. It was a good arrangement, for it enabled us to cover pretty well the whole of our trapline with traps at a time when the fur was at its best. In the last two or three years Veasy was often alone at the cabin, running his traps, and we never worried or fretted about his being safe. He was strong, and he was healthy, and there was no Indian in the Chilcotin who knew how to take better care of himself in the woods. The woods would never harm Veasy, of that we were sure. But now, with my own legs failing me, I thought, "Hope the boy's all right."

The blizzard hauled up to me a few minutes after I'd left the fire. My tracks of the morning were soon hidden, and it was only by sense of touch that I was able to keep the snowshoes on the pack of the trail beneath them. I could see nothing of the trail itself.

I'd never known anything like this before. I was becoming weaker by the minute, and the temptation to quit, build another fire and sit by it and rest, and maybe sleep for a few minutes, was almost irresistible. But no, I couldn't do any such thing as that. I had to keep moving slowly along, although now it was willpower and not strength that kept the snowshoes moving.

The blizzard passed by and the air became still. Now I had to stop every hundred yards and rest a few moments. But I rested standing on the snowshoes; I was scared to take them off and sit down. If I did that I might never get the snowshoes to moving again. I had to keep going.

Night closed in long before I reached home. Only instinct held my snowshoes to the trail. Instinct and a sort of stubborn determination that I wasn't going to let the woods lick me. A landmark here and there that might have told me in what direction I was going now told me nothing.

A building took outline from the darkness. I stopped, rubbing my eyes and staring at it. And stood there a few seconds before realizing that it was our own barn. I kicked out of the snowshoe harness, leaning the shoes against the logs. No need for the snowshoes now. I was home, or at least would be if I could just summon enough willpower to drag myself along the trail from barn to house.

Lillian must have been seated at the sitting room window, staring out into the night and watching for me. Lillian always worried a bit when night shut down with Veasy or me long overdue out of the woods. So many things could go amiss.

She heard me coming up the trail and was at the back door to meet me when at last I reached it. At once she saw that something was radically wrong.

"Eric, you're sick, what is it? What's wrong?" she cried anxiously.

"I feel sort of bad." I staggered into the kitchen, flopped in a chair and muttered, "Nothing for you to fret over. I'll be fine by morning."

Supper was on the table, but there was no hunger in me. I drank a cup of tea, shed my clothes and had misty recollection of Lillian helping me to bed and covering me with blankets. I lay there, still shivering despite the two hot water bottles that Lillian slipped under the blankets with me. Three weeks were to pass before I had strength enough to leave that bed again.

By morning I was delirious, completely out of my head. My clothes were saturated with the sweat that had drenched my body in the night. A medicine chest of sorts was tucked away back on one of the cupboard shelves, yet seldom had there been need to rummage among its contents. The medicine chest contained some quinine capsules, cough syrups and bottles of liniment. But little of anything else. We never had allowed thought of serious sickness to plague our minds, never since coming to the creek to live. A common cold or minor headache had so far been about all in the way of sickness that Lillian had had to contend with. Now that possible serious illness had stalked onto the scene, the quinine capsules were the only medicine in the chest that seemed likely to do any good.

Lillian managed to get some of the capsules down my throat, but sitting by the bedside during the long hours of night, covering me with the blankets again whenever I threshed around in the bed and tossed them aside, she knew that more than quinine was needed.

Night gave way to dawn. Lillian stood aimlessly at the bedroom window, watching a cold sun clear the treetops and wondering what to do. Then suddenly she remembered that today was Wednesday.

That realization fetched some relief to her tortured mind. It was Wednesday, and tonight Veasy would be back and she'd not be alone. Veasy's traplines were so arranged that on Wednesday and Saturday he was back home for an overnight stay, so tonight he would be home, and tomorrow, if so it had to be, he could drive the sleigh out to Riske Creek for help. The village of Williams Lake, thirty miles to the east, now boasted a doctor, so if the worst came to the worst Veasy could go to Riske Creek and phone into Williams Lake for a doctor. And haul him into Meldrum Lake on the sleigh. No Jeep or car could buck the snow on Island Lake Flats.

The thought of Veasy being home at nightfall buoyed Lillian up through the dragging day. At four in the afternoon she went to the barn and fed and watered the horses. A cow and a calf moose came trotting out of the woods as she forked hay down to the horses. Within seconds a half-dozen were milling around the barn. She forked hay to them too, scattering it out in the snow, and when all were eating made a dash back to the house. Lillian never had been able to forget the moment when Old Cantankerous collapsed lifeless almost at her feet. The incident had left her with a nervousness about any moose, cow or bull. But the moose paid no attention to her as she fled back to the house. They were far too busy squabbling with one another over the hay.

Five o'clock, and the oil lamps lighted, the woodbox filled and buckets of fresh water carried from the water hole at the lake. I had been unconscious all day, now lying very still, now threshing about in the bedclothes as the sweat oozed from the pores of my skin.

Six o'clock passed, but still no sign of Veasy. It had been pitch-dark for well over an hour. Now Lillian's thoughts were wracked by added anxiety: why wasn't Veasy home? Every few minutes she went outside, standing very still, listening. Veasy had a saddle horse with him at the cabin, and he'd be riding it home tonight. Yet why couldn't she hear the crunch of hoofs against frozen snow when she went outside and listened? Then too, there was generally a whistle on Veasy's lips when he neared the house. Why couldn't she hear that whistle now, when she wanted so much to hear it? What had happened to prevent Veasy from coming home? A dozen or more things could have happened, but as quickly as thought of one entered her head she swiftly pushed it away again. Veasy would be home, soon; he just had to be home. Nothing would happen to Veasy.

The hum of an airplane motor sounded from out of the night. Soon she could see its lights. The plane, maybe a Canadian Pacific Airways plane hauling passengers from Prince George to Vancouver, passed directly above the house. By now Lillian was accustomed to hearing planes fly over the house. They more or less followed the course of the Fraser River north or south as the case might be. Once upon a time, when they first began flying that route, Lillian would pat down her hair, wipe her hands on her apron and go outside and look up at them, as if the pilot or passengers could look back down at her and note whether her hair was slick and neat, or her hands perfectly clean. But after the novelty of it all wore off, whenever the planes went by she kept on with her housework and paid them no attention.

But now she rushed out into the night as soon as she heard the plane and stood there, staring at its winking lights, thinking, "There are people in it just like me. If I could only signal them. And maybe if they knew that Veasy wasn't home—" Then, realizing the craziness of her thoughts, she stamped a foot in the snow, set her teeth and tried to dam back the tears that wanted to flood her eyes.

Then the plane lights went out and its engines purred into silence. And Lillian was alone again, pacing the snow, indifferent to the cold that needled her face and ears, crying aloud, "Veasy, why don't you come!"

Seven. Eight. Nine. How slowly the hours crawled by. Lillian picked up a book but quickly laid it down again. She threaded a needle and tried to busy herself with some knitting. But that made no sense either. Tonight nothing made any sense.

A half-dozen times she ran to the door and out into the night when she thought she heard sound of a horse approaching the house. But it was only the moose that she heard. Having eaten their hay, they were now browsing willows a stone's throw away from the house.

A few minutes after ten she again heard the crunch of hoofs against snow. This time she was certain that it was no moose approaching the house. Moose didn't make that much noise even when they were trotting. She stepped away from the door a few paces, straining her eyes into the night, and calling, "Veasy, is that you at last?"

A horse took on form and colour from out of the night. The horse was a blocky roan, and as soon as she saw it Lillian recognized it as Veasy's. For a quick second relief and joy rushed through her. Then her legs trembled, a cry forced from her lips. The horse was without saddle, bridle or rider. Only a halter was on its head, the lead rope looped around the animal's neck.

"If anything goes amiss out here in the woods when you're on horse-back, jerk the saddle and bridle off your horse and turn him loose. He'll come home and let us know you're in trouble."

If Lillian had heard those words once, she'd heard them a hundred times. They were instructions I'd given Veasy when maybe rightly he wasn't quite old enough to be out in the woods on horseback alone. And when he grew older and began running lengthy traplines of his own, they became more of an order. "Turn the horse loose and he'll trail home." And somewhere Veasy had recently done just that, and now the horse was home, letting Lillian know there'd been trouble.

She stood in the snow by the horse's head, her mind a turmoil. All was very still about her. The moose had wandered away from the willows and were now probably bedded in the thickets, unseen and unheard. The air was crisp with the sting of a near-zero temperature. The tremulous cry of some faraway coyote suddenly split the night, melancholy and mournful. Then the cry trailed off and all was silent again save for the measured breathing of the horse.

A flood of questions swamped Lillian's head. Where had the horse been turned loose and how long ago? And why had it been turned loose? Once free to travel at will, the animal certainly wouldn't dawdle in the woods or on any trail. Instead it would start off at a fast walk in the direction of Meldrum Lake and the other horses it knew so well that were now in the barn. She ran a hand down its shoulder, then along its back. There was no frosted sweat on the hair as there probably would have been had the saddle been taken off in the woods. That seemed to indicate that the animal had been taken out of a barn and turned loose.

"He's down at the cabin," Lillian persuaded herself. "Unable to ride home himself but still able to turn his horse loose to let us know he's in trouble."

It would be eight or nine hours before another dawn broke, and Lillian could not abide the thought of waiting upon the daylight. She had to get down to the cabin now, at once. That decision acted as a stimulant of sorts.

Going back into the house, she stoked the heater stove with wood and closed its dampers. Then she scribbled a note and put it on a chair by my bed in case I came to my senses before she got back. She put on her warmest winter clothes, pulled a parka over her head, turned down the wick in the coal-oil lamp, set it on the kitchen table, lighted the barn lantern and led Veasy's saddle horse away.

Gipsy and Ben, the work team, stood side by side in the double stall of the barn. Lillian took their harness from its peg, threw it on the team and hitched them up to the sleigh. Then jumping up on the seat, she brought the whiplash down on their rumps, and the horses moved off through the night at a fast trot.

The road to the cabin hugged beaver marshes most of the way. The lantern on the seat beside her dimly showed the blazes on the trees ahead, which denoted the course of the track. As her eyes became tuned to the darkness she discerned fresh tracks in the snow ahead of her. These, she knew, had been made by Veasy's saddle horse. Now she became certain that she'd find him at the cabin.

The team slowed to a walk. She laid the whips across their backs and again they broke into a trot. Again the whip fell and they started to gallop. Ordinarily, and in cold blood, Lillian could never have driven any horses as she drove the team that night in her wild dash for the cabin. The snow was deep, and there was many an up and down to the road. Sweat lathered the horses, and their flanks heaved and fell. But steeling her heart to all else but the desperate need of reaching the cabin as quickly as possible, Lillian had no pity on the horses. She laid the whip down on their backs in harsh demand for every ounce of speed and endurance that was in them.

A fine snow was falling when she came to the cabin. She jumped from the seat, hitched the lines to a stump and ran inside. It was icy cold there in the cabin, and on one of its bunks lay Veasy, fully dressed. His flushed face and vacant eyes told of the fever that was in him.

Shaking his shoulder, Lillian said softly, "Veasy, it's Mother. I've come to take you home." At the sound of her voice his eyes opened, and he stared blankly at the lantern. Trying desperately hard to steady her voice, Lillian asked, "Can you manage to walk as far as the door? Ben and Gipsy are outside with the sleigh."

"Door?" he murmured. "Sleigh?" Then his eyes found hers and he smiled wanly. "Gee, Mom, I'm sick."

With Lillian's hand steadying him, he managed to get off the bunk and reach the door. After a minute of rest, leaning against the jamb, he moved outside to the sleigh and tumbled into the box. Lillian returned to the cabin, gathered an armful of blankets and bundled him up in them. Then she hoisted up into the seat, put the whip to the horses and started out on the longest five miles of her life.

As the horses broke into a trot, she suddenly swayed in the seat, almost dropping the lines. Regaining her grip on them and holding both in her right hand, she clutched the side of the box with her left, in order to support herself on the seat. She'd not had a moment of sleep last night, not a moment of rest all day. On the way to the cabin the horses had almost taken the bit between their teeth when galloping down a very sheer pitch in the road. It had required every single ounce of her one hundred and fifteen-pound weight to retain her hold on the lines and stop the horses from running away and perhaps smashing sleigh and box to splinters. Now a sharp and deadly reaction set in. She felt tired, weak and a little dizzy. She took a firmer grip on the lines, a still firmer one on the side of the seat. Her lips pressed tightly together. Her eyes, which had momentarily closed, forced open again. "You can't get sick yourself," she told herself. "You just simply can't!" She "whoa'd" the horses to a stop and sat huddled in the seat, repeating over and over again, "You can't get sick yourself." The cold began seeping into her body but still she sat there, until the weakness and dizziness began to leave her. Then, releasing her grip on the seat, she whipped the horses into a gallop.

She reckoned that almost two hours had gone since she turned down the lamp at home and went to harness the team. Now that Veasy was in the sleigh box with her, weak and sick but there just the same, her every worry was about me, alone and delirious at the house.

Within an hour, and by following the road, she would be back. But if she took a chance out on the ice of the beaver ponds she could make several shortcuts and knock minutes off the journey. In winter, as soon as we were sure that the ice was safe for travel, we would shortcut over it wherever there was a large enough loop in the road to warrant a shortcut. But unless we were reasonably certain that the ice was safe enough to support a team of horses, we shied away from it.

In the early winter of 1947, heavy snows fell on the ice before it had an opportunity to attain much thickness. The weight of snow had settled what ice there was, and beneath the snow many an air hole had opened up, unseen, but there just the same. In time the water being forced up from the holes would spread all over the ice and eventually freeze solid again. When that happened, the lakes and beaver dams were safe enough for any kind of travel. But as long as they were in the process of flooding, the ice was treacherous, strong as a paved roadbed here, but thin as a sheet of glass there. But now every minute was so precious, so vital. That thought was the deciding factor: she turned the team away from the track, out onto the ice.

Three inches of flood water lay beneath the snow. The horses balked for a second or so when they realized they were now on ice. But Lillian urged them on, and snorting, they splashed through the flood water.

They navigated the ice of one beaver pond without mishap, and now Lillian decided to risk it all the way. She'd hold the horses to the ice of the beaver ponds wherever she possibly could, and so cut the time it would take to get back home.

The team travelled the length of two beaver ponds safely and were halfway across a third when suddenly there was a sickening crash, and the ice gave beneath them, and they were floundering in dark water. They reared up, lunging, trying to get their forefeet on solid ice, but the more they struggled, the deeper they sank in the water.

It was now around 1 A.M., and pitch-dark except for the thin light of the lantern. The sleigh runners were still on sound ice, but Lillian realized the utter futility of her ever hoping to get the sleigh moving again now. Her thoughts and her strength must be dedicated to saving the horses. For without the horses, the only other way of getting back home was afoot. And Veasy hadn't the strength to walk fifty yards.

Lillian set her teeth. She had to get the horses out, just simply had to. There was a double-bitted axe in the sleigh, and grabbing it she stepped out of the box and onto the ice. The flood water was above her ankles. The old ice cracked as she crawled along its rim to the heads of the frightened team. Speaking quietly to the horses, she cut the martingales and pole straps with the axe. Then she uncoupled the lines and took the bridles from the horses. She tried to unhook the traces but couldn't, so she cut them with the axe, too.

Now that the team was free of the sleigh, she brought the whip down on Ben's back, and snorting and puffing the gelding lunged up and managed to hoist his front hoofs onto ice. Lillian allowed him to rest there a moment, to regain his wind, but as soon as he started to slide back into the water she again used the whip. With one huge lunge Ben heaved straight up from the water, this time with all four feet on the ice. He lay there a minute, then slowly got to his feet.

But with Gipsy it wasn't so easy. The mare was considerably older then the gelding, and her first wild lunge had drained her of wind and strength. She now lay very still in the water, flanks heaving and falling, eyes closed, chin on firm ice, but lacking the will or the strength to make the one effort necessary to bring her front feet out of the water.

Ben stood shivering and trembling, body frosting over. Taking the lead rope from his halter, Lillian crawled to the edge of the water and fastened one end of it around Gipsy's neck. She next took several half hitches around Ben's tail with the other end. Then: "Ben!" she shouted with all her might, using the whip for emphasis. As the gelding lunged forward Lillian brought the whip down on Gipsy's shoulders. The mare's front feet contacted firm ice, and before the horse could slip back again Lillian again urged Ben on. And soon Gipsy was dragged out of the water and onto ice that supported her weight.

Taking the harness from the horses, Lillian dumped it in the sleigh box. She knew that the sleigh could be chopped out whenever the flood water froze solid again. Somehow she managed to get Veasy up on Ben's back and cover him with blankets. Veasy lay there, hands clasped in the horse's mane. Then, pulling herself onto Gipsy's back and leading Ben, Lillian trotted the horses home.

For four days and nights Lillian hovered between my bed and Veasy's, utterly worn out herself but unable to find rest in sleep. For if she did close her eyes for a minute or two, the torment and uncertainty that was needling her quickly brought them open again. Finally the fever—caused perhaps by an attack of viral pneumonia—abated and both Veasy and I began to mend. But not until Lillian was certain that all was going to be all right did she stretch out on the bed alongside me and sleep for sixteen straight hours.

.~

It was the end of the first week in January, almost three weeks since Lillian had made her unforgettable dash for the cabin. The team stood at the edge of the ice, hitched to willows. There was no flood water now; all was solid ice. All, that is, save for a few feet around the sleigh. It had taken Veasy and me an hour or more to chop the sleigh clear, but at last the job was done.

"Go get the team, son," I bade him, and hitching the chain at their doubletrees to the end of the tongue, I murmured, "Giddup," and tightening the traces, the team hauled the sleigh out of the water.

I stood there, looking at that dark hole in the ice. Slowly I turned to Lillian and said, "I was just thinking about Cal Wycott." Wycott was a half-breed, riding for Charlie Moon. Three winters ago he had been spurring his horse up the middle of Meldrum Lake—it had snowed heavily two days earlier—when suddenly the ice gave way, and he and the horse were in the water.

Later that night Wycott dragged into our house, afoot, clothes a sheet of ice. He'd spent an hour or more trying to save his unfortunate horse, but all to no avail. The horse perished there in that ice cold water.

Now I shook my head. I looked wonderingly at Lillian. "Just how, I would like to know, did you manage to get them out?"

"Remember what I told you, long, long ago, when we were riding our one hundred and fifty thousand acres to see what they had to offer us?" And she laughed aloud as she reminded me, "One can do most anything if they've just the will to try."

Chapter 27

Water! It leaped down the gullied hillsides, quickly filled shallow ponds wherever it could find a minor depression in the awakening floor of the forest. No matter where one might be at the moment, whether anxiously watching the beaver dams or perched upon a boulder at the crest of some naked hogback, all other sounds that made up the symphony of the wilderness—the piercing lament of a coyote, the sharp bark of a fox, the insane chatter of a loon, the soft grunt of a cow moose—were subordinated to the clamant rumble of the freshets as they hurtled toward the river.

Water! It nourished man's crops, quenched his thirst, turned his turbines, cleansed his skin, bore the products of his industry across the length and breadth of the universe. It guarded man, it restored him with the healing balm of its bounty. But water could destroy as well as heal, snuff out a life as easily as give birth to one.

Only a week or two ago, the wilderness about us had been silent, immobile beneath the solid mass of snow that had crushed it for so long. Then, with scarce a warning at all, had come the metamorphosis. All that clutching depth of inanimate whiteness became a crazed, muddy liquid that swept down through the land in noisy, threatening tide.

Even the most ancient of the ancients said that they'd never seen such a winter before, although once in a while one would scrub his chin with the palm of his hand, gather his dimming wits and vaguely recollect: "The winter of '91–'92 was a real hell-born heller, but I don't hardly believe it was a patch on this one." And that was a statement indeed, because usually no matter how hostile or long-lived a winter might be these days, you could pretty well bet your boots that there was at least one Methuselah around, who'd come to the Chilcotin when it mostly belonged to the Indians, whose mind would wander back across the years trying to recall a worse one. Of one thing, though, I am certain: that winter of 1947–48 was the cruellest winter we'd lived through since we first came to the creek.

From the fifth of January through to the twentieth of February it seldom got any warmer than thirty below, even at high noon, and at sundown the mercury would drop like a plummet just as far down the glass as it could possibly get, to the fifty minus mark, or maybe sixty below if the thermometer would let it, and stay that way until along in the following morning. And the wind puffed down from the chops of the north with an appetite on its tongue that nigh cut a man in half as he faced it, then neatly quartered the halves. And the snow lay so heavy and deep on the game trails that when I flushed a deer from the thickets about my snowshoe paths through the woods, about all I could see of the animal above snow level was its head and a thin line of its back.

By the middle of March a half-dozen moose calves were curled up in the snow within a couple of hundred yards of the house, frozen hard in their beds as they lay there. Down on the sidehills that sheered off to the Fraser River, there was scarcely a fir tree of any size that didn't claim at least one fawn deer as a casualty beneath it. There was no shortage of deer browse along those sidehills, but the snow lay so deep and heavy about them, it was impossible for the fawns to paw down through it and get at a mouthful of feed. So they bedded under the spread of the trees where the snow wasn't quite so deep and lay there, bellies shrunk, the iron clutch of the cold freezing the blood in their veins.

Even many of the cattle, belly deep in hay on the feed grounds, lost all will to survive against the relentless pressure of that cold, and those that didn't die limped around come morning with frozen hocks, ears or tails. And after a bit the hocks began to peel, or the ears and tail to drop off. There's never been a winter like it since we came to the creek to live.

Nor spring either, for that matter. There wasn't a smear of bare ground in sight anywhere when on the twenty-fifth of April we loaded the fur on the pack horses and lined out for Riske Creek. Two or more feet of snow still smothered the hayfield, and it was a solid snow too, and first thing in the morning when the frost was on it you could gallop a horse over it just as though the horse was cantering along a hardtop highway. It was the kind of snow you'd maybe expect to find at this time of the year in the higher mountains, but not down where we were, at the three- and four-thousand-foot levels.

It was the twenty-fifth day of April, 1948, and still we hadn't heard the honk of a single goose, and there wasn't a bluebird or robin in the country. And it all seemed crazy for us to be riding out to Riske Creek on horses with the fur when rightly we should have been taking it out in the Jeep. But no motorized vehicle could buck that much solid crusted snow, and no horse-drawn one either. We'd kept a sleigh road of sorts open to Riske Creek until the end of January, then overnight, and where there was no timber to make shelter, it had all blown in, and the drifts on Island Lake Flats piled up twelve and fifteen feet deep. And now, although May was almost within beckoning distance, the drifts would still be there, and even to get out to Riske Creek with horses that were lugging no sleigh behind them we'd have to follow the high ridges in order to outwit the drifts.

"The old creek will be running wild when all this turns to water," I sang out to Lillian, tailing one pack horse behind the other and tightening the cinch straps.

"The sooner it runs, the better I'll like it," she flung back. "I'm that sick of snow I never even want to see a Christmas card again." And for the umpteenth time since March was peeled from the calendar, she complained, "Isn't it ever going to come spring?"

"Spring?" I repeated, grinning. "There'll be no spring this year. All of a sudden like, the snow will start to melt and by then it will be summer." And things turned out I wasn't far wrong at that.

This morning a little of winter still clung to the wind. It drifted in from the northwest, sharp and probing, and Lillian was bundled up in a creamy turtleneck sweater and a bright red mackinaw coat that she'd made from the remnants of an old one of mine. Lillian could take a coat or pair of pants of mine that I figured should rightly be thrown out on the trash pile, and with a few snips of the scissors and half a spool of thread make a real smart garment for herself from it. It was a trick she learned in the lean years, when dollars were scarce as diamonds, and when no scrap of cloth was thrown away if needle, thread and know-how could put it to use again.

Veasy bridled his roan gelding and buckled the throat latch. He legged into his batwing leather chaps, buttoned his sheepskin coat, fixed his ear flaps so they half covered his ears and then stood by the horse's head, straight as a ramrod, all five feet eleven and a half inches of him. The bridling of the horse and the pulling on of his chaps had been done almost mechanically, as if horse, bridle and chaps were leagues away from his true thoughts. Nowadays almost everything Veasy did was done mechanically, although none the worse for that. And every once in a while Lillian or I would see him stop in the middle of what he was doing and stare off into space, as if right that very moment his mind was over the hills and far away, busy with things that had no bearing at all on what he was doing at the moment. But I never trespassed on his inner thoughts and neither did Lillian. In his own good time Veasy would come right out and tell us what it was that he saw over the hills and far away, and although we rather dreaded the moment of his telling us, we knew that someday he'd have to.

If the winter had snuffed out the lives of no one knew how many deer and moose, and left many a rancher short on his last fall's count of cattle, it hadn't treated us too unkindly. Between them the two pack horses toted some eleven hundred muskrat pelts, good for a dollar and a half apiece. The marshes had flooded over in late February and promptly

285

frozen tight again. And the muskrats had retopped their push-ups, and since scarcely a flake of snow fell in March, one could stand at the edge of a marsh and see push-ups everywhere without looking for marker sticks. The way the winter clung on, refusing to let go, kept the ice sound and solid too, and we'd trapped right up to the twentieth of April, and might have been trapping yet if Veasy and I hadn't got tired of tending the traps and skinning the catch, and Lillian of tacking the pelts to the stretcher boards.

It took us thirteen hours to get through to Riske Creek what with having to twist around here, bypass there, to avoid getting our saddle stock belly deep in the drifts. There we tagged up our bundles of fur, shipping the lot off to the auction sales. Eleven hundred muskrat pelts was just too much fur to haggle about with any local trader. And with the fur on its way to the sales, and after two or three days of lazing around at Riske Creek, listening to and participating in discussions all relating to the hardships of the winter, and when in hell was it ever going to come spring, we saddled up the horses and returned home to our creek.

There was no spring at all in the true sense of the word. It was as if winter, ashamed of itself for having plagued everybody and everything for so long, suddenly died, leaving summer to come along to fill and tamp the grave. The first string of geese headed north high over the house along toward the end of the first week in May. Then the robins came hopping along, and a pair of bluebirds followed them with bits of last year's grass right there in their beaks, ready for the nest building. And crowding the bluebirds came the swallows, and right on their tails the hummingbirds. Never in our memory had so many migratory birds come back so close on one another to our wilderness to nest. Usually the robins were two weeks ahead of the bluebirds, and the latter a week ahead of the swallows. But in that spring of 1948, each crowded in on the other, all in frantic haste to get the nests built in the least possible time, ready for the eggs.

By the middle of May the thermometer, which such a short time ago had told a bitter story of fifty or sixty below, now said eighty above in the shade when we went and took a peek at it. Snowdrifts ran away as water even as you watched them. Meldrum Creek lifted four feet in one night, fed as it was by a thousand lusty rivulets pouring away from the forested hillsides. And as it was on Meldrum Creek, so was it on countless other creeks, some named, some yet to be named, that ran down through the land to make common rendezvous with a single mighty river.

It made us uneasy to stand outside the house at sundown and listen to the almost deafening roar of the creek as it hurled itself at the facades of the beaver dams and sluiced over their tops. There were so many dams, so much water tumbling down the creek, probing here, seeking there, watchful for a weak spot somewhere in the dams that could be breached and pushed aside.

And what if the beaver dams gave, unable to withstand the shock of water battering them any longer? What would happen down in the valley at the mouth of the creek where folks were plowing their garden patches, or harrowing their hayfields, or drilling down a crop of oats, if the beaver dams were pushed aside and the tens of thousands of acre-feet of water they contained was suddenly free to run off in one mighty avalanche down through the land and into the Fraser River? If those beaver dams gave, the garden patches and the hayfields and the acres of newly sown oats would all be lakes.

There was scarce a pause between the runoff of the snows at the three-, four- and five-thousand-foot levels and that at far higher altitudes. All became water at the selfsame moment, and into the Fraser River poured the water.

Not for a half-century or more had the Fraser overflowed its banks and inundated the reclaimed lands about its mouth, where, in the spring of 1948, thousands of people were at work, tilling and seeding their farms, secure in their belief that the dikes and embankments that had been built since last the river went on the rampage were now formidable enough to bridle and hold it in check no matter how high might be the crest of its flood water. But the very ground upon which so many of their homes sat was stolen from the river in the first place. Drained and diked, and moistened by subirrigation, the soil produced bumper crops of hay, grain, vegetables and fruits, but that soil was mostly silt, deposited there in years long gone by the flood waters of the river itself. And in that late May and early June of 1948, the river was again to claim its own.

Fed and fattened by a thousand minor creeks, as well as by the flood waters of such major rivers as the Nechako, the Cottonwood, the Quesnel, the Chilcotin and the North and South Thompson, the Fraser inched ever higher up the dikes, seeking a spot to breach them. Like ants busy about a hill, mankind swarmed along the tops of the embankments, working the clock around with sandbags and dump trucks and earth-moving equipment of every design in an endeavour to strengthen the barricades and subdue and contain the rampant sweep of the river. But all their labour was in vain. For forty years man had been the master, the river his servant. Now, for a moment, the river was again the master, and man stood baffled and impotent before the impetuous strength of its flood.

Levees became sodden with the weight of the water probing them. Seepage occurred in countless different places. Rivers inched slowly higher. Now it was lapping at the tops of the dikes, and unable to deny it any longer, the embankments gave way and a turgid tide of water hurled through them, inundating the reclaimed lands beyond.

Once more the Fraser Valley was a lake. Homes emptied as people fled them. Dairy and other cattle drowned in pastures where so very recently all had been placidly grazing. Houses and barns floated hither and thither like bits of wood on a beaver pond. Boats must travel over roads that but a day or so ago had been travelled by a procession of automobiles. The tracks of both the Canadian Pacific and Canadian National railways rested beneath several feet of water, and the city of Vancouver was cut off from rail traffic with the rest of Canada to the east. And on the rivers and creeks that fed the Fraser, storage and other dams deemed formidable enough to withstand the shock of no matter what weight of water came against them were pushed aside as the incoming tides of the ocean push aside the sand.

∻

In that spring of 1948 we reckoned there were some two hundred beavers on Meldrum Creek, and in that moment of dread uncertainty, when the breaching of but a single major dam would probably result in the breaching of every dam below it, we could do little but pin our every hope and faith in the beavers themselves. Yet it hardly seemed possible that the beavers could defy such a cataract when man had so hopelessly failed to do so.

But those beavers did not fail us. From bank burrow and lodge they came. From eventide until sunrise they worked without rest at the almost impossible task of raising their dams so that each might play its own individual part in taming the flood waters of the creek and holding them back from the river. Immature yearlings, full-grown males and mother beavers so heavy-bellied with young that they floated high up in the water, one and all they came. They came that the waterfowl overhead should always have somewhere to nest. They came that the fish should not perish in the polluted puddles of the creek channel. They came that the mink and the otter and the muskrat should never want for food. And they came that perhaps somewhere, a man, a woman and a nineteen-year-old boy should not have to look behind them and see all that they counted so dear disappear beneath the silted waters of the cataclysm.

A breach in a dam here was repaired almost as quickly as it occurred. A weak spot there was sought out and strengthened that the water could not force a passage through it. Every beaver dam along the creek held, defying all that the flood might do in wanton attempt to breach it. Not only did the dams hold; so much of the surplus water was harnessed and stored in front of the dams that the overall flow of the creek where it eventually arrived at the river was no greater than in any normal spring. Such was the miracle of the beavers of Meldrum Creek in that disastrous spring of 1948.

~

For every one of its more than 170 million people, the United States of America consumes an average of fifteen hundred gallons of water daily. All told, the nation uses up 231 billion gallons daily, more than enough water to float the combined merchant fleets of the entire world.

To raise a single bushel of corn by irrigation, about ten thousand gallons of water are required. About two hundred thousand gallons of water are necessary to grow one ton of alfalfa hay. Industry itself in the United States now uses about eighty billion gallons of water daily, and it has been forecast that the amount required to meet those needs by 1975 will be about two hundred billion gallons daily.

Although some 1.5 quadrillion gallons of water falls annually on the United States, in many sections of the country a serious water shortage now actually exists or is impending. Despite the omnipresent threat of serious water shortage both for agriculture as well as industry, seldom a year goes by but that some major river overflows its banks, flooding the lands about it, drowning the livestock pasturing them, destroying their crops and driving the residents from their homes.

Well might man think deeply about what happened on Meldrum Creek in that disastrous flood year of 1948. The antics of any main drainage artery itself are governed almost entirely by the antics of all lesser arteries that feed it. No colony of beavers can dam the flow of a mighty river, but they can and will dam the flow of the multitude of lesser watersheds that flow into it. On Meldrum Creek the beavers allowed none of the flood water to find its way to the river and so add its mite to a major drainage system that could neither use nor contain it. Instead they stored it on their dams for gradual release, in a way that instead of harming man would benefit him.

~

The sultry heat drenched our faces with sweat; our lungs heaved frantically for air. We'd tied the horses at the foot of the promontory, then scaled its final three hundred feet of almost sheer rock afoot. Once in a while I looked back at Lillian a few yards below me, stretched out a hand and asked, "Need any help?" She was bareheaded, her white blouse unbuttoned. A miniature rivulet of perspiration ran down her forehead. There was a rent in the right leg of her slacks that wasn't there when we began the climb. She shook her head and puffed, "I'm coming along nicely."

Veasy was way ahead of us, going up the rock like a steeplejack up a chimney. Once in a while he too turned and looked below, and his voice floated down to me: "Need any help?" Wolfing a mouthful of air, I sang back, "We're both coming along nicely."

Finally we dragged out on top and lay there in the full glare of the July sun, resting, and replenishing our lungs. We were 4,750 feet above sea level, almost a thousand feet higher than any of the hilltops around us. Far to the northeast, ten or more miles distant, was a long finger of water: Meldrum Lake. There were many other patches of water there too, linked to one another like a long crooked chain: the beaver marshes. And still farther away, a sheer dark trench split the land: the Fraser.

I steadied my breath. I could hear the voice of the river, if only very faintly. It was just a low placid murmur as the water sped down through the land to an ocean that a month ago was digesting the silted, debris-littered, swollen contents of many mighty rivers. But now the voice of the Fraser was no longer as thunder in my ears. The freshets had passed on. The river had had its fling.

From the trench of the river my eyes came back to the links of that crooked chain. Perhaps if the flood water of Meldrum Creek had had its way about things, there would be no links in the chain. A few years ago, yes, then the water would have rushed down through the creek channel without obstacle to prevent its reaching the river. But in the spring of 1948 the beavers were there waiting: waiting first to challenge, and then to halt the flood in its tracks and throw it back upon the marshes.

Chapter 28

When the moment of parting came, it came as neither a surprise nor a shock to Lillian or me. It was something we'd been expecting and steeling ourselves to meet since Veasy first acquired the habit of suddenly looking up from what he was doing and gazing off into distance, as if somewhere beyond the horizons were places he had to visit and get acquainted with.

Although it was something Lillian and I hardly ever discussed between ourselves, we both knew deep within us that the wilderness could not hold Veasy forever, that someday he'd have to leave it, for a year or two anyway, perhaps longer, and see for himself just what was going on over the hills and far away. And I knew and Lillian knew that when the moment of his decision arrived, neither of us would utter a single word in an effort to deflect him from his purpose.

It was in late October of 1951 when Veasy finally made up his mind. The lakes and beaver marshes were nicely freezing, and I figured that given a couple of nights of real hard frost, the ice should be sound enough for us to get onto it afoot to start staking the muskrat push-ups. We were in the sitting room listening to the evening news as it came in over the radio. Much of the news was of the fighting in Korea, and after a while, and if you listen to too much of it, even news of battles being won or lost acquires a sort of staleness—that is, when none of your own flesh and blood is taking part in the battles.

The news ended, and I was scouting around the air waves for a little worthwhile music when Veasy suddenly interrupted with: "Do you mind shutting it off for a few minutes?"

I glanced at him sharply, at the same time doing as he asked. The sultry voice of a blues singer in San Francisco sheered off as if the lady had dropped dead at the mike. I turned to Veasy. "What's on your mind, son?" I asked.

It came quietly but steadily. He said: "Think you and Mum can get along here without me for a while?"

With almost imperceptible movement Lillian straightened a little in her chair. She folded her hands in her lap, and her eyes wandered to the window. If the proverbial needle had dropped, we'd have each heard it fall.

After a little I said almost too casually, "Don't see why not." And with a measured breath: "For how long?"

"Three years perhaps." And the way Veasy said it told me that he'd got it all figured out in his head, and there was nothing at all to argue about. So I held silence, letting him take his own good time about telling us what he wanted to do, and where he was going to do it.

"I'd sort of like to get away from these woods for a while if you and Mum can carry on without me," he went on. Then slowly: "I was thinking about joining the army."

Lillian's lips came together and her eyes shifted to me. Somehow I avoided them. "So," I thought, "it's the army, is it?" Involuntarily I shook my head. After the complete freedom of his life in the wilderness, I somehow couldn't picture Veasy in any armed forces, doing almost everything that had to be done at someone else's order. Still, he was nearing twenty-three, he could shoot the eye out of a deer standing a hundred yards off in the woods, and if he wanted to join the army then that was his affair, certainly no one else's.

I aimed a glance at Lillian. Her eyes were still on my face, saying nothing at all. If maybe her mind had suddenly been plunged in turmoil, none of it showed without.

"When do you figure on going?" I asked serenely, as if we were merely discussing a trip to Riske Creek for the mail.

"You really think that you and Mum can carry on things here without me?" he persisted.

"Why of course we can." And looking to Lillian for confirmation: "Can't we?"

"I don't see why not." Lillian tried ever so hard to say it casually, but somehow she fumbled the words a little.

"Then I might as well take off whenever you've got time to drive me out to Williams Lake," he said in a tone of finality. "I suppose I'll have to go down to Vancouver to join up."

Thus was the unit broken, as we each had known that someday it must. The three of us drove out to Williams Lake in the Jeep on the last day of October. A little snow was on the ground, just enough for me to be able to discern the track of a weasel or coyote when it paralleled or crossed the road. There was a Greyhound bus service now shuttling between Vancouver and points far to the north, and we went down to the depot in Williams Lake, chatting about this and that with one another until the driver sat down at the steering wheel and the moment of parting had come. We said goodbye to Veasy, got out of the bus and watched the vehicle until it went around a bend in the road and we could see it no longer.

I stole a glance at Lillian. Her teeth were set, and the colour had almost all gone from her cheeks. With an impulsive little gesture she thrust her hand into mine. It felt very warm and moist. And because I knew that it would be better if the tears came, instead of her trying so mortal hard to dam them back, I said softly, "Once in a while a real good cry does no one any harm." And that's how it was. She moved over to the Jeep, flung herself into the seat and let the tears come.

I got in behind the wheel and started the motor. "Do you good. Only try to hang onto some of them. Someday he'll come back again and you'll need a tear or two then, won't you?"

She wiped the tears away with her handkerchief, steadied her breath and said, "What makes you think he'll ever want to come back to the trapline again?"

I forced out a laugh. "Don't they all come back to the wilderness? You just wait and see, that's how it will be with Veasy. He'll have his fling in the army, maybe see a bit of the world, and after a while he'll get sick of what he's seen and be hungry for the woods again. A lot of things raised in the woods get an itching to leave them after a while, but most of them come back. Now, let's you and me go home."

I put the vehicle in gear and depressed the gas pedal. We drove a half-dozen miles in silence, then, coming to a long upward slope in the road, I geared down a notch and said meditatively, "Take the bluebirds, for instance. There's a pair of them nest in the eaves of the house every spring. Then the eggs hatch out, and after a while you see the young ones perching around on the cottonwood trees, not quite sure of their wings, and the old birds packing them grubs and other tidbits. But when the youngsters have learned to fly real good, they have to get out and rustle their own grub because now the old birds won't do it for them." The crest of the hill was reached and I slipped back into high. "Then along about the middle of September," I continued, "all the bluebirds pull out, head-ing south, and seems hardly likely that you'll ever see feather of them again. But you do, don't you? Next spring they all come, and mighty happy to be back, too. Same way with the geese and the ducks and the robins: they all pull out and all come back. That's how it is with the wilderness: a lot of things born and raised there get up and leave it for a spell, but they can't leave it for keeps as long as there's life in their bodies. Someday they have to come back. That's how it will be with Veasy. Sure, we've lost him for a while, but someday he'll come back, you just wait and see if he doesn't."

Of course we missed him more than we missed anything else on earth. We missed him in so many ways. Sometimes when Lillian went to set the table for breakfast or maybe supper, she'd place three sets of knives and forks mechanically like, then with a swift impatient gesture sweep one set away and put it back in the knife box. We missed him sorely at night when we were there in the sitting room alone, not caring to listen to the radio because if we did, pretty soon along would come a tune that only a short time ago Veasy had been humming or whistling when he went about the chores. Even the fresh track of a real small fisher cat in the soft snow went almost unnoticed. Until now, sign of a real small fisher was worthy of much discussion at night because the fisher cats were the most valuable fur-bearers on the trapline, and if you caught a real small one with dark silky fur, you could figure that the pelt was good for a hundred dollars anyway, maybe a hundred and a quarter if the fur was exceptionally fine. So whenever we saw a track, Veasy and I would plan a strategy together, deciding just where to set down the traps so that we'd be sure of catching the fisher when next it passed that way. And every now and then Lillian would throw in her two bits' worth of advice, maybe just to have us understand that she knew a mite about catching small dark fisher cats too. As a matter of fact, a fisher had once gotten into Lillian's traps, and the skin fetched her one hundred and twenty dollars at the auction sales. But that, I teased her, was sheer beginner's luck. "You know darned well that you set the trap for a mink without so much as a thought of a fisher getting tangled up in it, didn't you now?"

She evaded the question with: "But I caught the fisher, didn't I?" And since she was just that very minute tacking the pelt to a stretcher board, there wasn't too much I could say.

But now, with Veasy gone from the woods, even the track of a real small fisher didn't amount to very much one way or the other. If I mentioned it to Lillian she'd just nod her head, saying little, and if she did say anything it was said absent-mindedly, as though she didn't give a nickel whether we trapped the fisher or didn't.

And that's pretty well how it was with me when it came time to stake the muskrat push-ups. I began with Rawhide Lake, and there the push-ups were so close together it seemed that I'd no sooner cut one bundle of marker sticks and toted them out on the ice than I must go back to shore and cut myself another bundle. Every now and then I'd stop and look up and down the ice, half expecting to see Veasy moving through the bulrushes at the other side of the lake, sticking his markers into the push-ups. I'd always gone down one side of the lake or marsh, and Veasy down the other. But now I was alone, and there was no sense in my stopping and looking around for Veasy. He wasn't there, and I had all of the lake to myself.

Back from the lake a ways was a clump of fir trees, and apart from the other a few yards was a tree with a four-foot girth, with bark six inches thick and with stout drooping boughs. Beneath the tree was a scatter of limbs that had been broken off by winds or by the weight of winter snows. I'd tied my horse close to that mighty fir tree because that's where Veasy and I always tied our horses when we were staking the push-ups in Rawhide. Now, consulting both the sun and my belly at the same time, I thought it was time to eat my lunch. I dropped my bundle of marker sticks on the ice and lit out for the fir tree to build myself a campfire. I reached the tree and glanced around for a real dry piece of wood good for whittling shavings. My eyes came to rest on a single staple driven into the hard bark of the tree. Part of a leather thong was still hitched to the staple, though why the squirrels or pack rats hadn't chewed it up long ago was more than I could say. Just then it seemed that Veasy was right there under the tree, skinning a muskrat that was hitched by the tail to the staple. When trapping muskrats at Rawhide, Veasy generally managed to get a half-dozen skinned out while I was ruminating over an after-lunch cigarette.

For a fleeting second I could almost see him there, peeling the hide from the muskrat, then he was gone. Just then a timber wolf howled, sad, dismal and lonely. The wolf was quite a ways off in the woods, maybe a dozen miles away. The voice of a timber wolf carried a long way in the wilderness on a really calm day. I had just the right piece of kindling stick in my hand and was patting my pockets for my jackknife when the wolf went to crying. As its laments tailed off into depressing silence, I dropped the wood and murmured, "The hell with it. I'm going home."

Without another thought of Rawhide Lake and all the muskrat

push-ups that yet had to be staked, I flung into the saddle and trotted the horse all the way home.

Lillian eyed me with surprise when I stalked into her kitchen. "I didn't look for you back this early," she said. "Aren't there many muskrats in Rawhide this year?"

"Maybe more than there's ever been before." And a bit sheepishly I went on to explain: "It was too lonely out there on the ice, and every once in a while I'd forget and start looking around for Veasy."

Lillian moved her head in a gesture of understanding. "It's like that here too. Things seem altogether different now that he's gone. And I keep forgetting too—" She broke off, smiled faintly and then went on, "I started to make a prune pie this morning. Veasy always was hungry for my prune pies, though you hardly ever ate a slice of them. I started pitting the prunes before it came to me that there wasn't much sense in me baking a prune pie anymore."

"Not much sense in me staking muskrat push-ups either," I said moodily. "Maybe I'll just run a line of mink traps up and down the creek, put out the old fisher and lynx set in the woods. We can take two or three hundred muskrats in late March when the snow has gone from the ice and I can see the push-ups without their being staked. Not much sense in me wearing myself to a frazzle trying to catch a lot of fur when—"

"You can tend the mink traps on horseback, can't you?" Lillian cut in.

"Until the snow gets real deep, yes. Then it's easier to run the traps on snowshoes."

"Then until the snow *does* get real deep, I'm going with you whenever you tend the traps," Lillian declared.

When next we heard from Veasy he was a private in the Royal Canadian Regiment, based at a training camp in Ontario. He'd signed up for a three-year hitch in the army. And Ontario was thousands of miles away from Meldrum Lake, B.C. Every once in a while he wrote a letter home. As regularly as we could get out to Riske Creek with mail, I wrote him of almost all that was going on in the woods. But I made no mention of the fact that this winter there would be mighty few push-ups staked, or that I'd only got twenty or thirty mink sets out around the beaver marshes when rightly there should have been twice that many.

We didn't see hair nor hide of the boy again until Christmas Eve of 1952. Then he was given seven days of what he in his letter referred to as "embarkation" leave. Embarkation! The word stirred my memory. In World War I two of my brothers had been with British troops in the crater fields of Passchendaele and at the blood baths of the Somme. One had been killed in action a few days before the November 1918 armistice. I knew of what was meant by the term "embarkation" leave, and the word had a sinister, disquieting flavour to it.

"What does he mean by embarkation leave?" wondered Lillian. And because I knew it was no use beating around the bush I told her outright that Veasy was going overseas. "Germany, maybe," I hinted lightly. "Guess maybe his outfit is going to relieve other Canadian troops over there." I glanced at the letter, letting on that I was reading it. Then, with forced assurance, I told her, "Sure, he's going to Europe. Do him a pile of good to see something of England and France, and a little bit of Germany. A real holiday, that's what it will be to him." But there were Canadian troops in other parts of the world than Germany, and Korea was one of them.

Lillian slipped into an apron and began rolling her sleeves. I raised my eyebrows. "What are you aiming to do?"

She said: "I'm going to bake a couple of prune pies."

We drove out to Riske Creek to meet him the day before Christmas. In that early winter of 1952 the weather had treated the wilderness with a kindliness that wasn't always its lot at such a time of the year. A scant six inches of snow covered the game trails, and out on Island Lake Flats there wasn't a single drift. The air was clean and as clear as spring water seeping out of the moss. It was fifteen above zero and the tires of the vehicle made a pleasant crunching sound as they broke tracks through the snow. Before leaving the house Lillian had spent almost all of an hour fixing herself up. She wore the neat gray suit that was only lifted off its hangers in the clothes closet on extra-special occasions. Three or four years ago Veasy had taken three unusually large weasels in his traps, all spotlessly white save for the black tip at their tails. He'd sent the skins away to a furrier and had them made up as a neckpiece for his mother. Of the hundreds of weasels that we'd taken in our traps, Lillian declared that there never had been such weasels as those three. This morning the weasel stole was around her neck.

I fidgeted around the Jeep, brushing off the seats and polishing the windshield. I stalked in and out of the house, stamping my feet and aiming suggestive glances at the clock. Finally, and with impatience, I asked, "You fixing up to go visit the Queen?"

She retorted, "You wouldn't want Veasy to see me in slacks and all untidy-like, would you?"

"That I wouldn't," I said fervently.

He was waiting at Riske Creek when we drove in. I had to look a couple of times to make sure it was really Veasy standing there, smart as a Grenadier Guard in his well-tailored uniform. I greeted him: "Khaki sort of suits you."

"I prefer overalls myself," he quietly came back, and there was a quality to the way he said it that told me yes, he really did prefer overalls.

Then I hurried into the store, not because there was any occasion for hurry but because I reckoned that Lillian would want to have Veasy all to herself for a minute or two anyway.

Soon we were halfway across Island Lake Flats, on the way home. Veasy was at the steering wheel because he always could handle the Jeep a shade better than me. "You off to Europe?" I suddenly asked.

"No." There was a long silence. Then: "Korea," he said quickly. And the word sank into our hearts.

Seven days' embarkation leave. But that was from the moment of his stepping away from the training base in Ontario. He'd used up three of those precious days just getting to Riske Creek. It would take another three days for him to get back to his base, which only gave him one full day at home. But still, that day was Christmas, the best day of the year. The way I saw it, we were God Almighty lucky he was able to spend this

Christmas Day with us before taking off for Korea. For Korea seemed awfully remote and pretty frightening to Lillian and me.

Veasy and I took a long hike along the ice of Meldrum Lake on Christmas morning. "I figure there are a dozen active beaver lodges in the lake this year," I said. "How about you and me going around just to make sure?"

It wasn't that I really wanted to count the beaver lodges but because I knew that Lillian always did like the house to herself Christmas morning, what with all the cooking to tend to. And if we stuck around the house, every once in a while wandering into her kitchen, lifting a saucepan lid here and there, maybe giving her a bit of unsolicited advice now and then, she'd sniff and grumble, "Now what does a man know about cooking the Christmas dinner? Why don't you go and set some rabbit snares or a trap for that coyote that was howling its head off last night?"

That night we sat around the radio, listening to a church service being broadcast from Vancouver. Lillian always did like organ music, and now the organ was accompanied by a real choir. And our stomachs were so full of turkey and plum pudding, and mince pie and cake, that any sort of talk was a matter of huge effort.

I went and sprawled out full length on the lounge, eyes partly closed. My thoughts shifted back over the years, to some twenty-two other Christmases that we'd spent deep in the heart of a wilderness. It was calm and peaceful there in the sitting room, and the church service came in soft and subdued. The cat had jumped up on the lounge and flattened out alongside of me, purring easily and contentedly. Its belly was full of turkey too. Spark, our Labrador retriever, lay by the heater stove, nose on paws. I thought, "Queer how that dog can stand so much heat on his belly." Spark's stomach was full of moose meat because dogs prefer moose meat to turkey, even on Christmas Day. Veasy had picked up a book that Lillian had given him for Christmas and was riffling through its pages.

Twenty-two Christmas Days! Didn't hardly seem possible that so many had come and gone, and all spent back here in the woods. My eyes came open, shifted around the room and came to rest on Lillian. She was seated in an easy chair by the radio, arms folded, listening to the church service. And looking at Lillian I knew that it must have been that long. Only that many years could have lined her face as it was lined and sprinkled her hair with the gray that was in it now. "Shucks," I thought, "who are you to think about Lillian's hair beginning to gray—you're getting as gray as a badger yourself." And mighty darned quick I'd have to start wearing glasses, because last fall I could no longer see a deer standing stock-still in the woods a hundred yards off. No, I couldn't see the deer at all until it picked its hoofs up and started to move away. When first we came to the creek, I'd have seen the deer there even if most of its body was behind a bush. So Lillian's hair was graying and mine was graying too. And maybe come spring I'd take a trip to the Outside and go hunt up an optometrist, and maybe he could tell me why now I couldn't see a deer when it was standing still in the woods watching me.

Twenty-two years is a tidy stretch of time when all have been spent in a wilderness, shut off from the rest of the world. But apart from the graying heads and failing eyesight—and that would have happened almost anywhere—the years had treated us fairly. They owed us nothing at all; we owed them much. And not a one of them had been in vain—you only had to travel up and down creeks, marking the occupied beaver lodges, to be quite sure of that.

My eyes closed again. The organ music stopped and the preacher was starting the sermon, solemn and serious. His voice had a sort of mesmerizing cadence to it. Spark moved off from the stove a few feet, then flopped down again. The cat flexed its paws. Korea. Veasy was going to Korea. Why should Veasy be going there to mix in with their disputes? Why wasn't the whole world peaceful as it ever was at Meldrum Lake? "And the Lord Jesus Christ—" The preacher's voice droned on, mixing in with my thoughts. Twenty-two years, and the Lord Jesus Christ had seen us safely through all of them. And that's how it would be with Veasy when he was fighting in Korea. The Lord Jesus Christ would see to it that Veasy came back to us all in one piece. Of that much I was sure.

Chapter 29

Had it not been for the radio, Lillian and I might have never known that Veasy had taken part in a single battle. But on the fourth of May, 1953, the radio told us of the battle that had been fought the day before, and according to the news commentators it was one of the fiercest and bloodiest battles of the whole Korean War. But then news commentators often exaggerated a little, and maybe the battle hadn't been quite as bloody as some of them tried to make out. Just the same, they wouldn't have stated that the 3rd Battalion, Royal Canadian Regiment, had borne the main brunt of the battle unless that had been so. And we knew that Private Veasy Eric Collier was part of the 3rd Battalion, Royal Canadian Regiment.

It was knowledge of that that took the colour from Lillian's face as the news came in over the radio and left her a grayish white. And made her set her teeth just as she'd done when the bus went out of sight around a bend in the road, carrying Veasy away from her with it.

It was knowledge of that that compelled me to snatch at my breath while my troubled mind groped for the words I wanted. And when they came to my tongue, I moved over to her side, laid my hand gently on her shoulder and told her, "Now don't you go to worrying. He'll come back, just you wait and see if he doesn't." That's what I said at the time because there was little else I could say.

Three weeks later the large brown envelope with Department of National Defence printed on its left-hand corner arrived at Riske Creek. I didn't bother opening it until late that evening, when we were back home, and when all other envelopes had been opened and their contents read and digested. Large brown envelopes from any government department seldom had much of interest in them.

We were in the sitting room, and the sun was about at the setting. Lillian was seated on the lounge, resting. A few minutes ago she'd been working in her flower garden, setting out some plants. There was a smear of dirt on her forehead, and a streak of blood on her chin where she'd squashed a mosquito. I picked the envelope up from the table with scant interest and slit it open. Inside was a sort of scroll-like affair, eighteen inches long and seven or eight wide. I tensed with a dreadful premonition as I began reading the printed words that danced before my eyes. When I reached the end of them I exhaled a pent-up breath.

Lillian glanced at me sharply with question in her eyes. "It's from Department of National Defence," I explained, "about Veasy."

"Veasy!" The word was loaded with anxiety.

"Now, now, there's nothing for you to get alarmed about. Here, you'd better read it yourself." And I began to get up from my chair.

"No," she insisted. "You read it to me."

So, word for word, I quietly began to read:

Award of Mention-in-Despatches to SK 13874
Private Veasy Eric Collier, 3rd Battalion, The
Royal Canadian Regiment.

I paused a moment, trying to steady my breath, and when I had it under control again, I continued.

During the night 2/3 of May, 1953, C Company, 3rd Battalion, The
Royal Canadian Regiment, sustained a heavy attack by superior ene-
my forces accompanied by an intense artillery bombardment. Private

Collier was on duty as a relay station operator in No. 7 Platoon position of "C" Company which bore the brunt of the assault. Throughout the action Private Collier remained calm and efficient, keeping his wireless sets operating at maximum efficiency. On three separate occasions when his aerial was shot down, he exposed himself to heavy enemy fire to re-erect the damaged aerial, and subsequently when the Assistant Signals Officer and his Platoon Commander were obliged to leave the Command Post, he continued to keep communications open and remained on the position until ordered to leave. This soldier's gallantry and devotion to duty in keeping communications operating contributed in a large measure to the successful conduct of the battle.

I laid the citation down on the table and got up from the chair. Lillian had dropped the little file, or whatever it is that women use to clean their fingernails, on the lounge, and her hands rested in her lap. She sat there very prim and straight, and gave me not so much as one quick glance as I went out through the door and down to the lake. Though there was a stiffish breeze at the time, I had no eyes for the wavelets jigging on the water. In fact, instead of open water I saw ice and a dusting of snow on the lake, and the spruces and pine trees around it were weighted down with snow. And a child was moving up the ice toward me, short, stout little legs pushing the skis over the snow. And I saw something else there too: behind the child, a hundred yards behind, padded five lusty timber wolves, and when I saw them, the crisp winter air I was breathing into my lungs became pregnant with terrible danger. "Keep coming, son—steady—just like that. Don't let them bluff you, don't panic. Steady—steady—steady—" And the child hadn't panicked, and a few minutes later he was there at my side, showing me a dandy mink that he'd taken from his traps.

The vision melted. The ice was gone, and there was no snow on the evergreens as the breeze swayed their tops. But the words "don't panic" still sang in my ears. Perhaps that's how it had been over there in Korea when Veasy was fixing the aerial. He hadn't panicked, when such panic might have changed the whole course of the battle, because of all the things that the wilderness had been able to teach him, above all not to panic was one of them.

~

That summer, we irrigated the hayfield, cut the crop and hauled it away to the corral. Then, after what seemed to be only a very brief pause, it came season to dig the potatoes, gather the other vegetables and stow them away in the root cellar.

We hunted no geese that fall, although flocks of a hundred or more settled down on the beaver ponds, tarrying a while before continuing their southward trek. "Eric, it's been two years or more since you last shot a goose," Lillian commented with surprise.

I stroked my chin. "That it has. You think I should go shoot one now?"

"No." It was an emphatic no, too. Lillian loved the geese. Even in those other years when the price of a Christmas turkey had to be spent on more urgently needed things, Lillian had to steel herself into flushing the geese and putting them over my gun.

The lakes became ice overnight, then snow rustled down from the north. "Remember the bear dens?" I asked, pulling a chair up to the heater stove and patting my pockets for tobacco pouch and cigarette papers.

She made a little grimace. "I'll never forget them."

I rolled the cigarette, lit it and teased, "Were you ever even a bit scared?"

"Always."

I winked. "Me too." And after a long puff at the cigarette: "You'd rather have store lard, wouldn't you?"

"Now that we've the money to buy it with, yes."

Not too many traps were set out in cubbies that winter. Just enough to give me exercise, a run of two or three miles on the snowshoes every afternoon.

I trapped a few muskrats in March. Not too many, although the marshes were dotted with push-ups. Enough to give me the exercise I had to have. And maybe enough to inform me that for some reason or another the snowshoes were heavier now than they'd been five years ago.

The winter clung on as our winters so often did. It was mid-April when I chained up all four wheels of the Jeep, backed it out of the old log cabin that had been converted into a garage and steered it through the snow still quilting the hayfield. For a hundred yards the vehicle painfully bulldozed its way through that snow, then the wheels started to spin, and we seemed to be marking time. "We're into a drift," I commented without any surprise at all.

Lillian poses with the Colliers' Labrador retreiver in front of the one-room, sod-roofed cabin that they lived in for sixteen years. At this point, the cabin served as a garage for the Jeep.

Lillian's eyes clouded with disappointment. "Eric, you don't think we can make it across Island Lake Flats yet, do you?" she asked.

"Veasy maybe could. But me—" I shook my head. "I wouldn't like to even try. Maybe we'd get stuck and be afoot out there in the snow." I never had much faith in myself when it came to driving the Jeep over a questionable passage.

"Veasy." She said it so softly I could scarce hear her. "Veasy," she repeated. "I wonder where he is right this very moment."

It was close to a month since we'd last been out for mail. We went out on horseback, and it was a tedious, miserable journey what with all the drifts and crusted snow making travel terribly slow. Seemed that nowadays riding bothered Lillian, did something to her back. But it was saddle horse or nothing. I didn't like trying to buck heavy snow with the Jeep.

There'd been a letter from Veasy at the post office then, mailed in Inchon, Korea. The boy had heard rumours that his battalion might be returning to Canada, though just when he didn't know. That was in mid-March.

Now, backing out of the drift and re-garaging the Jeep, I said, "If the next three or four days are warm ones and the snow melts some, we can maybe then get out with the Jeep and try again."

Lillian was very quiet for the remainder of the afternoon. It was a quietness born of her disappointment. And she was worrying about Veasy.

After supper we both strolled down to the lake and walked out on the ice. The ice hadn't started to rot. It would still support a six-horse freight outfit. I stopped, looking toward the south, listening.

"What is it?" asked Lillian.

I grinned sheepishly. "I thought I heard geese. Must have been something else. Guess these old woods were fooling me again."

"I do wish the geese would come back," she sighed. "Then we'd know for sure that it was spring."

"What the heck—?" I dropped down on one knee, shading my eyes with a hand and peering intently at the southeast end of the lake.

"You see something?" Lillian was looking now.

"Yes, in the fir timber. See? Coming toward the ice. Moose maybe. No, not a moose. Say, it's a horse. With a rider too. What the heck—?"

"He's riding out on the ice." Lillian too shaded her eyes. "Look, he's reining the horse right up the middle of the lake."

"He knows the country," I said. "Knows that the ice is safe yet."

We could see the rider's red mackinaw coat and blue denim overalls. He sat loosely in the saddle, left leg crooked around the horn, as cowboys often ride when the seat of the saddle begins getting hard. "Not scared of the ice at all," I muttered again.

Then the rider waved his arm. I waved back in reply. "Who the heck?" Then recognition came to me. I heaved up from the ice. "It's—it's—"

"Veasy!" The name shot from Lillian's lips. All the disappointment vanished like a snowflake on a campfire. "Veasy!" And she raced along the ice toward him, flinging herself into his arms as he came down from the saddle.

I grasped the lad's right hand, pumping it. My eyes raked his outfit. The mackinaw coat and overalls were far too small for him. The horse was an ancient gelding, a sorrel, with little fat on its ribs. "Where'd you steal the outfit?" I asked.

"Borrowed them from one of the ranchers. I got to Williams Lake last night, hitched a ride to Meldrum Creek with the stage this morning. Left down there around four this afternoon and have been pushing the poor old sorrel mortal hard through the woods to get here before dark." He laughed. "Of course you never got my telegram?"

With uplifted eyebrows I said, "Did we ever get a telegram back here in these woods?"

"Didn't figure you would when I sent it from Vancouver. We docked there three days ago and—"

I didn't give a hoot whether the ship docked at Vancouver or Montreal. "You through with the army?" I interrupted.

"Will be in about three weeks."

That's all I wanted to know. I said, "Veasy boy, you go on ahead to the house with your mother, and I'll look after the horse."

I reached for the bridle lines and was about to hoist into the saddle when I suddenly stiffened, left foot in the stirrup, right still on the ice. I looked to the south and said tensely, "Listen!"

"You and your listening," scoffed Lillian impatiently.

"I hear geese," I whooped.

It was only a faraway murmur at first, one that we could hear for several seconds before the dots showed against the horizon. The murmur became a raucous, strident clamour; the dots took on definite shape. There were two hundred or more of them, the formation of their squadron etching a perfect V against the blue vault of the sky. They passed high over our heads, beating steadily northward.

I swung up into the saddle and headed for the barn, musing, muttering happily over and over again, "They all come back to the wilderness!"

Chapter 30

It was a June evening of the year 1956. Though the aftermath of an incarnadine sunset still lay on the forests, long strips of shadow were already reaching out here and there across the lake and lay as dark fans upon the water. The evening patrol had come away from the lodge a half-hour ago, and a few minutes after the beaver broke surface, I thought I heard a soft thud or two as if the beaver's sensitive guard hairs had detected a trickle of water escaping through the dam that rightly shouldn't be escaping at all. But, since the dam was a half-mile from where I sat, and out of sight too, I couldn't be sure whether the beaver had plugged such a trickle or not. I could only presume that he had.

This was the third night in succession that I'd walked through the screen door, quietly closed it behind me, crossed the strip of hay ground between house and lakeshore, and squatted down at water's edge, eyes and thought fixed on the large cottonwood that still somehow managed to remain upright at the other side of the bay. The tree stood some fifteen feet back from water's edge and about fifty yards from where I sat. Even in the failing light I could still see the dark, packed and narrow path between it and the water, and the scattering of white chips surrounding the tree. The path had been indented into the soft and muddy ground by the old beaver's weight, and the chips chopped from the tree by his chisel-edged incisor teeth. By rights the tree had no business standing there at all, since so many chips had been whittled out of it that even a slight puff of wind would start it swaying and send it crashing down. But for the last three or four days there had been no wind at all, and a few more chips would have to be taken from the tree before it went down.

The screen door swung gently on its hinges, closed softly again. A second or two later Lillian perched beside me. Though the longest day in the year was only a week away, the air began to chill as soon as the sun went down, and she was bundled up in a soft, woolly sweater and had tied an old silk handkerchief around her head.

Without pulling my eyes from the cottonwood tree I said, "Hullo. You going to watch too? It will surely go down tonight. If the beaver takes another dozen chips out it just has to go down."

"And maybe lodge," stated Lillian thoughtfully.

I tried to suppress a chuckle. "You believe in seeing the dark side of things as well as the bright, don't you?"

"Where beavers and cottonwood trees are concerned, yes." Then, smiling a little herself, she observed, "There's a mosquito on your cheek, and it's having a feast."

Absent-mindedly I palmed my right cheek. "No, not the right cheek," she pointed out. "The other one." Which only seemed to prove that if we'd accomplished little of anything else in the last twenty-five years, we'd at least learned to ignore the itchy sting of a mosquito.

But she was absolutely right about the cottonwood tree, and it was the tantalizing doubt about it that had fetched me down to the lakeside these three nights in a row to sit there quietly in the grass until it was so pitchy dark there was no sense in my sitting there any longer. I wanted to be there at water's edge when finally the tree went down.

Inland from the cottonwood, and only twenty feet away from it, stood three large, tall and stately spruces, huddled in a clump. Should the cottonwood fall away from the water and into the spruces, it would hang up, and all the persistent work of the beaver would avail it nothing. It was an old cottonwood, one that perhaps had taken its first peep at the sun a half-century ago. Its bark was gray with age, and it was two feet through at the stump. Almost every night for the last week, the beaver had waddled up the path from the water, gone erect on his hind webs and, moving around and around the tree, gnawed out the chips. Had there been any lean to the tree at all, it would have gone down three or four nights ago, but there was no lean, and the tree would have to be cut right through before it would topple. Then the chances were even that instead of falling into the water, as the beaver wanted it to, it would go the other way and hang up in the spruces. When beavers felled a tree they did not undercut it as a man would; they just went around and around it, slicing out the chips and trusting entirely to chance that it would fall where they wanted it to.

At the mouth of the bay and out in the water a few feet was the beaver lodge. Short lengths of aspen, some peeled of their bark, some yet to be peeled, littered the water around it, and often at sundown if you watched the lodge real closely, you'd see the mother beaver surface, pick up a length of unpeeled wood, then swiftly dive again. And a few seconds later you'd hear the soft, hungry grunts of the kits as their perfectly formed incisor teeth gnawed away at the bark.

Again the screen door opened, then closed with a jarring bang.

"You two going to sit there all night?" Veasy called.

It was darkening fast now. I could scarcely see the foot of the tree, though its top still stood out against the skyline. "You want to go in?" I asked Lillian.

She replied, "I'd like to sit here just a few minutes longer."

"Put the coffeepot on the stove and give us a call when it's ready," I sang back to Veasy.

∻

As Veasy's footsteps thumped back through the sitting room, my thoughts returned to the cottonwood tree. If it fell as the beaver wanted it to, it would go down in the water, and after a while, when the little ones in the lodge were old enough to get out in the water and hunt up food for themselves, they'd be able to swim in to the tree, reach up with their paws at a limb and go to shucking it of its bark without having to get out on land at all. So long as they were in the water, no skulking coyote or razor-clawed lynx could harm them, but on land such little fellows as they were too clumsy and inexperienced to escape the tooth or claw of any watchful predator that was out for an easy meal. Maybe that's what the old buck beaver had in mind when he began to whittle away at the tree: to fall it into the water so the little ones could eat in safety.

Veasy and I had trapped a hundred beavers in the spring of 1956. Neither of us really liked trapping the beavers because, as I told Lillian, "They do far more good in the water than as fur on some woman's back." But there were so many beavers on Meldrum Creek now, and we were forced to trap them just to hold their numbers in check. So many beaver colonies that if man didn't check their further increase with use of his steel traps, they'd go to killing one another as beavers will when they become too numerous, or maybe disease would become rampant in the colonies, as disease ever will where any wildlife population is outbreeding its food supply.

In this spring of 1956 our trapline and two nearby had yielded some four hundred beaver pelts. That seemed like an awful pile of beavers to trap when only some fifteen years ago there was scarcely a living beaver to be found throughout all the Chilcotin. But now the beavers were pushing out every which way, wherever there was a watercourse for him to follow, and many an Indian trapper was catching beavers too. And wherever there was a good-sized beaver pond, there were so many ducks of all kinds that in the fall of the year they lifted from the marshes at sundown in clouds that hid the skyline. And sleek, velvet-furred otters preened their guard hairs atop the beaver lodges, and moose came down to the ponds to drink and wallow just as in Lala's childhood the elk had come. Though there weren't too many trout in Meldrum Creek yet, there were one or two beaver ponds and the odd stretch of foam-flecked creek where you could drop a baited hook and catch a plump, red-fleshed rainbow on almost every other throw. In early July the ranchers pushed close to three thousand head of Hereford cattle onto the timbered summer ranges about the creek, and the grass grew so high and lush around the beaver ponds that the cattle waxed fatter every day as they cropped it, and never a one perished in the slimy muck of a boghole. Far below us, in the valley at the mouth of the creek, a rancher with weather-tanned face and work-calloused hands, a spade over his shoulder and a bit of a tune on his lips, moved slowly along his irrigation ditch, turning the water onto his alfalfa fields and thinking to himself, "There'll never again be a shortage of irrigating water on this creek as long as the beavers take care of things."

~

"I'm getting cold." Lillian's complaint suddenly interrupted my thoughts.

I got up and flexed my legs. "Too dark to see anything now anyway," I retorted.

"Coffee's ready!" Veasy's clarion summons erupted from behind the screen door.

I grabbed Lillian's hand and pulled her to her feet. "Come on, let's go." I peered into the night, looking for the top of the cottonwood. Not a limb of it was to be seen over there in the darkness. Maybe it would still be standing there with the dawning.

We were almost at the screen door when from out of the night and across the bay there came the grate of a beaver's teeth as he gnawed the chips from a cottonwood tree. I held Lillian's hand a little tighter. "Wait!" I breathed tensely.

One—two—three— The night was that calm and still I could almost count the toothings of the beaver as he notched deeper into the heart of the tree. Six—seven—eight— Then, following a few seconds of pent-up silence, I beard the almost explosive crack as the tree started down. With a resounding splash it settled in the water. Then all was quiet again.

We stood there in the night, rigid, looking toward the lake. Suddenly a tumultuous splash shattered the silence. It was the old beaver's tail, flailing the water. My eyes found Lillian's. We smiled at one another. I cleared my throat. "Something attempted, something done." That's all I could think of to say. Yet somehow those words expressed everything. And we joined Veasy in the kitchen and sat down to our coffee.

About the Author

Eric Collier was born in Northampton, England, in 1903. He moved to Canada in 1920, where he worked at several jobs in the interior of B.C. He married Lillian Ross in 1928, and a year later son Veasy was born. The Colliers eventually settled at Meldrum Creek, where they built their own cabin and lived off the land, Eric eking out a living as a trapper.

By the late 1940s, Collier had become well known for his wildlife expertise and his advocacy of humane trapping methods. He also began writing articles for such publications as *Northwest Digest* in Quesnel, the Williams Lake *Tribune* and *Outdoor Life* in the U.S. In 1949 he became the first non-American to win *Outdoor Life*'s Conservation Award. It was, in fact, *Outdoor Life* staff who encouraged him to write a book about his experiences.

Collier moved his family to Riske Creek in 1960 and sold his trapline in 1964. He died at Riske Creek on March 15, 1966. Lillian moved to Williams Lake, where she died in 1992. The Colliers' second cabin at Meldrum Creek, built in 1946, is now a historic site after being restored in 1994.

Also in the Classics West Collection

The Rainbow Chasers
1-894898-30-3

Harmon's Journal 1800-1819
978-1-894898-44-7

Klondike Cattle Drive
1-894898-14-1

The Ranch on the Cariboo
1-894898-02-8

Packhorses to the Pacific
1-894898-13-3